Alberta Remembers

Recalling Our Rural Roots

Karen Brownlee

Text by Ken Tingley

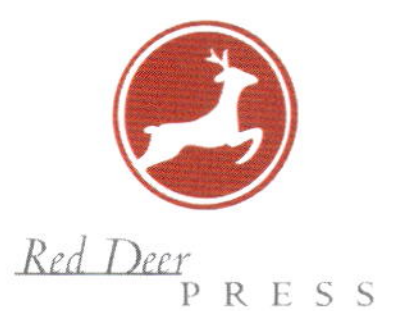

Red Deer Press

Published in the United States in 2006
5 4 3 2 1

Published by
Red Deer Press
Trailer C
2500 University Drive N.W.
Calgary Alberta Canada T2N 1N4
www.reddeerpress.com

Credits
Edited for the Press by Dennis Johnson
Cover and text design by Erin Woodward
Printed and bound in Hong Kong by Codra for Red Deer Press

Acknowledgements
Financial support provided by the Canada Council, the Government of Canada through the Book Publishing Industry Development Program (BPIDP), the Alberta Foundation for the Arts, a beneficiary of the Lottery Fund of the Government of Alberta and the Alberta Historical Resource Foundation.

National Library of Canada Cataloguing in Publication
Brownlee, Karen
Alberta Remembers / Karen Brownlee.
ISBN 0-88995-325-2
I. Title.
PS8587.A3723T86 2005 C812'.54 C2005-902478-X

Artist's Dedication

To Ray, Robyn and Logan, with my love. To the four generations who have worked on and dreamed of the land: Michal (Mike) and Irene Hazuda, the Vaselenaks, the Brownlees, the Determans and the Kingsburys for our rural Alberta heritage. With thanks for God's direction in my work, my family and my life.

–KB

Author's Dedication

To Sheila, my wife, an invaluable member of the team on this book, and to our parents, Frank and Margaret Tingley and Bob and Norah Whitson, whose farming heritage and love of the land inspired my interest in agrarian history.

–KT

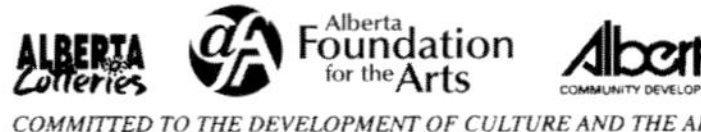

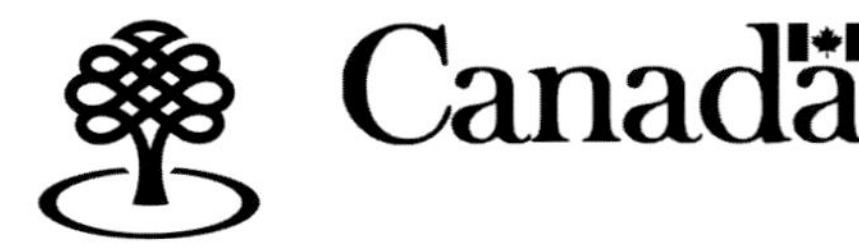

The Canada Council for the Arts since 1957 | Le Conseil des Arts du Canada depuis 1957

Acknowledgements

I wish to thank the following who assisted with the publishing of this book: The Alberta Foundation for the Arts, Visual Arts Project Grant; The Alberta Historical Resources Foundation Heritage Preservation Partnership Program, Publishing; Harold and Doreen Lissel; Southland Transportation Ltd./Pacific Western Transportation; Mike and Irene Hazuda; Dave and Carol Cruickshank; Bill Cade; Greer Homes Ltd.; Rick Casson, MP Lethbridge; Lethbridge Ironworks Ltd.; Young Parkyn McNab LLB Chartered Accountants; Gary and Beverly Duell; Office of the Mayor, City of Lethbridge; Doug McCallum and Johnna Kubik; Brian and Linda Brownlee; Agricore United, Beans and Speciality Crops; Sheila and Kenneth Tingley; Dr. Wes Fournier; Bridget A. Pastoor, MLA Lethbridge East; KPMG LLB Lethbridge; Campaign to Re-elect Clint Dunford; Canbra Foods Ltd.; Sylvan Learning Centre; Kathy Thrall; Ralph and Velda Sjovold; Schwartz Reliance Insurance; Tompkins Jewellers Ltd.; Kawneer Ltd.; Randy Thiessen.

The following individuals were instrumental in providing me with encouragement, guidance and faith in completing a book: Morry Katz; Ross Bradley, Paul Pearson and Judy Hayman of The Alberta Foundation for the Arts; Parlee McLaws, William (Bill) Pieschell, Q.C.; Roger Penner Professional Corp.; Kenneth and Sheila Tingley, Bill Cade; and Dennis Johnson, Managing Editor, Red Deer Press, and all staff members.

My heartfelt gratitude to Dr. Daniel Gallacher, Curator Emeritus, The Canadian Museum of Civilization; Ms. Jane Ross, Curator of Western Canadian History, The Royal Museum of Alberta; Cecil and Leta DePratu; and to Neil Webster of New Venture Photographics for photographing the artwork.

Thank you to the wonderful people and organizations who played a significant role in the development of the Rural Prairie Community series: Ross Bradley of The Alberta Foundation for the Arts; Morry Katz; Harold and Doreen Lissel; Alex Gepneris of Tollestrup Construction Inc.; Shirley Hutchison of Imperial Wilson Ladies Wear; Guy McNab; Ann Elle of Sylvan Learning Centre; James Enman of Scotia McLeod; Elmer and Virginia Brownlee; and Dilene Sorochan of TD Wealth Management.

Heartfelt thanks to the following who have shared their friendship, time, energy and resources in furthering my arts career: Ray, Robyn and Logan Brownlee; Mike and Irene Hazuda; Donna and Brian Gallant; Erin Demers and Don and Pat Demers family; Darren Gilbertson; Aaron Hagan; Betty Comperen and Rick Hart; John and Helen Vaselenak; Lemonia Kollias; Elizabeth Ginn; Father Howard Keon; Father Don O'Gorman; Chris and Gloria Oates of COGO Productions; Gail Holland; Karen Davis; Cheryl Bradley and Lorne Fitch; Jim Spurrill; Sudaene Warren; Joan Stebbins, Curator, and Marilyn Smith, Director, and all staff of the Southern Alberta Art Gallery; Adriane Cooke; Fred Greene; Dr. Ches Skinner; Robert Bogle and Dr. Lissel Lewke-Bogle; Pat Horrocks; Brian Kenwood of Advance Glass,; Stephen Smart; Chris Kitzan; Wally and Dee Ryrie; Brian Bourassa; Sheila Buelow; Debra Scott; Madelaine Lukenda; Barbara Lacey; Stan Perrot; Bob and Kathy Wilson; Margaret Lewis; Travis Coleman; Phyllis McClafferty; Kathy and Bob Wilson; R.J. Konefall and family; Joan and Sig Weiser; Liz Allen; Andie Wicherts; Jean Pilch; Brent Laycock; Debbie Orr; Bob Webb; Barb Martin; Dr. Ray Huel; Dr. James Penton; Dr. William Baker; Dr. James Tagg; Pauline McGeorge; Herb Hicks; Bob Hicks; Charlie Crane; Carl Granslow; Dr. Josephine Mills; John Daminato; Juanita Willis; Karin Richter; Shirley Wyngaard, Suzanne Lint and the staff of the Bowman Arts Centre; Linda Carney; Allen Jensen; Claudette Kettle; Dr. Ed Langford; Don Frache and Irene McCaugherty.

–KB

Thanks to Karen, whose vision was the force behind this book. Thanks also to all those who gave their financial support to the book; to Ms. Jane Ross and Dr. Daniel Gallacher for their written contributions; to Dennis Johnson and the staff of Red Deer Press for realizing the finished project; to The Provincial Archives of Alberta, which was a rich source of local history; and to Sheila, my wife, who provided invaluable editorial insights. Her interest in my work and unfailing support were, as always, an inspiration.

–KT

Foreword

–Jane Ross
Curator
Western Canadian History
Royal Museum of Alberta

Over the past decades Western Canada has undergone sweeping changes. Barely noticeable at first, but then with an accelerated pace, these changes have worked to alter the nature of our rural societies. Most pronounced have been the demographic and economic shifts that saw our rural population rooted in a traditional wheat-based economy move increasingly to the burgeoning cities whose economies are largely dependent upon the oil and gas industries and their spin-offs. New technologies that allow for bigger and bigger farms, better access to higher education and skills training, and the resultant plethora of jobs outside of the farm-based service sector have combined to pull young people to the urban centres and to reduce dramatically the number of farms. The traditional prairie economy and lifestyle have been further decimated by a host of government and corporate decisions such as NAFTA, continued rail line abandonment, the closure and demolition of the country grain elevators in favor of new centralized terminals, the disbanding of marketing boards once created to protect the family farm by ensuring equitable access to markets and fair market prices and, not least of all, the 1995 cancellation of the Crow Rate, a subsidy to the railways that reduced the producers' cost of grain shipping. These upheavals are felt not only in the farmyards and farmhouses across Alberta, but in our communities, where they signal irrevocable changes. The regionalizing of services such as schools, hospitals and post offices further encourages the move to larger centres. The result is a landscape emptied of small family farms and sleepy hamlets. The depopulation of the countryside places the remaining communities and farm families at risk as the social capital—the communally shared knowledge and skills—and networks wither.

Karen Brownlee recognizes the pressures that are remolding traditional prairie farms and communities. I first became aware of her ties to the land, to small town life and to a lifestyle we have all taken for granted and which has all but disappeared while curating the exhibit "Finding Our Way Home: Alberta's Disappearing Grain Elevators" at the Royal Museum of Alberta in 1997–98. In addition to a select number of photographs that illustrated themes I wanted to explore and artworks by other artists and artisans, I wished to underline the importance of the grain elevator within the context of their communities and as a symbol of a passing way of life. I was immediately taken with Karen's ability to capture the moment in her renditions of everyday occurrences in our towns and villages, whether it be a parade down main street, shopping at the Co-op or enjoying a cappuccino at an old heritage railway station.

Karen and I discussed the richness of community life. We pondered the future of our small towns. And I was delighted when Karen's enthusiasm for the project resulted in the first 22 watercolours of what is now her Rural Prairie Communities series. By illustrating everyday scenes characteristic of almost any small town in Alberta, she has documented not only the passing symbol and architectural form of the grain elevator, but, perhaps more importantly, a way of life now threatened by outside influences and decisions. While rural societies now often feel impotent and frustrated, Karen's paintings, with their bright, vivid colours, also capture the resilient spirit of the farming communities and their determination to not only survive, but thrive. For the majority of Albertans who live in cities and whose way of life seems so far removed from our country neighbours, Karen's paintings remind us of our society's roots and what is valuable in life: a sense of community and a feeling of belonging.

Foreword

My search for grain elevator images to include in the Canadian Museum of Civilization's *Canada Hall* permanent exhibition led me to Karen Brownlee's paintings. Initially, our need was for pictures of the historical prairies, including landscapes and buildings. The original curator, Steve Prystupa, aimed at variety rather than stereotypes to depict Canada's western interior and thus amassed a diverse collection of potential photographs, drawings, paintings and other elements.

As our research took a sharper focus due to both storyline and space constraints, Steve and the designer, Ian Gregory, culled those images that caught the essence of smaller communities. Because their ultimate display structure would be a full-scale grain elevator *circa* 1939 complete with didactic and interpretative exhibits, it struck me that we also needed special artwork that would focus on such buildings yet contain additional subject matter. About then, Karen Brownlee's Rural Prairie Communities series came to my attention in artnote form, and I saw immediately how her work could fill that gap. Curating the exhibit had fallen to me, and I contacted Karen, who, in turn, generously provided us with a complete set of 35mm slides of her paintings for both study and display consideration.

Having been born in Alberta and having spent boyhood summers largely at Clover Bar with my grandparents on the Canadian National mainline east of Edmonton, I had strong memories of small prairie towns. A special recollection was seeing the elevators looming up from the horizon whenever I could hitch a ride on my grandfather's railway speeder. The huge red structures and close-by town would flash alongside, only to drop away behind us—wondrous indeed! Karen's watercolours not only captured such locales, but took me back five decades and more.

Still, my task was history, not simply nostalgia. The *Canada Hall* is organized along geographical and chronological lines, and is underpinned by sociocultural and socioeconomic experiences. Its theme structure and storyline elements focus chiefly upon ordinary people and everyday life, from the earliest settlers in New France to modern-day inhabitants of our western shores and northern territories. Wilderness, frontiers, rural settings and urban life are portrayed historically for each major region of our country, including the Prairie West, housed in our grain elevator with its extensive displays entitled "King Wheat."

In examining Karen's work, I saw clearly that it was devoted to much more than a record of grain elevators, no matter their importance; it was the unique small town settings she also included that really attracted me and my colleagues to her art. Karen Brownlee's paintings mark the zenith of small towns in Alberta while foreshadowing, through the prominence of elevators in each picture, a main element of community decline and even disappearance. She was inspired to paint these locales by the loss to prairie producers of the Crow's Nest Pass Agreement that, since 1897, had held the CPR to reduced freight rates on eastbound wheat and westbound flour and settlers' effects. Whatever long-term effect this dramatic change will have on the prairie economy is not yet known, but it certainly has hurried the elimination of branch lines serving small towns, and with the rails gone, the elevators, worth only salvage now, are demolished, too.

Once the elevators are gone and grain is hauled to larger and more distant handling centres, one important economic reason for the existence of small towns is lost. After the elevators are gone, it can only be a matter of time before other businesses and services decline. Karen's watercolours feature all these elements of small town economic and social life, and they provide definitive documents of a place and time that are highly valuable references as well as extremely pleasing visual art. We included adapted examples of Karen's watercolours in the exhibit. We hope as well to show some of her originals in the "Acres of Dreams: Settling the Canadian Prairies" displays commemorating Alberta and Saskatchewan becoming provinces in 1905, and ultimately to add a selection of her work in the Canada Hall web site. This book—a tremendous record of Karen's contribution to our knowledge, recollection, understanding and feeling about the nation's small communities—is a wonderful resource.

–Daniel T. Gallacher, Ph.D.
Curator Emeritus
Canadian Museum of Civilization

Introduction

–Ken Tingley

Brocket

Brocket is a hamlet about 15 kilometres northeast of Pincher Creek in southwestern Alberta. The Canadian Pacific Railway (CPR) established a station there in 1897–98 along the Crowsnest Pass route to the Pacific coast. It was named for Brocket Hall, the English seat of Lord Mount Stephens, the famous director and financier of the CPR. For over a century, the grain elevator was a feature of Brocket, a focus of commercial and social activity, and a landmark overlooking the Oldman River winding through its deep valley below.

As my wife and I passed through Brocket on a summer trip west to the Rockies, we suddenly noticed that something was very different. Looking back, we realized that where there had once been an elevator, now there was only open Alberta sky. We both felt a little shock at the sudden loss of that familiar landmark.

For decades grain elevators like the one at Brocket have been disappearing from prairie communities all over the West. Thousands of prairie people have felt that same mixture of sadness and resignation we felt on looking back at the town. For many, these elevators were an integral part of their lives and a potent element of their memories of growing up and struggling with the land to make a go of it. Ironically, many of the towns that no longer possess a grain elevator sport its image on their welcome signs at the side of the highway or on their chamber of commerce literature.

Small town elevators owed their existence to the Crow's Nest Pass Agreement of 1897, which established fixed rates for the movement of grain on the prairies. When the Crow Rate was abolished in 1995, Alberta artist Karen Brownlee immediately recognized that it would inevitably lead to the abandonment of branch lines, the loss of grain elevators and the irrevocable transformation of the character of the western towns that had grown up along the railways and around the elevators for a century.

In many ways the 20th century had made western Canada, transforming it from the sinecure and hinterland of the fur trading companies to the "last best west" of settlement and agricultural growth. The grain elevator was the symbol and physical reality of that transformation. Karen Brownlee set out to capture the spirit of small town life in Alberta before the sweeping changes following the loss of the Crow Rate took hold. The result was her ambitious Rural Prairie Communities series of paintings. That series is the subject and essence of this book.

Early History of Elevators

Elevators are inextricably woven into the fabric of prairie development. Before their wide-scale introduction, transporting grain from the West was a difficult and complex undertaking. The first recorded shipment of wheat from the prairies occurred in 1876 when R.C. Steele of Toronto, one of the founders of the Steele, Briggs Seed Company, travelled to Winnipeg to purchase seed wheat. Although he needed 5,000 bushels, he was able to purchase only 857. His purchase was sacked and shipped through a circuitous route south from Winnipeg by steamer on the Red River to Fisher's Landing in Minnesota, where it was taken by rail to Duluth, by boat to Sarnia and finally by rail to Toronto. Shipments of wheat to Great Britain, the first exports of Manitoba wheat, were made in 1878–79, again using the Red River and American railway lines. With the completion of the Canadian Pacific Railway from Port Arthur to Winnipeg in 1883, James Richardson & Sons shipped the first cargo of wheat, 10,000 bushels, from Port Arthur to Owen Sound. The Canadian Pacific Railway began the construction of a terminal elevator at Port Arthur that year and completed it in early 1884. In 1884 the first sacked shipment of 1,000 bushels of No. 1 Manitoba Hard wheat was carried over the all-Canadian route to the East Coast.

The prairie provinces emerged relatively suddenly with the transfer in 1870 of Rupert's Land and the Northwest Territories from the Hudson's Bay Company to the newly formed Dominion of Canada. The instruments of government and orderly development arrived before most settlers did. After 1869 the surveyors with the Dominion Land Survey created a matrix of townships and ranges west of the First Meridian. This Herculean task was followed by the creation of the North-West Mounted Police to bring law and order to the West and the extension of a transcontinental railway to transport settlers and their effects.

Harold Adams Innis observed that settlement in the Canadian West "differs fundamentally from settlement in Eastern Canada and in the old world." Much settlement preceded the railroad in the East, but in the West,

> [u]rban centers were created in direct relation to the railroads and the convenience of elevators for grain shipment, e.g., approximately eight miles apart with loading platforms four miles. These centers became distributing points for supplies, e.g., agricultural implements, lumber, coal and general merchandise. Larger centers flourished at divisional points located approximately 110 to 130 miles apart, depending on accessibility of water and the efficiency of engines, at which point engines and train crews were changed. The largest centers were dependent on the location of branch lines and junction points, of terminal points, and the stimulus to population afforded by government buildings, educational facilities, and wholesale houses. . . .[1]

With the framework of survey and railway lines in place, orderly development could follow, and the stage was set for the great wheat boom and for the coming of the grain elevator and all that it would ultimately come to symbolize for the West's rural population.

Elevators in the Rural Prairie Community

Before the advent of the grain elevator, farmers hauled their grain to loading platforms or warehouses along rail lines to await the availability of boxcars to transport it east. Loading platforms were simple timber shelters with earth ramps constructed beside local sidings. Platforms were constructed at the height of the floor of a boxcar, which could be "spotted" alongside to allow a farmer to shovel grain directly from his wagon. Warehouses were basic flat sheds containing low bins in which grain could be stored for later transport by rail.

These early grain-handling facilities allowed the first wheat farmers to build up carload quantities of grain at sidings in the expectation of the arrival of railcars. They were cheap to build and provided shelter from the weather, but grain could be loaded in or out of these early storage facilities only by shovel or manpowered truck. They were primitive measures that soon proved inadequate to meet the rising tide of western wheat following the completion of the Canadian Pacific Railway across the western Canadian plains. Mechanization of grain handling was needed to exploit the rich agricultural resources of the prairies.

Efficient handling of large volumes of grain came with the development of the grain elevator, which combined larger storage capacity with mechanized processing. The traditional grain elevator so well known to prairie dwellers was typically a narrow 70- to 80-foot tall warehouse containing 16–18 bins for storing 25,000 to 35,000 bushels of grain, though later examples would house up to 100,000 bushels. Constructed of thick, stacked planks to withstand the enormous pressure of thousands of tons of grain, they were erected on concrete foundations with amazing speed by crews travelling from town to town as the wheat economy boomed.

At the heart of the elevator's grain handling system were metal cups attached to a power-driven vertical belt that "elevated" grain to the building's distinctive gable, where gravity would deposit it into tall bins through spouts operated from

[1]H.A. Innis, cited in G.E. Britnell, *The Wheat Economy.* Toronto: University of Toronto Press, 1939.

below. In the most simple terms, an elevator's basic features, in addition to the elevating "leg," are storage bins, a weighing and unloading platform with a receiving hopper under it, and a hopper-weigher for loading railcars. This entire assembly became known as a grain elevator, or just an elevator.

The Canadian Pacific Railway, wishing to exploit the vast agricultural resources of the West but not wishing to launch another costly building program, offered free leases and shipping monopolies to those agreeing to construct elevators with a minimum capacity of 25,000 bushels. Given this inducement, elevators sprang up quickly along railway mainlines and branch lines. By 1913 elevator design had become standardized into its classic form, the defining element in the West, breaking the skyline in a way that would become familiar to generations of western Canadians. By 1938 some 5,700 elevators would dot the prairie landscape, one every 8–10 miles along the railway lines. Though some elevators were operated by individual proprietors, they were more commonly owned by large corporations. These became known as line elevators.

Along with granting monopolies to the line elevator companies, the CPR prohibited the use of the old flat warehouses for grain storage and refused farmers the opportunity to load their wheat from loading platforms. Railway "blockades," or car shortages, were another instrument used by the CPR to reinforce the line elevator companies' control of the grain trade. It was not uncommon for independent operators to be denied railcars, forcing their customers back to the line elevators. Farmers were thus compelled to accept the line elevator companies' price, grades and dockage. Hugh Boyd, in his classic *New Breaking,* describes the outcome of the CPR's concessions to the line elevator companies:

> Private interests were glad to accept, for they were given free sites. Moreover, the railway undertook not to allow loading of cars through flat warehouses or direct from farmers' wagons; the elevator got all the business. By the close of the century 447 country elevators were operating, 281 of them being owned by five companies. . . . The coming of these elevators would have been most welcome to Western farmers but for the privileges under which they carried on. The grower no longer had any choice in the matter: the elevator bought his grain or stored it, in either case on its own terms. And the charges for storage he considered much too high. Seldom now could he get a "special bin" so as to preserve the identity of his own grain until he was ready to ship it east and obtain the inspector's official grading; instead he had to accept whatever grade the local operator offered him.
>
> Then, too, the elevator firm combined warehousing and dealing in a way which aroused the grower's indignation still more. Revenue from handling was not thought sufficient for a company's welfare, so most elevators speculated as a profitable sideline, buying from a host of farmers who needed cash badly, and later, when the market had recovered from the usual fall pressure, selling at a higher price.
>
> Competition, it was said, ensured fair dealing, but farmers were skeptical. At single elevator points they had to agree to whatever price, grade and dockage were set by the buyer or else drive a weary journey to some other point. But even where more than one company was represented, the suspicion grew in farmers' minds that local prices were really set daily by a conference of elevator men at Winnipeg, and that occasionally better prices or grades were made up by overdocking or shortweighing.
>
> A few farmers here and there tried to run local elevators for themselves. This was an early attempt at co-operative business, but it did not go far enough. . . .[2]

[2]D.J. Hall, "The Manitoba Grain Act: An Agrarian Magna Charta," *Prairie Forum,* Volume 4, No. 1 (Spring 1979), pp. 105–120.

Throughout the early years of grain elevator proliferation, the volume of grain transported by the railways rose dramatically. In 1886 they carried only about 11 million bushels from the West. This amount doubled in the next four years and quadrupled by 1899. Farmers chafed under the shortcomings of an inadequate system and the monopoly power of the private line elevator companies:

> By 1899 resistance to what was considered by most settlers in the West as an unacceptable situation led to the establishment of a Royal Commission. This in turn led to passage of the Manitoba Grain Act in 1900. This legislation allowed the building of flat warehouses, instructed the railways to provide loading platforms at shipping points, and called for the fair distribution of box cars to all those who required them, and not just those dealing with the line companies. The railways managed to frequently provide more than their fair share of cars to the private elevator companies. Finally, in 1902 and 1903, the Manitoba Grain Act was strengthened through amendments. Thereafter, it was sometimes referred to as "the Agrarian Magna Charta."[3]

In spite of legislation, by 1905, the year Alberta and Saskatchewan gained provincial status, the private line elevator companies had captured almost complete control of the grain trade at country points. Thus, in the earliest days of agricultural settlement in the West, the elevator was more a symbol of the oppression of the farmer by the vested interests of the CPR, the grain traders and the line elevator companies than a symbol of progress and prosperity. Historian Vernon Fowke concluded that elevators were a great improvement over flat warehouses and loading platforms, but that "paradoxically, the rapid construction of elevators throughout the West immediately prior to the turn of the century was accompanied by an intensification of dissatisfaction with grain handling facilities and by an accumulation of distrust of their operators." Fowke listed the litany of complaints against line elevator agents:

> Against the local elevators the allegations were of short weight, excessive dockage, improper grading, unduly low prices, refusal to provide special bins, the mixing and substitution of grain, and other minor malpractices. Informants were of two opinions on the responsibility for such actions. Some held that the actions were performed by the local elevator operator on the basis of instructions from the head office of his company. Others regarded them as the sole responsibility of the local operator. The belief was common that the local agent was under such pressure from his employer to make his elevator show a profit that various sharp practices were inevitable.[4]

It would not be until the development of farmer-owned cooperatives that the elevator would be transformed into a more benign symbol of prosperity for Western Canadians.

The fight between the farmers and the line elevator companies became the stuff of legend. In 1901, after years of widespread frustration with dubious attempts to provide viable alternatives to the line elevator companies, the Territorial Grain Growers Association (TGGA) was formed to promote farmers' interests. The TGGA proved to be the first effective agrarian organization on the prairies. Through the leadership of men like E.A. Partridge, the Grain Growers' Grain Company (GGGC) was established in 1906 as the first farmer-owned cooperative on the prairies. Partridge excoriated the Winnipeg Grain Exchange as "the house with the closed shutters," a combine "with a gambling hell thrown in." In 1910 GGGC agitation led to the acceptance of the so-called Partridge Plan that called for government-owned elevators in Manitoba to break the monopoly of the line

[3]D.J. Hall, "The Manitoba Grain Act: An Agrarian Magna Charta," *Prairie Forum,* Volume 4, No. 1 (Spring 1979), pp. 105–120.

[4]Vernon Fowke, *National Policy and the Wheat Economy.* Toronto: University of Toronto Press, 1957.

companies. When the Partridge Plan failed for a variety of reasons, Manitoba's 170 elevators were leased back to the GGGC. The Saskatchewan arm of the GGGC, the Saskatchewan Co-operative Elevator Company, was formed in 1911 with ownership and control vested in the farmers' hands. In 1913–14 the Alberta Farmers' Co-operative Elevator Company (AFCE) followed suit with the province providing 85 percent of the capital to build elevators and guarantee bonds.

In 1915, with the Great War raging and wheat farmers struggling to meet the wartime demand for grain, a movement emerged to amalgamate the GGGC organizations in the three provinces. In 1917 the GGGC and the AFCE merged to form the United Grain Growers. By 1923 the UGG and the Saskatchewan Co-operative Elevator Company were operating some 900 grain elevators.

The Crow's Nest Pass Agreement

Located far from the commercial centre of Canada, wheat farmers felt isolated and victimized by the line elevator companies and railways. The line elevators set the price of grain. The railways set the price of transportation. To alleviate some farmer concerns, government ratified the Crow's Nest Pass Agreement in 1897. Rich mineral deposits were being developed in the Kootenay district of British Columbia at the time, and the CPR wished to extend its lines through the southern pass into the region. In exchange for this right and $3.4 million, the CPR agreed to reduce in perpetuity the freight rates on wheat and flour shipments to central Canadian markets as well as settlers effects and farm machinery being shipped to the booming agricultural West. In subsequent years, western grain farmers came to depend upon this benefit for which they had fought so hard. Vernon Fowke called it possibly the single most important political and economic fact of the Canadian wheat economy in its day. However, it is important to recall that it never was a farm subsidy: "on the contrary, it was designed to stimulate settlement and the production of exports for the benefit of the commercial interest of central Canada."[5]

[5]Vernon Fowke, *National Policy and the Wheat Economy.* Toronto: University of Toronto Press, 1957.

The plan to cancel the Crow Rate, which many in the West regarded as merely a scheme to divide farmers and bribe grain companies, involved a one-time payment to farmers of $25 per acre and railway incentive loading rates to grain companies on multiple-car unit trains. The cancellation of the Crow Rate effectively spelled the demise of small communities on branch lines that did not possess grain terminals, hospitals, schools and proactive municipal governments that could offer incentives to attract businesses to their communities.

In the southwest agricultural region of Alberta, very few communities have any prospects for growth in the future. Medicine Hat, Taber, Bow Island and Brooks survive, while 36 other communities have languished. An example of the adverse influence of rail deregulation is found in Empress, Alberta. On July 31, 1995, the community boasted a population of over 300, two wooden crib elevators (Alberta Wheat Pool and Pioneer Grain), a hospital and a school. Today the rail line and the elevators are gone, the hospital and school have closed, and less than 100 people remain—all the result of the cancellation of the Crow Rate.

The Wheat Pools

Developments in farmer-owned grain handling cooperatives and government-legislated freight rates were paralleled by experiments in government control of marketing. During the last years of the First World War, Canadian wheat export was controlled by the Wheat Export Company, which represented the British government, while a federally appointed Board of Grain Supervisors set grain prices. In 1919 the Canadian government replaced the Wheat Export Company with the Canadian Wheat Board, but the Wheat Board ceased to exist almost as quickly as it was formed when the government bowed to pressure from private grain traders to deregulate. Wheat prices on the Winnipeg Grain Exchange rose to $2.85 per bushel before plummeting in the deregulated market to just $1.07 in 1923. Having expanded their operations to meet wartime demand, prairie farmers were mired in debt, while inflation drove up prices on goods and machinery, and interest rates rose as high as 10 percent.

Prairie farmers promoted the renewal of the Canadian Wheat Board to support prices through the Council of Canadian Agriculture (CCA). In 1920 a CCA committee recommended that a central wheat purchasing pool be established similar to those used in the states of Washington, Idaho and Oregon by non-stock, non-profit cooperative wheat pools.[6] The object was to establish a system of national control to avoid the price declines that inevitably resulted from the over-selling of grain during the peak delivery time of harvest. That year conventions of all three provincial farmers' organizations on the prairies endorsed the CCA proposal. The legislatures of Alberta and Saskatchewan passed an act to push for a federal wheat board, but the Government of Manitoba, home of the Grain Exchange, declined to join the effort.

In 1923 the United Farmers of Alberta (UFA) determined to proceed on its own to reduce the distress of the province's farmers. Under pressure from the organization, a committee representing the UFA, the unorganized farmers, the press, the government, the banks and other interested groups began a membership drive with the goal of subscribing 50 percent of Alberta wheat acreage, a target easily achieved. The line elevator companies bowed to the inevitable and agreed to handle Pool wheat in a manner similar to that used by the Canadian Wheat Board in 1919. On October 19, 1923, the Alberta Wheat Pool opened for business, the first such endeavor in Canada. Its first year was successful, and the pool marketed over 34 million bushels of wheat at a cost of half a cent per bushel. The Wheat Pool began to purchase or construct local Pool elevators, which, by the 1960s, would number over 500. The success of the Alberta Wheat Pool encouraged the governments of Saskatchewan and Manitoba to establish Wheat Pools.

By 1928, with Pool organization essentially complete, the combined revenues of the Alberta, Saskatchewan and Manitoba Wheat Pools reached $323 million, making them collectively the biggest business in the nation and the largest grain-selling enterprise in the world. Membership in the three Wheat Pools would eventually climb to 140,000 farmers delivering wheat from 25,000 square miles to 1642 elevators.

The Esther Elevator: The Last of the First

The Esther grain elevator is the last of the first three Alberta Wheat Pool elevators raised in 1923. It is located in the Sounding Creek basin, a borderline farming district where crops have been uncertain for much of its history. Railways first opened the Sounding Creek area in 1910, when the CPR began building its branch line east from Lacombe to Coronation. During 1911–12 the Grand Trunk Pacific Branch Lines Company built its Dodsland Subdivision from Biggar to Loverna, Saskatchewan, directly east of Sounding Creek Flat. These drew the first settlers into this marginal area, which was quickly occupied by homesteaders.

One settler recalled how wartime premium prices for wheat drove the Sounding Creek economy. "We went at it in earnest and bought more horses and machinery. We had excellent crops, which we sold at a fair price. We figured that this was a Garden of Eden."[7] Despite such high hopes and a bumper crop in 1916, direct railway access was unavailable. With no elevator, the biggest problem remained the long hauls to distant shipping points. One farmer later remembered that "it was a mad rush every fall to get the grain to Loverna, before the price fell too badly and horses had to be shod to climb the slippery hills."[8] When post-war grain prices plummeted, the district around Esther became a very strong early

[6] Alberta Co-operative Wheat Producers Ltd., *Pooling Alberta's Wheat.* Calgary: Alberta Co-operative Wheat Producers Ltd., 1928, p. 7

[7] Ken Tingley, *Alberta Wheat Pool Elevator No. 3, Esther, Alberta, 1925–1979.* Edmonton: Alberta Culture, Historic Sites Service, 1982.

[8] *Ibid.*

supporter of the United Farmers of Alberta and the Alberta Wheat Pool. Organizer Aaron Sapiro gained enthusiastic support, and demands for railways, elevators and improved marketing became stronger by the year. It was this conjunction of climatic, political and cooperative events that focused attention on what was otherwise a rather isolated part of Alberta and led to the construction of Canada's first Wheat Pool elevators at Leo, Naco–Sedalia and Esther.

In 1925 a 40,000 bushel elevator was constructed by Voss Brothers at Esther based on a plan provided by James Miller of United Grain Growers. Sy Ness became the first agent. When the elevator opened for business in October, 60 loads were delivered the first day, with teams lined up for some time to await the official opening.

The Esther elevator rapidly became the economic core of the area, a very visible bulwark against the increasing distress besetting the region during the Depression. It closed only briefly in the summer of 1937, although it handled a meager 1,205 bushels the next season.

After the Second World War, the Esther elevator reached its peak of productivity with the addition of balloon annexes in 1940 and 1956. However, with the closure of the railway branch line in 1979, the elevator closed. Today it remains a stark yet dignified reminder of the importance of the elevator in prairie society, one of perhaps less than 1,000 still in existence. That number continues to decline as more small, aging country elevators are demolished to make way for in-land grain handling terminals, those concrete behemoths that many regard as a blot on the landscape.

The prairie grain elevator—variously dubbed the Prairie Giant, the Prairie Sentinel, the Gibraltar of the Prairies and the Castle of the New World—remains today largely a memory of a once proud prairie tradition. Almost daily it seems that another demolition crew arrives at another country elevator. More often than not, the entire community gathers to witness the fall of what was not simply a grain storage facility, but a place to meet and greet neighbours, a place of pride and accomplishment, and a place that more than any other encapsulated the soul of rural prairie experience.

The Making of an Artist

Karen Brownlee has roots in southwestern Alberta stretching back to 1893 when her great-grandmother immigrated to Lethbridge from Czechoslovakia. Karen's mother grew up on a farm near Coaldale, in the Readymade district, while both her husband, Ray, and his parents before him, were raised around Lucky Strike. Karen's parents, Mike and Irene Hazuda, were married after her father returned from overseas service in 1946. For four years he worked on farms around Coaldale and in 1951 bought a farm near the town. Karen Mary Hazuda and her sister, Connie Jane, were born before the family moved again in 1958, this time to the Sunnyside area.

Karen, now living in Lethbridge, received her Bachelor of Arts degree in clinical psychology with a minor in art in 1976 from the University of Lethbridge. She then broadened and deepened her technique through art studies at the University of Lethbridge, Lethbridge Community College and the Lethbridge Sketch Club. Karen was introduced to Sumi brush painting through a drawing class taught by Pauline McGeorge at the University of Lethbridge, where she discovered that Oriental painting techniques seemed to most reflect her temperament. While experimenting with various media such as conte, drawing pencils and the Chinese brush, she found herself particularly attracted to the brush and found her images becoming stronger. Training in Oriental brush technique was very structured, and this was satisfactory at the time. She then worked for a number of years under the guidance of Laotian Master Thep Thavonsouk and Hong Kong Master Chien Shek, both gifted teachers of the art of Chinese brush painting.

Karen worked with the bamboo and orchid brush to render lines of varying thickness, depending upon delicate differences in pressure applied to the brush. She also used the flower and bird brush to create form and wash. She painted on special papers including rice paper, Hsuan paper, an unsized handmade Chinese paper used for flower and bird paintings, Kozo paper used for washes and landscapes, and Casen paper, a thin unsized paper used for flower and bird paintings. These apprenticeship years spent studying northern Chinese and modern Taiwanese styles would greatly influence her later style.

Karen's first important show, "Images in Ink," consisting of 27 images, opened at the Bowman Arts Centre in Lethbridge in February 1982 and moved to the Red Deer and District Museum and Archives in October of that year. All her subjects were taken from nature and included landscapes, bamboo, studies of grapes, leaves and flowers, and shrimps, all rendered in Chinese ink, watercolour and natural pigment.

Karen's "Full Bodied Peony" was singled out by one reviewer. "Its petals are like pink explosions of mist, intense at the core and lighter near their edges, especially delightful when one views them from about a metre away."[9] At the Bowman show, "Coast Landscape (No. 103)" was described as "a reflection of her inner self, rather than an actual vista. The complicated and time-consuming process of repeated washes is carefully controlled without getting in the way of imagination, resulting in a delicate and timelessly elegant work."[10]

Karen held her first Edmonton show in September 1982 at the Shadows Gallery in Walden's Restaurant, exhibiting more paintings in the Chinese tradition. Soon Karen's paintings would appear in other solo and group exhibitions and juried shows in various Alberta communities, and her works would be purchased by the Alberta Foundation for the Arts and by a number of private collections.

Reflecting on those early years, Karen concluded:

> I think the concept I took away from Chinese brush was contrast. With Chinese brush painting you could have just black on white, but to render western perspective and depth, you almost need three values—white, grey and black. I think, generally speaking, my work is quite high contrast as a result of my training in Chinese techniques.

The high contrast of her presentation, her sense of composition and her techniques are lasting legacies of this early period of exposure to the rigorous standards of Chinese brushwork. The Chinese ideal of artistic expression elevating the artist above the merely commercial and encouraging the artist's personal growth and enlightenment also seem to have been introduced into her art at this time. This ideal continued to suffuse her work as she moved increasingly to watercolours and to subjects in her immediate environment. She notes:

> I guess I'm caught between traditional western painting and the Chinese brush painting with respect to ideas such as enlightenment and familiarity. I was told, for example, that one master spent his whole life becoming very, very good at painting orchids. In western culture few artists paint just one subject, but with that long familiarity with a subject comes the ability to find beauty and enlightenment in your immediate surroundings. You bond with that place in a dialogue that happens after investigation, observation and being there for an extended period of time. For example, when I started to paint on the beach in Waterton, the first day I didn't paint a lot because I was still getting a sense of space and place. It's like an accommodation that happens between the artist and the subject. I find that the more I become

[9]Kathleen Engman, *The* [Red Deer] *Advocate*, 9 October 1982

[10]Otto Rapp, Review, *The Lethbridge Herald*, 17 February 1982

> familiar with my subjects, the more I can express my love for them. I don't tire of them; they don't become redundant or repetitious, even though the forms may remain the same. Painting the elevators in my Rural Prairie Communities series has been an exercise in familiarity. One element of the composition remains constant, but each day the light striking the scene is different. Each day I feel the joy of getting closer and closer to my subject.

As the forces of globalization transform our landscape, Karen Brownlee shows us in her paintings what the rural human landscape means today and has meant in the past. Within the sense of loss implicit in her painting is a countervailing optimism. When you view her paintings, you see more than the apparently doomed elevators. You see rural prairie communities in their many and varied dimensions. In many of the communities, a generational continuity is evident. The elderly stroll along the streets, children play in the parks, farmers and merchants talk under the trees. The viewer feels that surely there will always be such people to carry on.

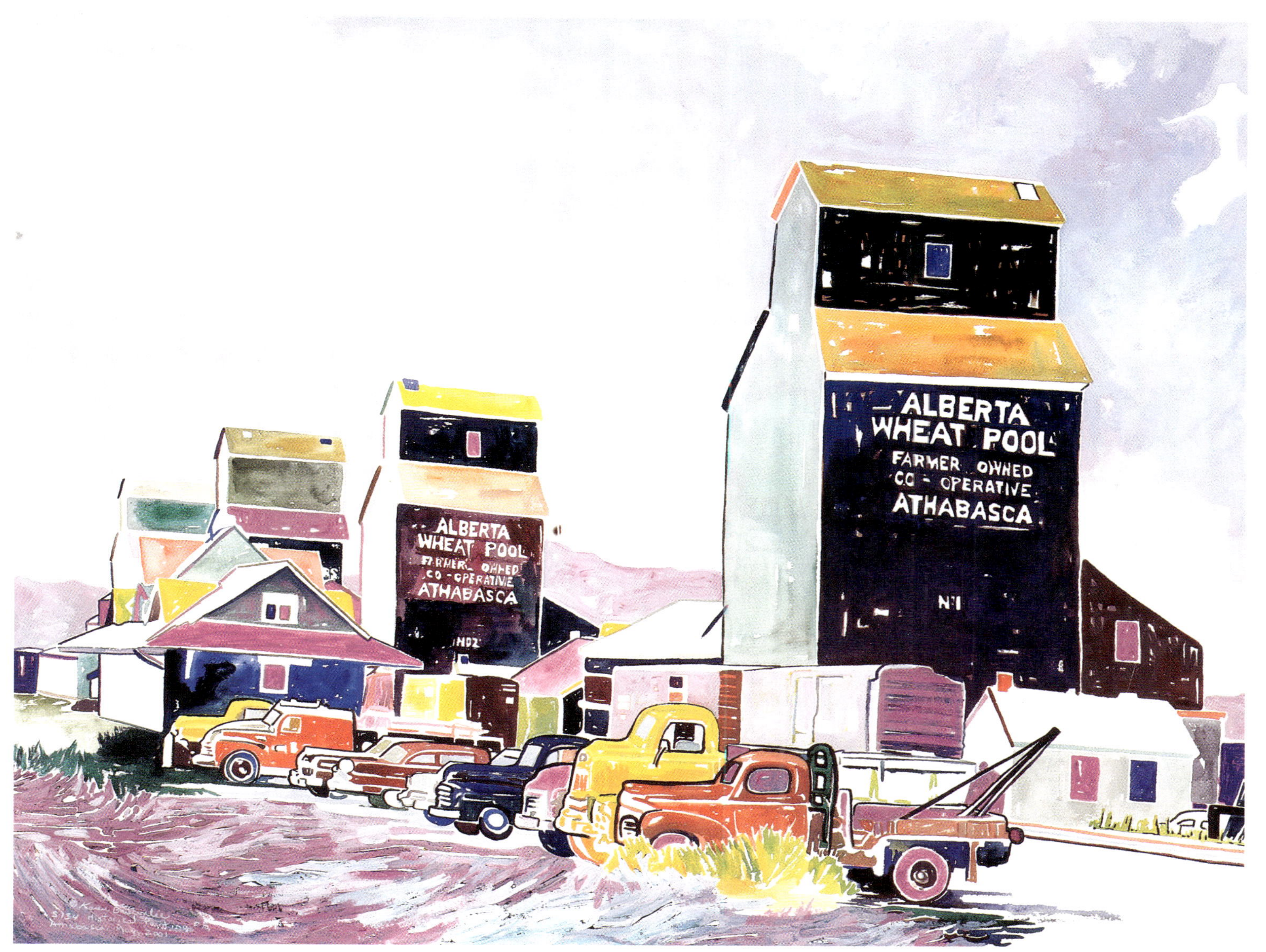

Athabasca Landing, the place where goods were transfered to riverboats for transport further north, was renamed Athabasca in 1913. The area, depicted here after the Second World War, was an important agricultural centre. A local member of the provincial government, J.R. Boyle, organized the establishing of Alberta's seventh and last demonstration farm near here in 1912.

Historical Painting #10, Athabasca, 2001, 28" x 21", Provincial Archives of Alberta, Public Affairs Bureau Pa. 147/3.

Agricore and United Grain Growers, large grain handling companies, merged in 2001. Communities lost elevators in the consolidation. In 2002 the *Smoky Lake Signal* noted that citizens wanted to preserve the one remaining elevator, a reminder of the many that once graced the town's skyline, as indicated in this impression of earlier times in Smoky Lake.

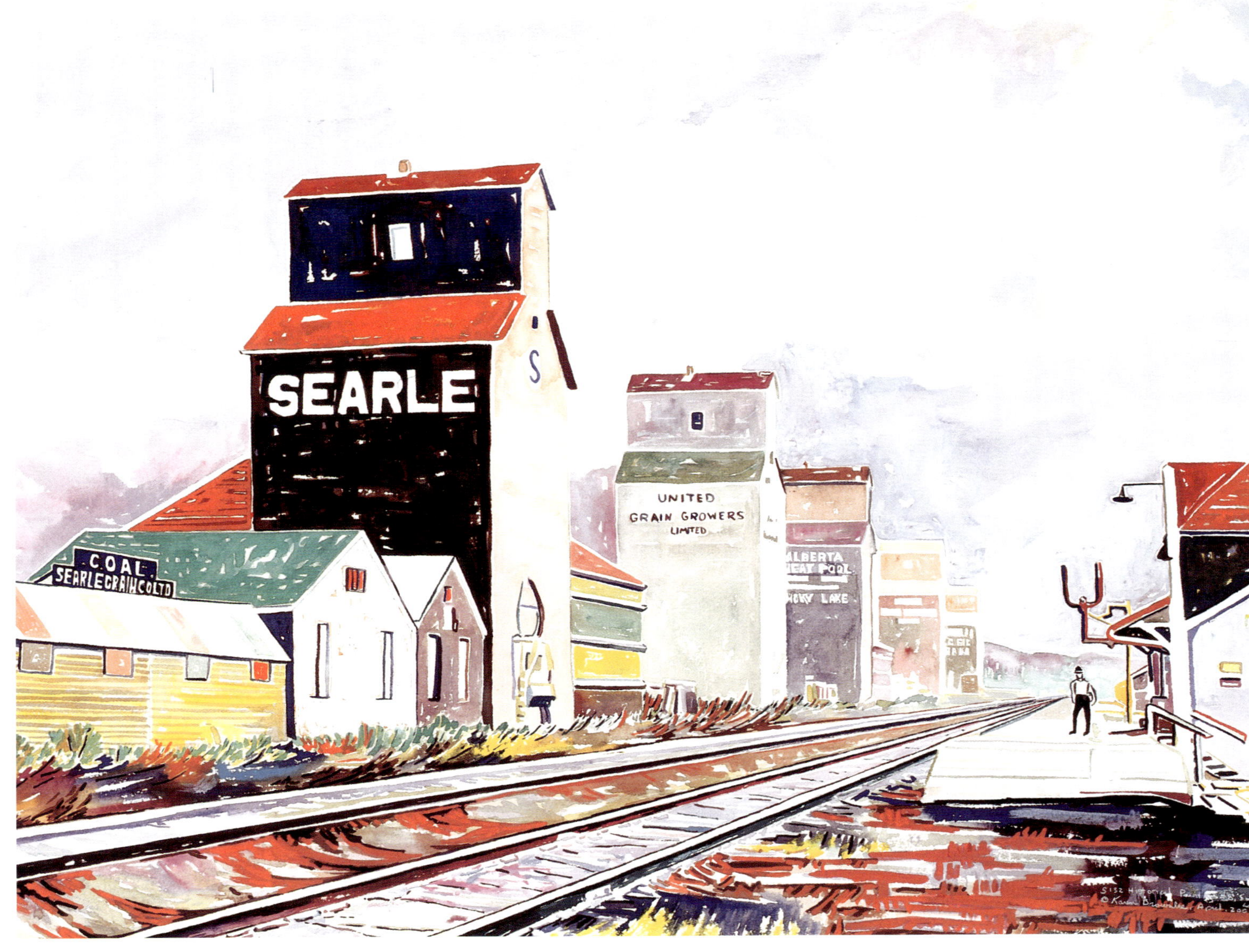

Historical Painting #8, Smoky Lake, 2001, 28" x 21", Provincial Archives of Alberta, Nicholas Gavinchuk Fonds G. 2811.

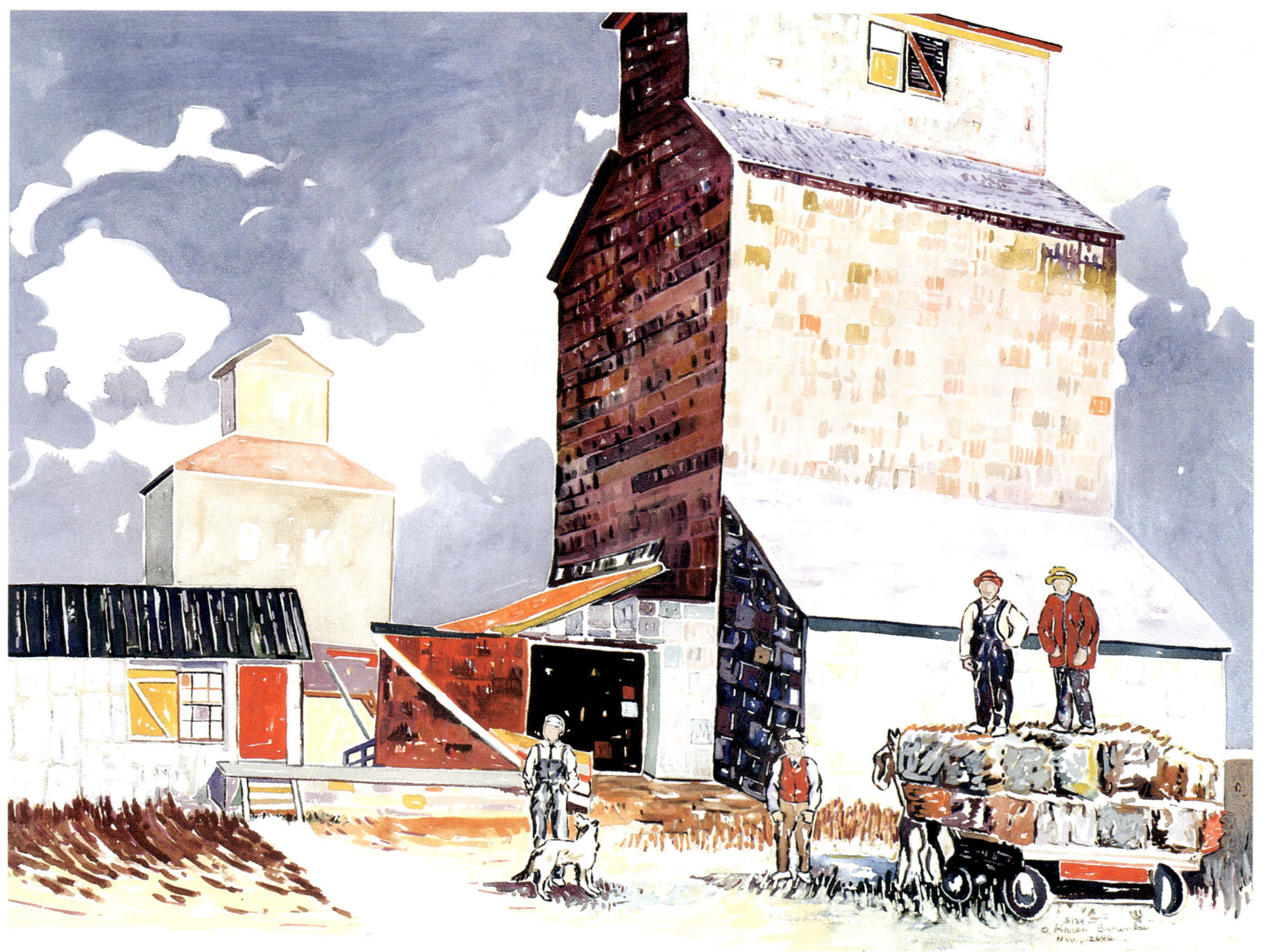

In the days before augers, farmers could save $17.50 per thousand-bushel car by loading their own grain. Bagged grain prevented loss and saved time, and at peak shipping periods, speed in loading meant a chance at better prices. This scene recalls, for the artist, her homesteading grandfather and uncles who hauled grain to the elevator by wagon.

Historical Painting #1, 2000, 28" x 21", Provincial Archives of Alberta, Miscellaneous Fonds A. 2857.

In the early days of the 20th century, agriculture used all available power. Mechanized farming, with steam traction and gasoline engines at the forefront, did not definitively supplant teams of oxen and horses for many years. The mix of transportation in this painting reflect for the artist stories told by her husband's family of the early days of farming.

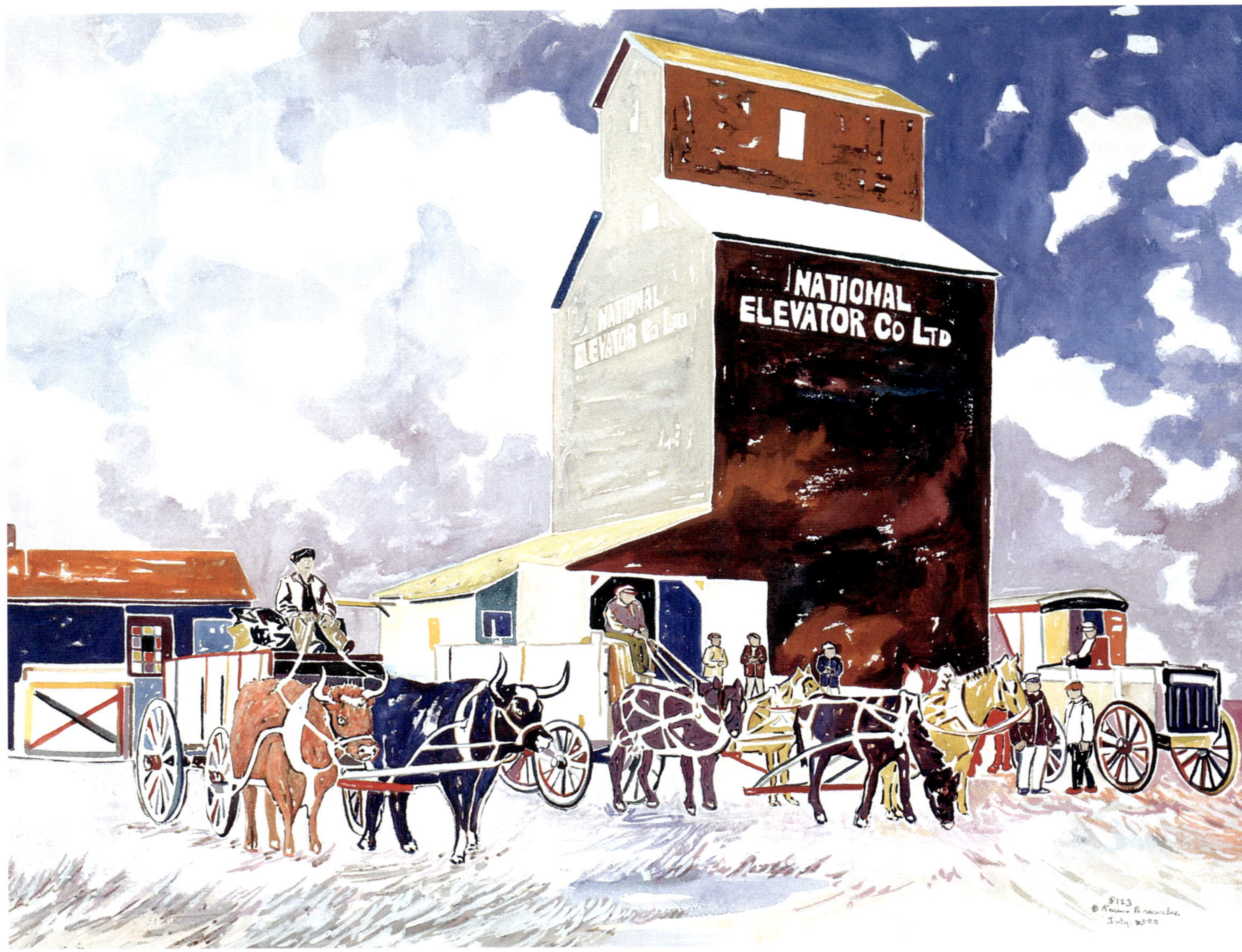

HISTORICAL PAINTING #2, 2000, 28" x 21", SIR ALEXANDER GALT MUSEUM AND ARCHIVES #2507.

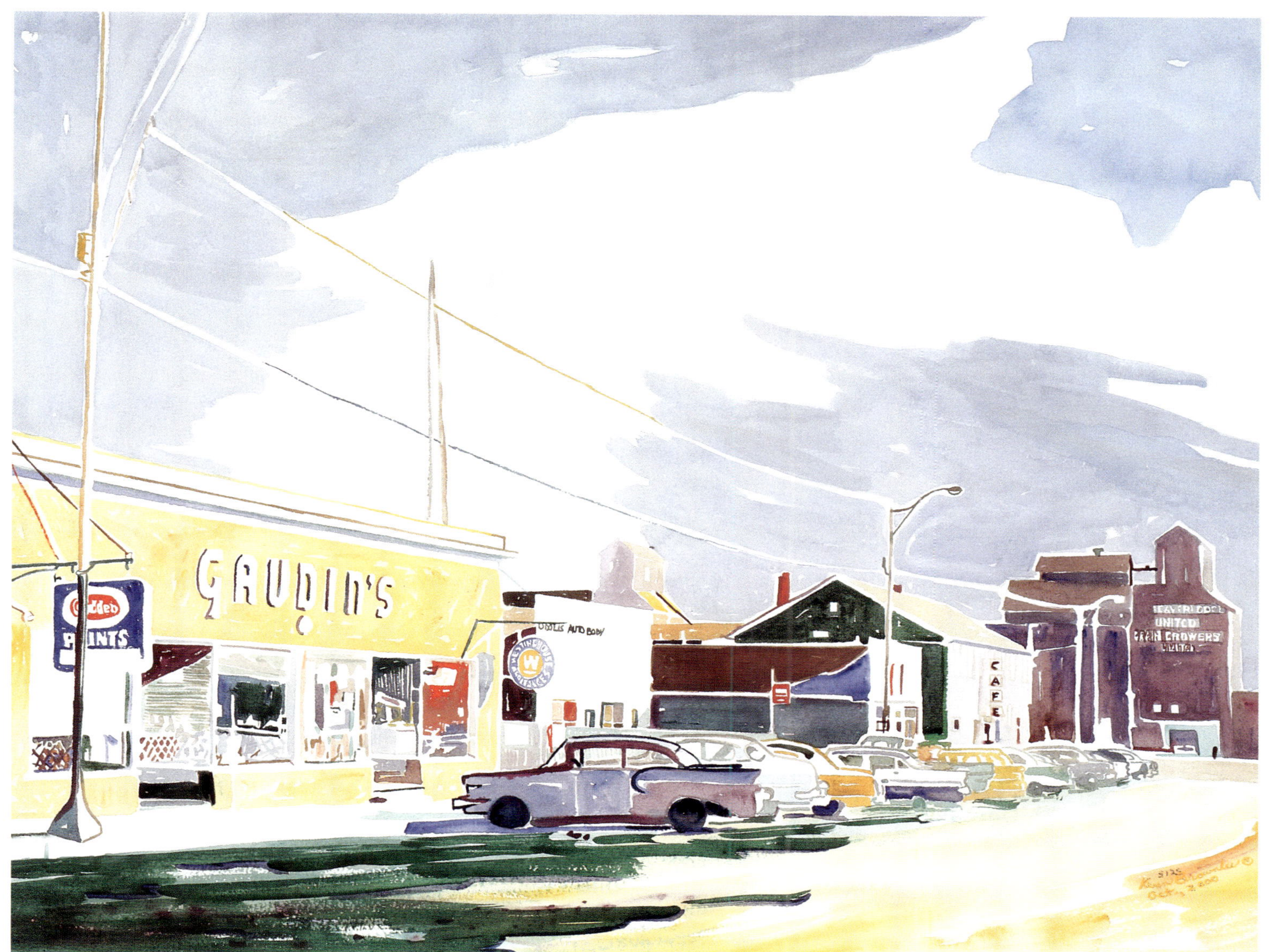

Beaverlodge's first settlers, including the Gaudin family, arrived in the early 1900s and used oxen as draft animals. Oxens' hooves tolerated the boggy ground on the Athabasca, Edson and Hinton trails better than horses' hooves. In 1954, around the time depicted here, the Canadian Forces Radar Station began operation on nearby Saskatoon Mountain.

Historical Painting #3, 2000, 28" x 21", Provincial Archives of Alberta, Fublic Affairs Bureau Pa. 132/6.

Freighters delivered grain to dumps, sometimes using six to eight horses to pull two wagons in tandem. Skilled teamsters positioned the wagons over two centrally hinged logs or planks, and a hand winch was used to raise the wagon to let the grain run out.

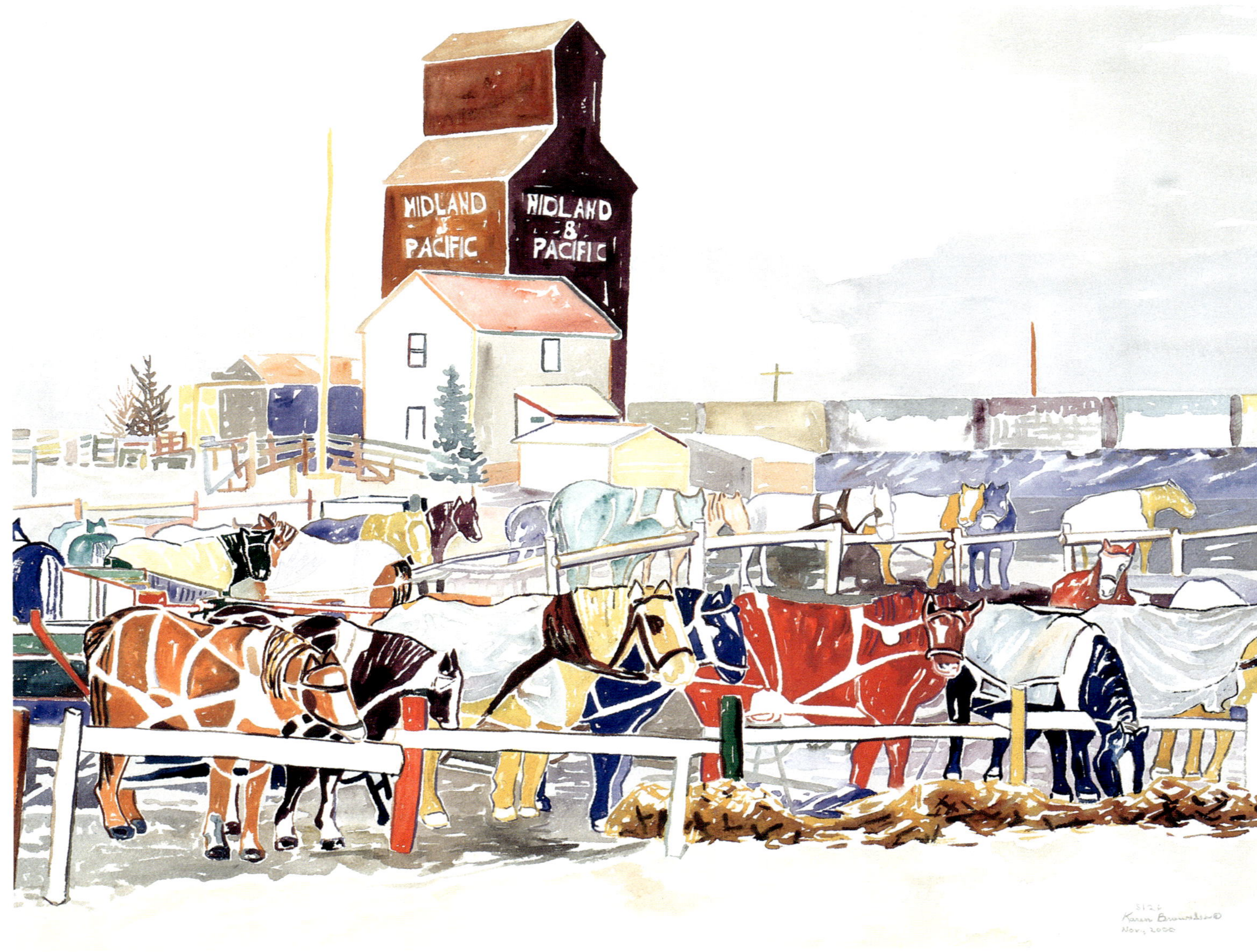

 Historical Painting #4, 2000, 28" x 21", Provincial Archives of Alberta, Nicholas Gavinchuk Fonds G. 1423.

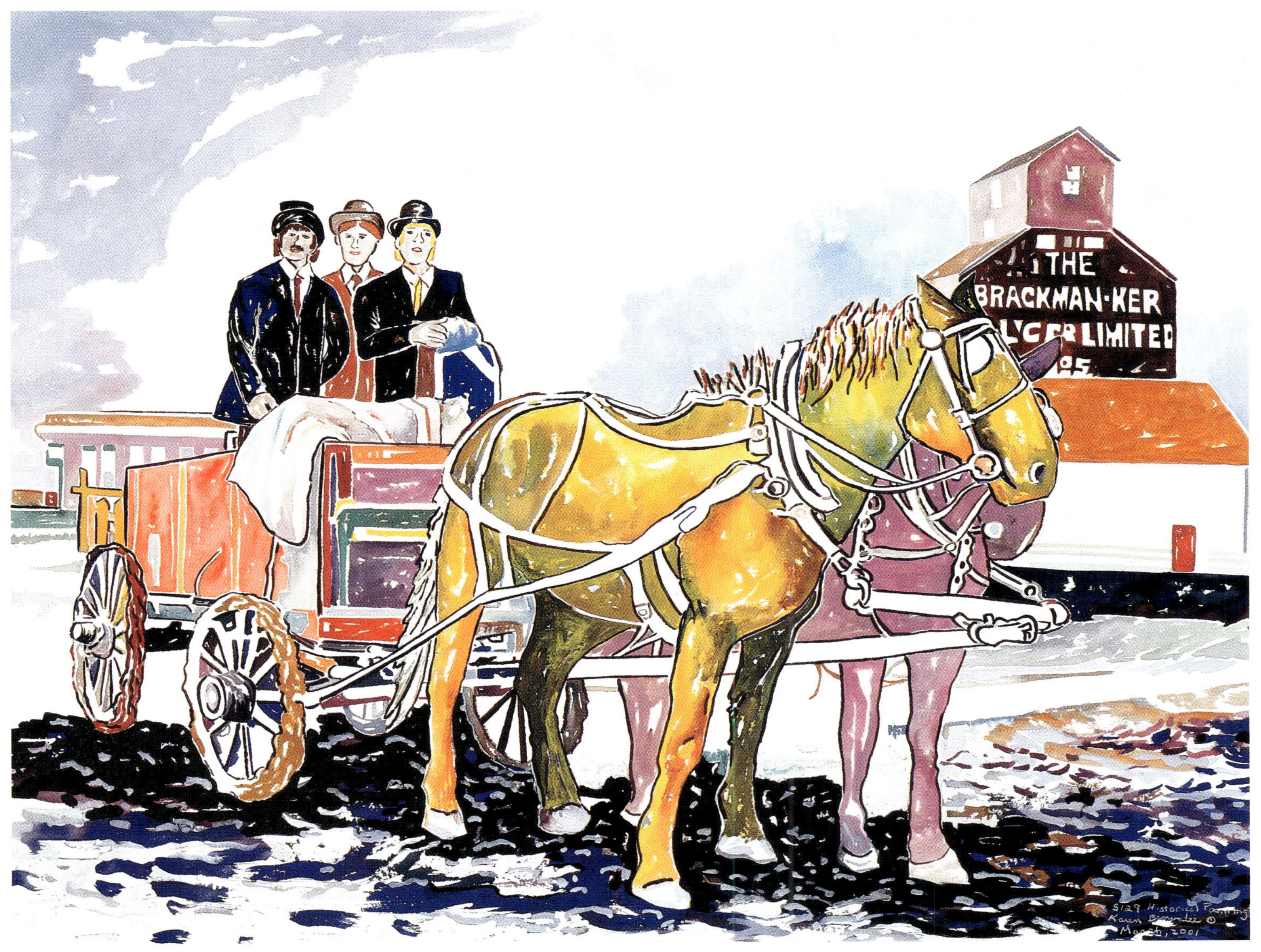

Brackman-Ker, a British Columbia company that shipped and milled grain, built the first elevator in Alberta. It was constructed in 1896 at Strathcona, the end-of-steel for the Calgary and Edmonton Railway across the North Saskatchewan River from Edmonton. The mill's urban location made this early secondary processing a sound business practice.

Historical Painting #5, 2001, 28" x 21", Provincial Archives of Alberta, J. A. Irvine Fonds I.R. 262.

During harvest, elevator agents worked long days helping wagon drivers dump their loads. With grain cars waiting on the siding, time was money, and families worked together. The artist recalls family stories about the communal efforts of her grandfather and his four sons hauling grain by wagon to the local elevator.

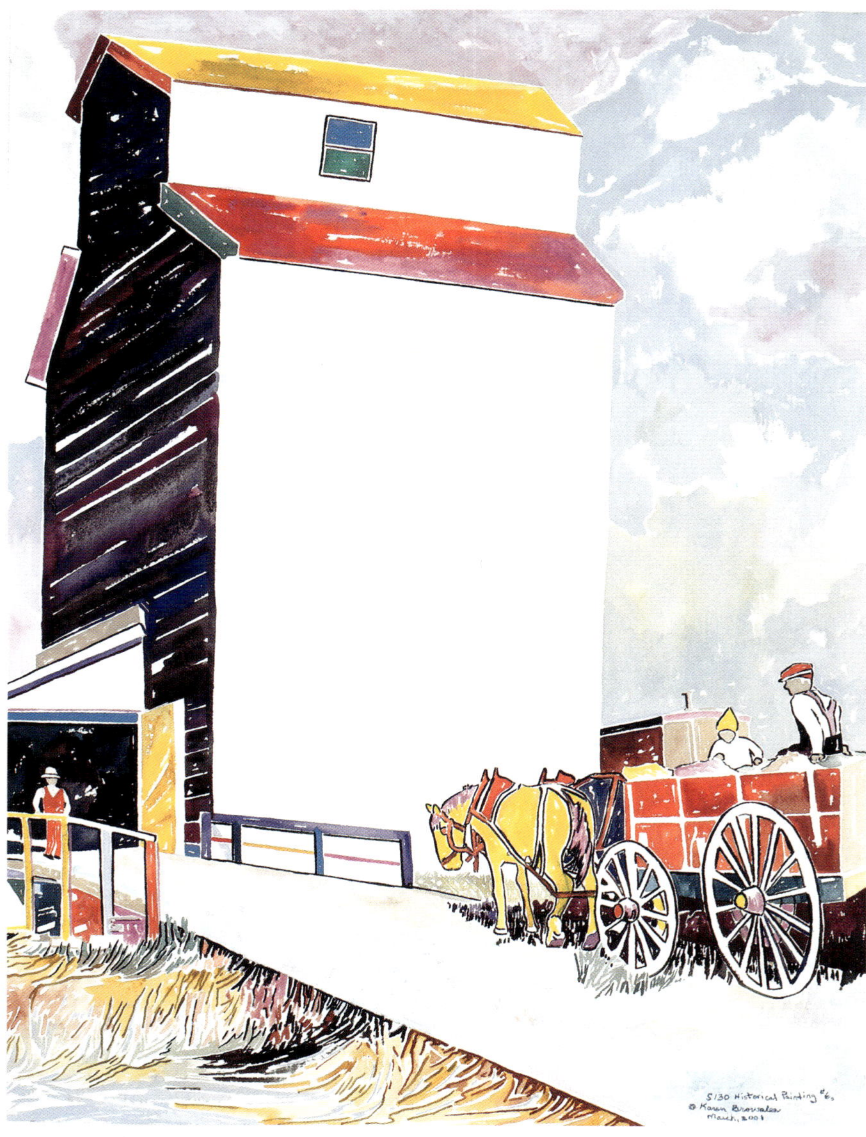

 HISTORICAL PAINTING #6, 2001, 21" x 28", PROVINCIAL ARCHIVES OF ALBERTA, MISCELLANEOUS FONDS A. 11, 158.

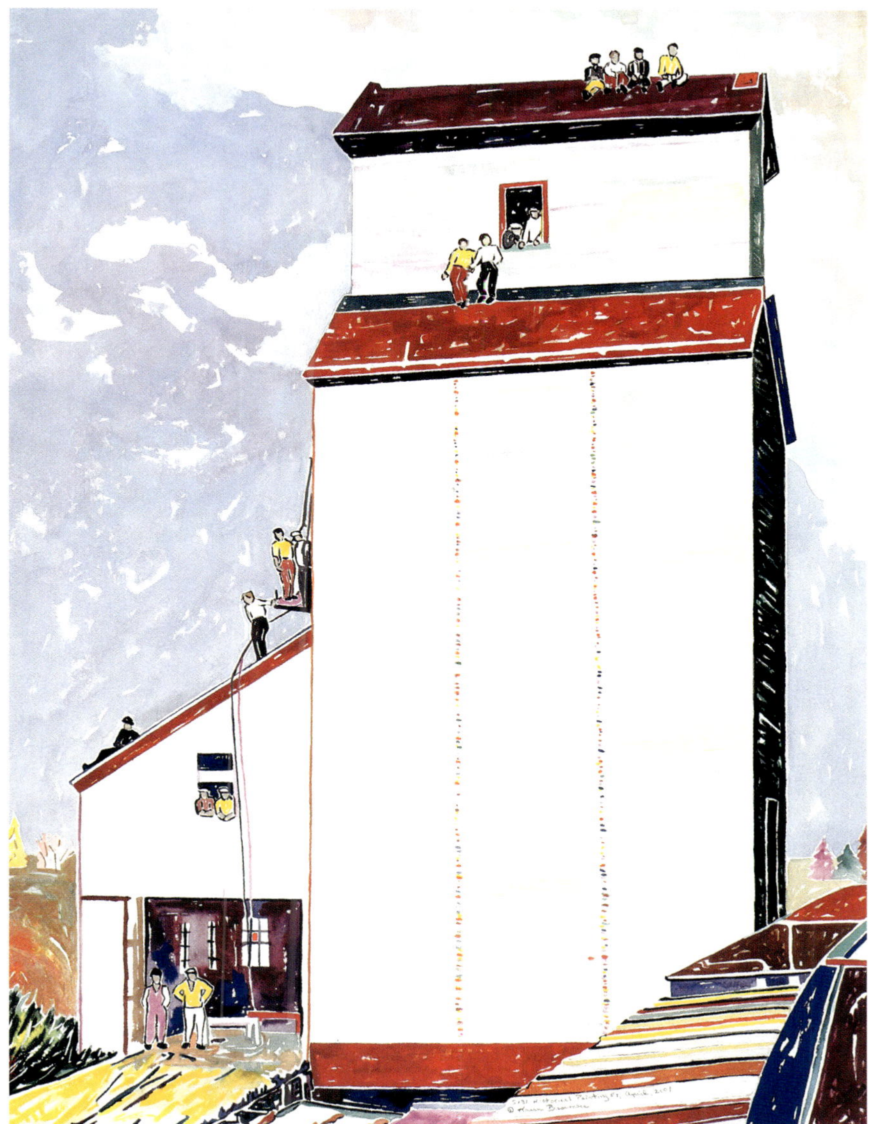

In the early 20th century, community members banded together to construct elevators. With the growth of large elevator companies in the 1920s, the standard design that would become an icon of prairie life came into use. Twelve-man crews could raise the towering wooden structures in about a month. The process of ascending the structure was hazardous, but the view from the top was exhilarating.

Historical Painting #7, 2001, 21" x 28", Provincial Archives of Alberta, Harry Bamber Fonds Ba. 71.

Following the Second World War, the Krause Mill Company in Athabasca loaded railcars and also produced flour. Stray sparks sometimes caused massive fires in the dust-filled interiors of the mill buildings. Elevators were among Alberta's first "no smoking" areas.

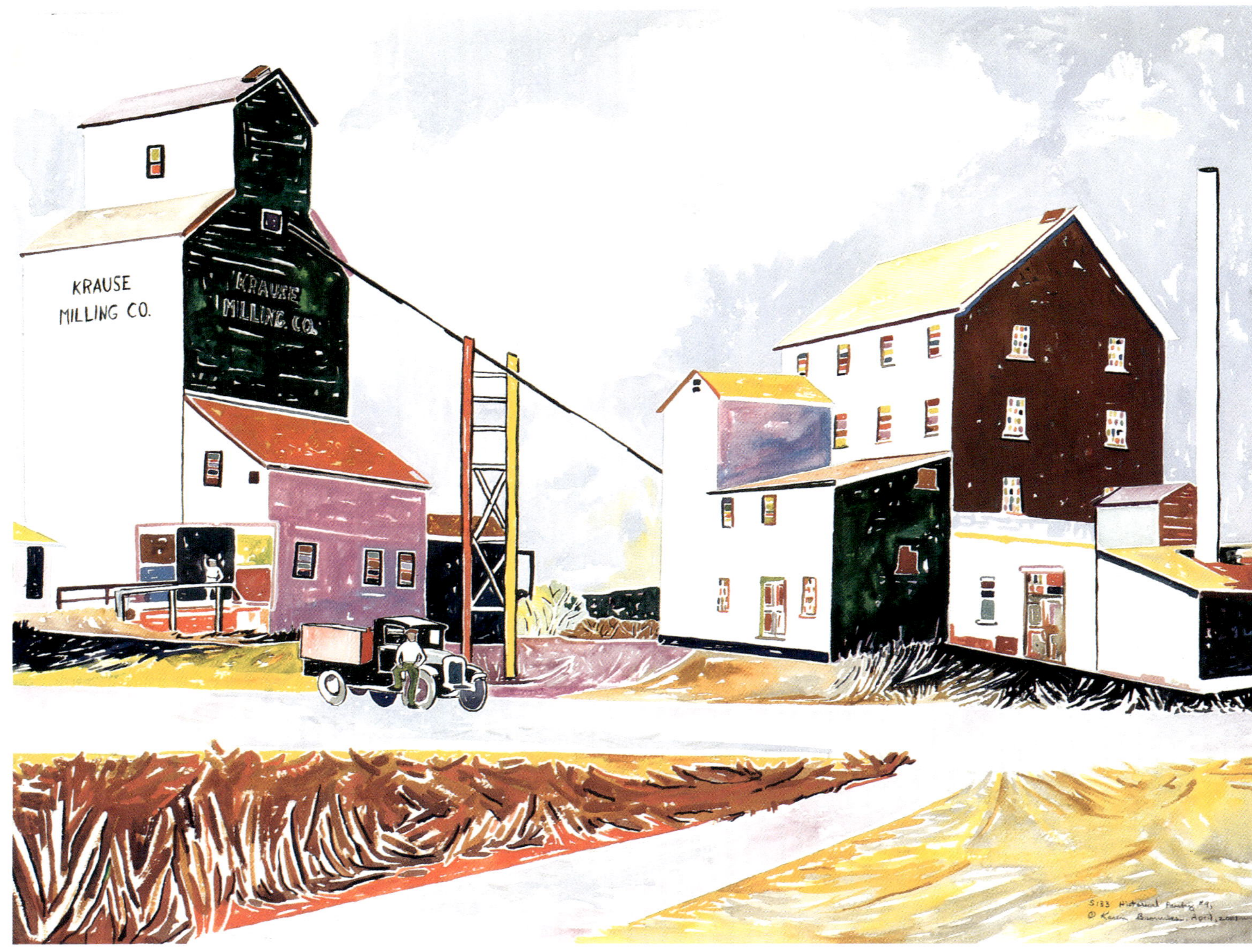

Historical Painting #9, 2001, 28" x 21", Provincial Archives of Alberta, Harry Bamber Fonds Ba. 70.

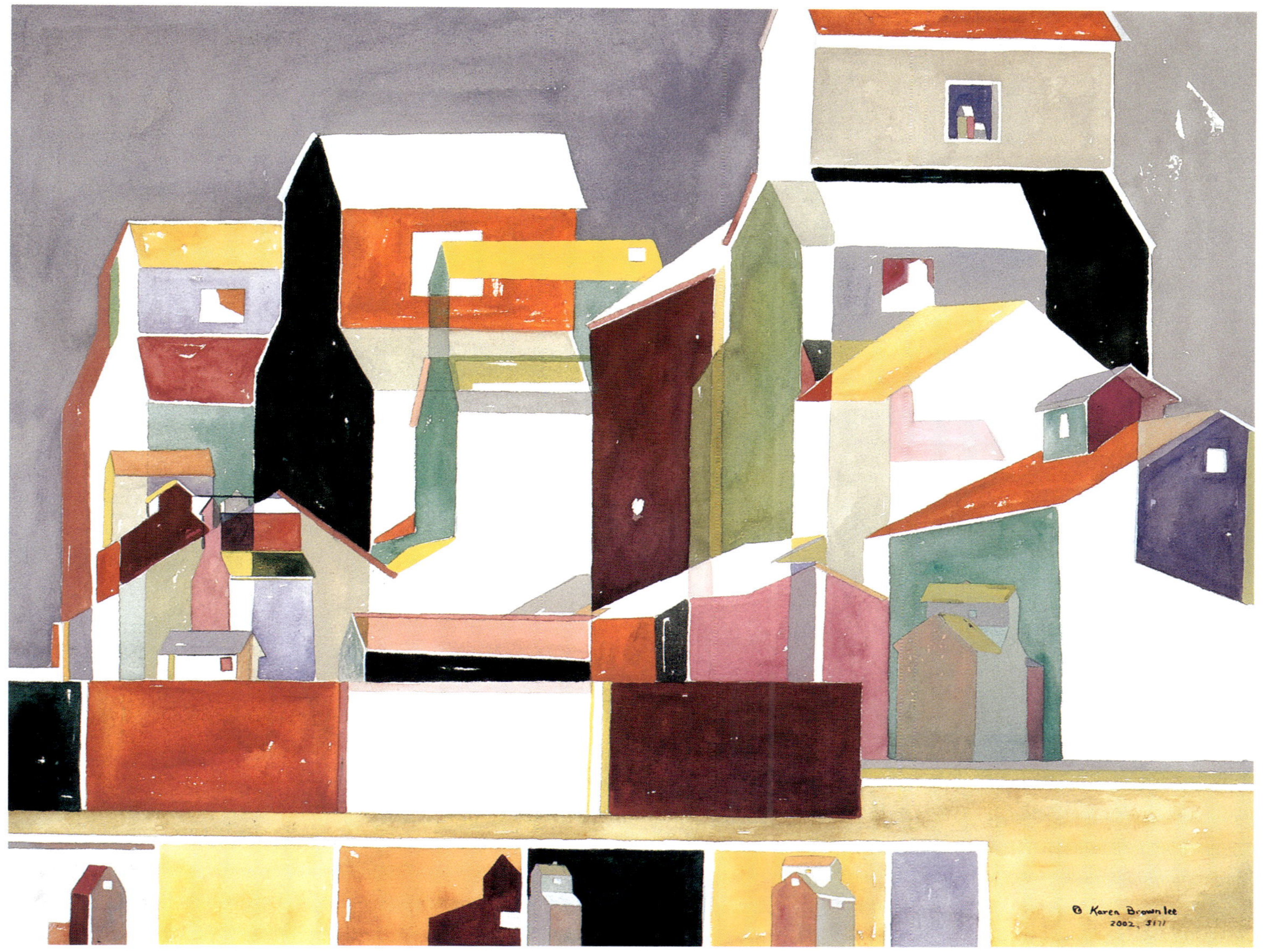

The first Canadian grain elevator, built in 1879 for Mennonites near Niverville, Manitoba, was round. It contained an elevating system, but creating the 16–18 storage bins needed was difficult. The narrow profile elevator, 70–80 feet in height, was adopted by 1913 and became the standard for most of the 20th century. Seen here in its elemental form, the distinctive gable at the top houses the elevating machinery.

Abstract Grain Elevators, 2002, 28" x 21".

In 1991 St. Albert purchased two elevators, one of which, the Musée Heritage Museum 1906 elevator, is the oldest working elevator in the province. Visitors can watch the "leg," a belt loop with 45 buckets, as it transports grain from the bins to the top of the elevator, where the distributor spout loads the grain cars.

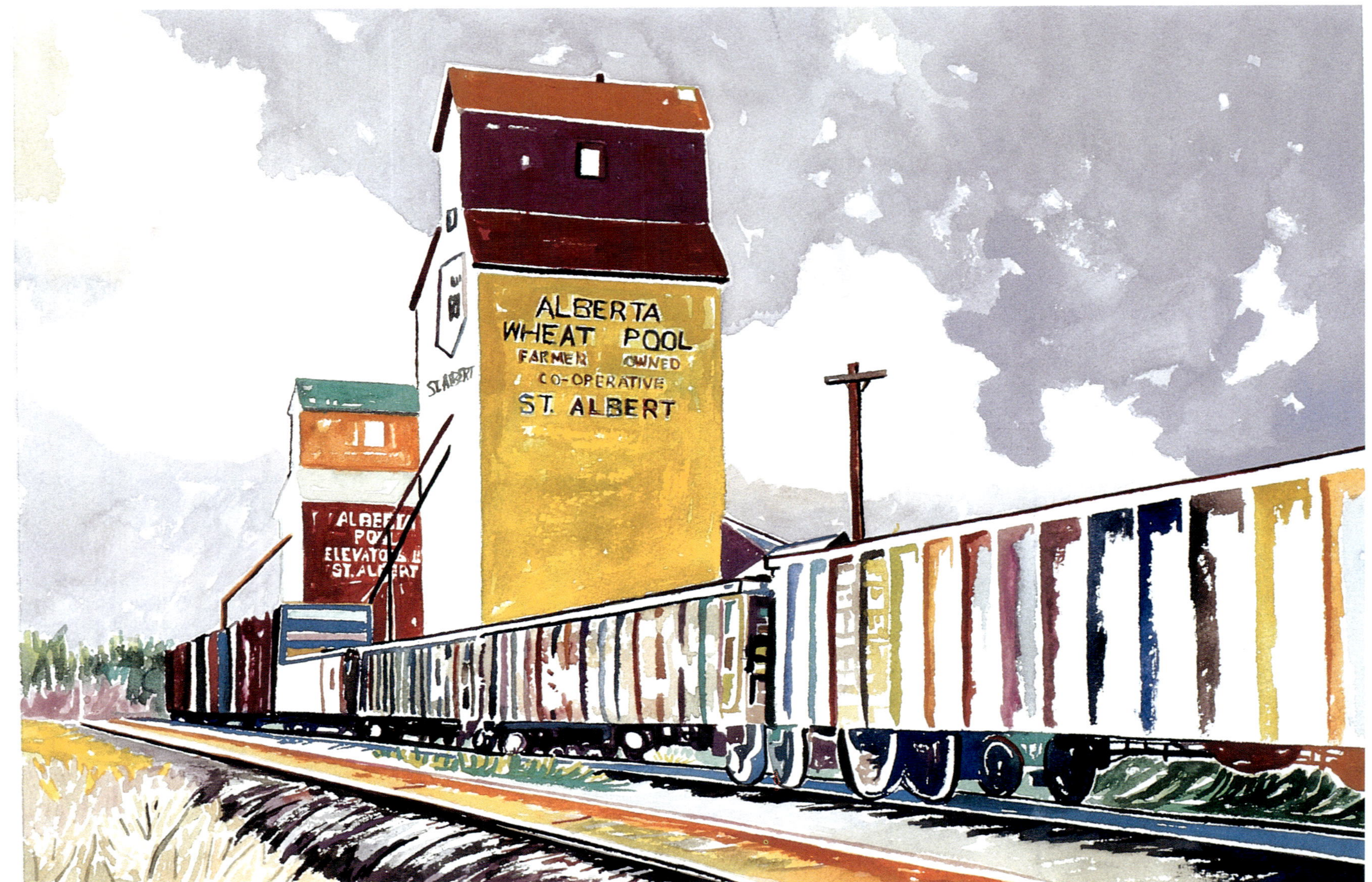

 St. Albert #2, 2001, 18" x 12", circa May 1999.

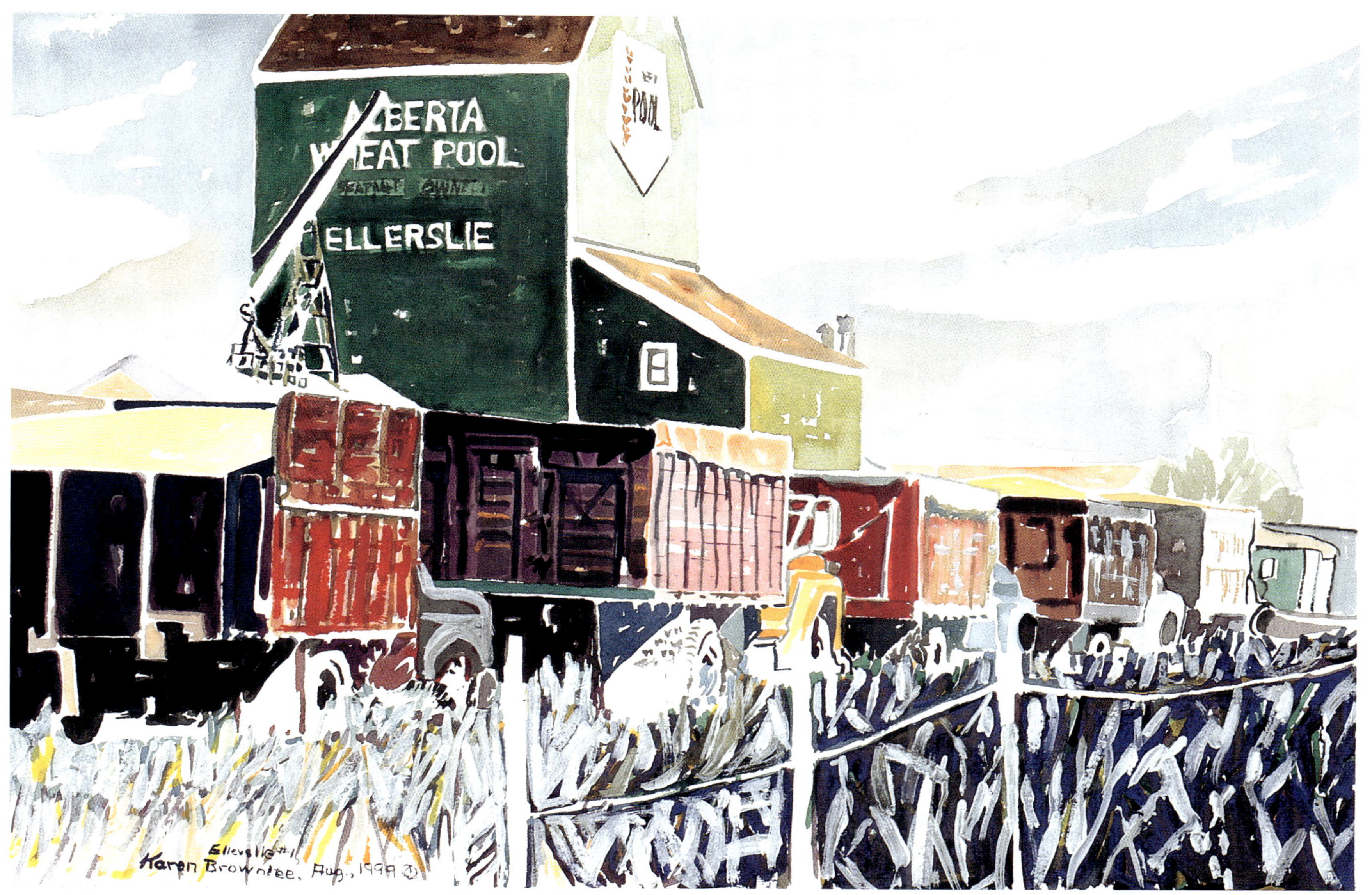

For one year, 1916, the Western Canada Flour Mills stood at Ellerslie, just south of Edmonton. Elevators reappeared here with the Gillespie Grain Company in 1921 and the Brooks Elevator Company in 1923. By 1955 the Alberta Wheat Pool owned both elevators. For years the Ellerslie elevators were important landmarks, signalling arrival in Edmonton for travellers from the south. Both are now only memories.

ELLERSLIE #1, 1999, 18" x 12", PROVINCIAL ARCHIVES OF ALBERTA.

This painting, based on a 1973 photograph, depicts the social role of the elevator in rural communities. Mrs. Helen Hibner recalled the Biblical quotes on Harry Sommerville's smaller brown elevator. The last to be seen before the elevator's destruction was Mark 8:36: "What profiteth a man if he gain the whole world but lose his own soul." As elevators disappear, many feel that part of Alberta's soul is also being lost.

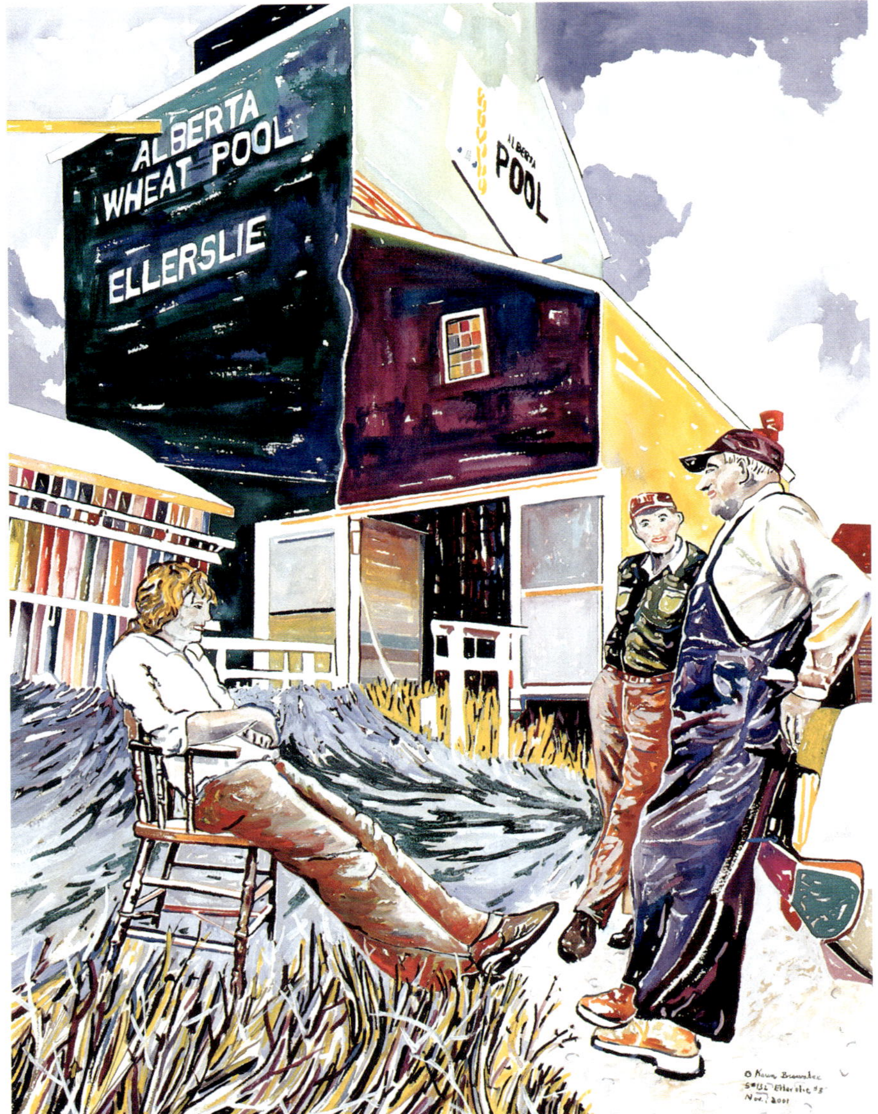

 ELLERSLIE #3, 2001, 21" x 28", PROVINCIAL ARCHIVES OF ALBERTA.

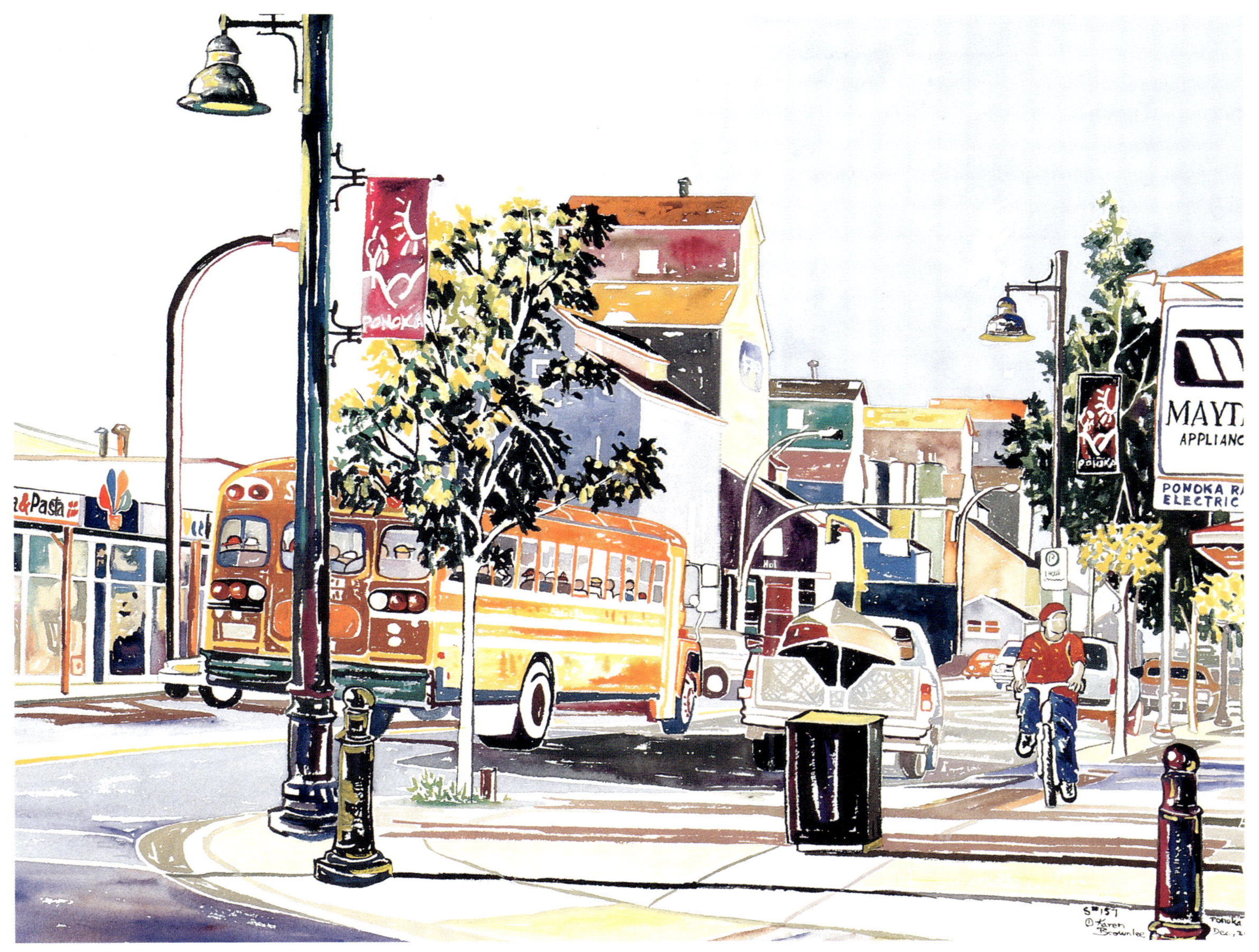

Ponoka was incorporated as a town in 1904, one year after the first telephone went into service at Campbell's Drugstore. The mix of urban features in the town with the more rural symbol of the grain elevator inspired the artist to refer to this scene as an urban view of a rural community.

PONOKA #1, 2001, 28" x 21", CIRCA SEPTEMBER 2001.

Elevators and agents figured prominently in Ponoka's local history. Wetaskiwin Produce, near the stockyards, was the first elevator in the town with Harry Smith, noted locally as a "whizz on figures," operating it. Fire was a recurring feature of elevator life here as elsewhere. Pioneer Elevator operated the Alexander and Tugman site starting in 1906, and rebuilding it after a devastating fire in 1909. By 1925 Ponoka supported four elevators.

PONOKA #2, 2002, 28" x 21", CIRCA SEPTEMBER 2001.

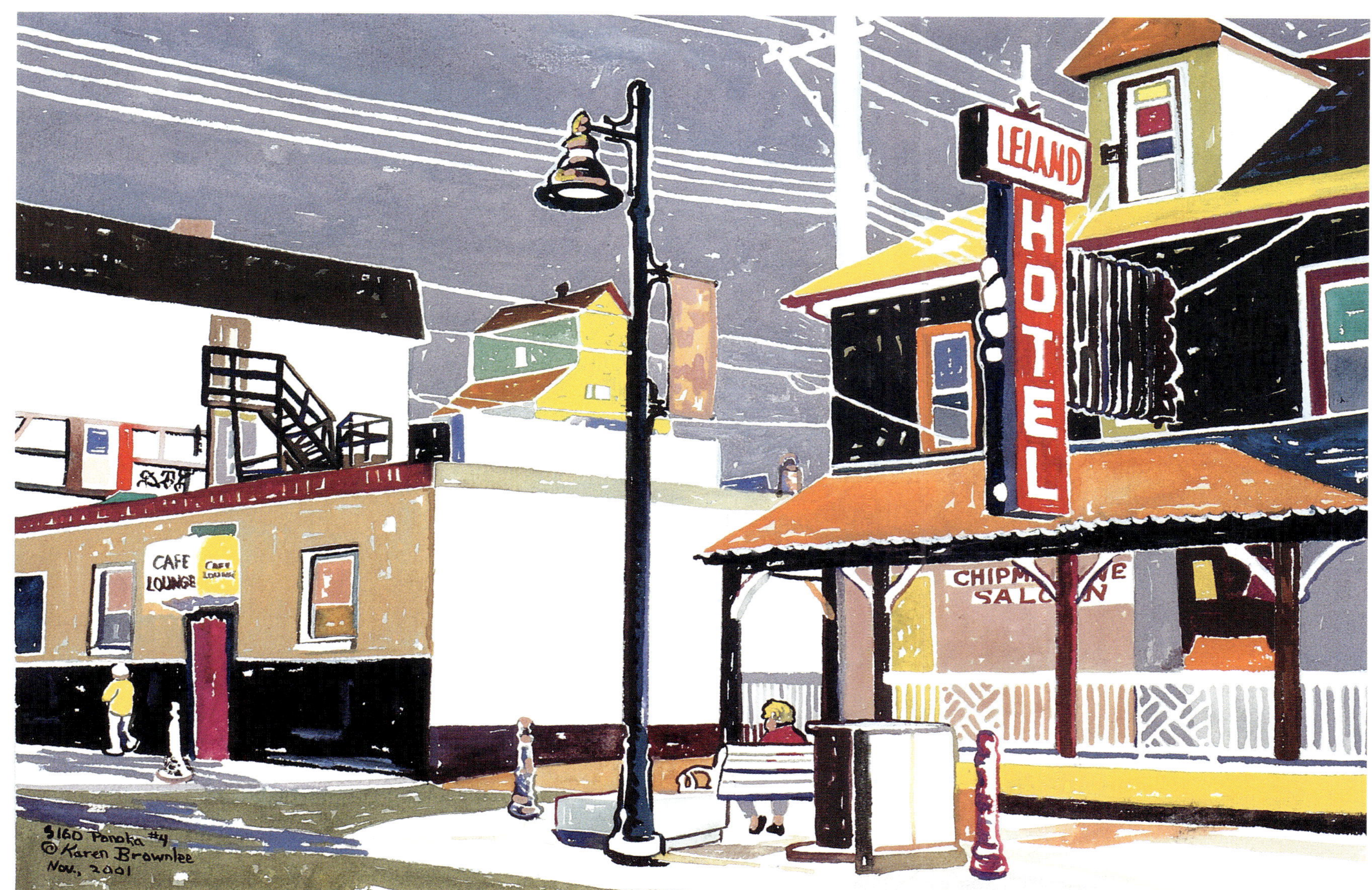

Ponoka is the site of a highly successful Alberta Main Street program. Since 1995 the city's Moderne architectural heritage has been preserved. The town's built heritage, from "boomtown" storefronts to the Provincial Building, designed by Douglas Cardinal, architect of the Canadian Museum of Civilization, is celebrated. Sadly, no elevators, symbols of the community's earliest agricultural days, remain.

PONOKA #4, 2001, 18" x 12", CIRCA SEPTEMBER 2001.

Farmers formed the Alberta Wheat Pool in 1923 in order to get fairer prices, and the fledgling cooperative raised its first three elevators in that year. This example at Esther is the only one remaining. Crops were always uncertain in the Sounding Creek basin. The dry climate, however, kept this elevator true on its foundation, raising hopes that it can be preserved.

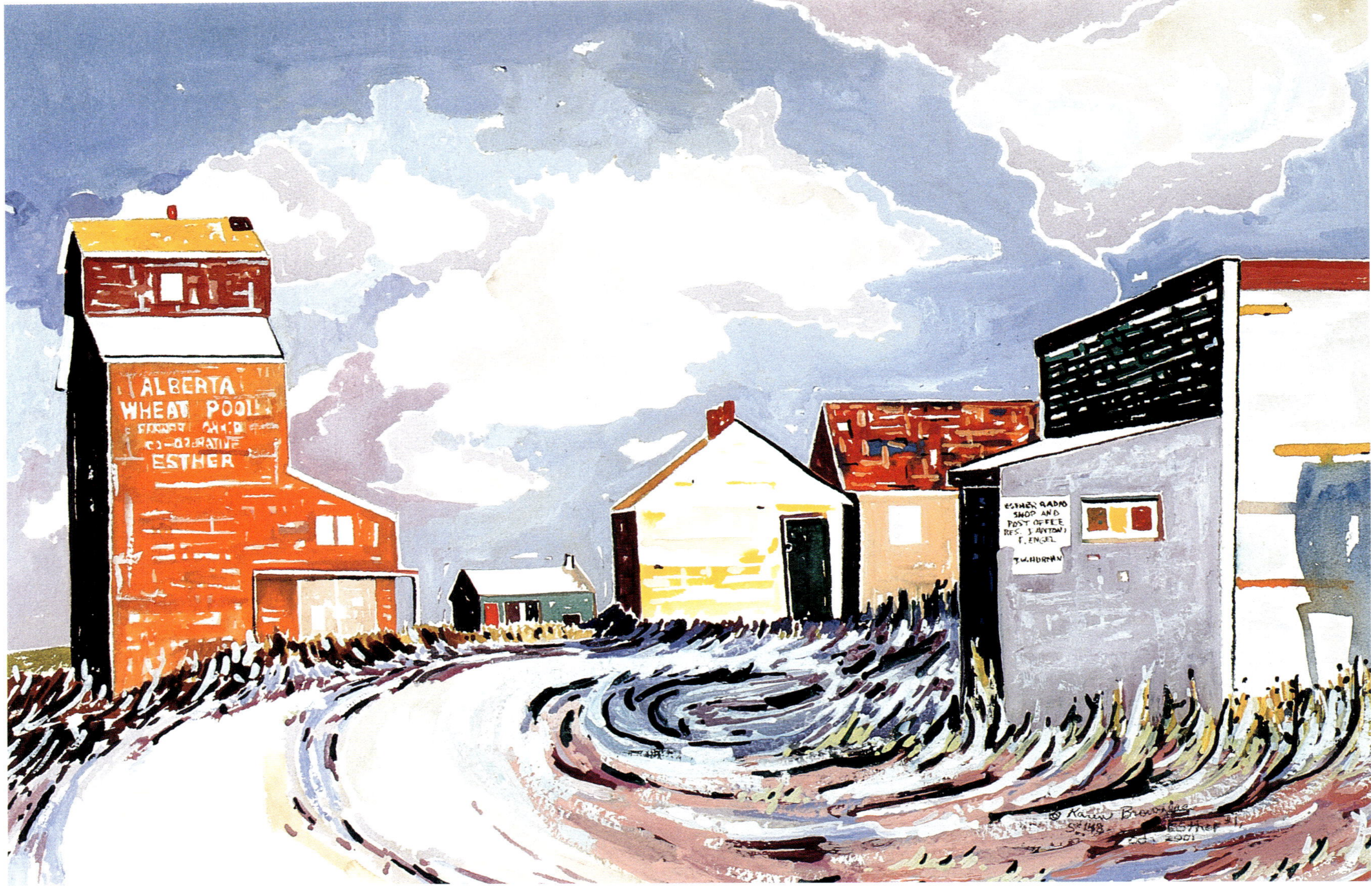

 Esther #1, 2001, 18" x 12", circa July 2001.

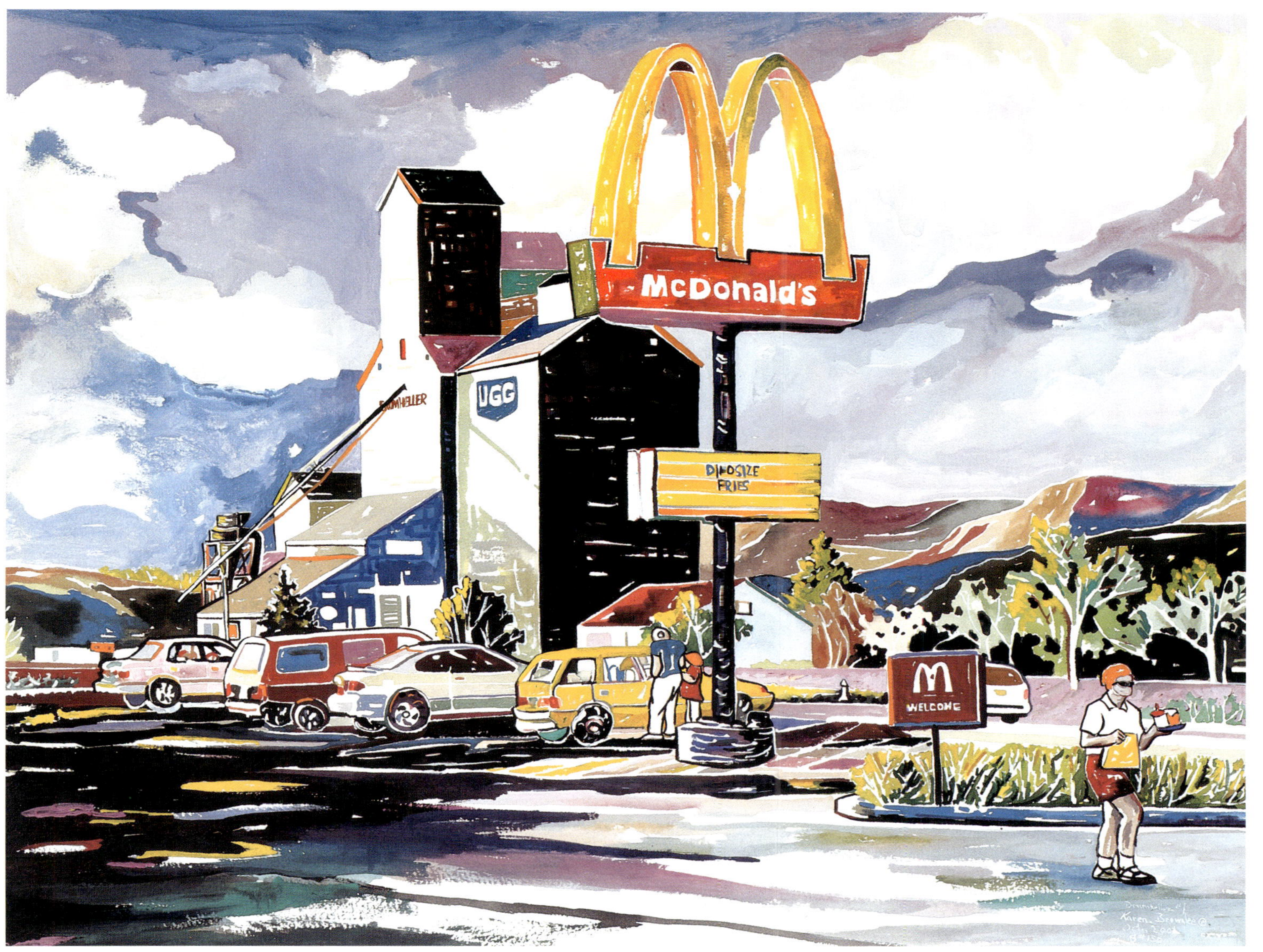

Thomas Greentree became Drumheller's first settler when he began farming here in 1902. The town, however, took its name from Samuel Drumheller, an American entrepreneur interested in the coal reserves of the area. Although Drumheller was an important grain shipment point, and elevators graced its skyline, mine tipples and behemoth dinosaurs are more associated with the present-day town.

Drumheller #1, 2001, 28" x 21", circa July 2000.

Before elevators existed in a town, grain was hand-loaded into railcars. Hogg and Little of Winnipeg built the first elevator in DeWinton in 1923. The project, a seed handling and distributing operation, was unsuccessful. Parrish & Heimbecker Grain Company of Calgary purchased the operation and turned it into a grain elevator, relieving farmers of the work of hand-loading grain for shipment.

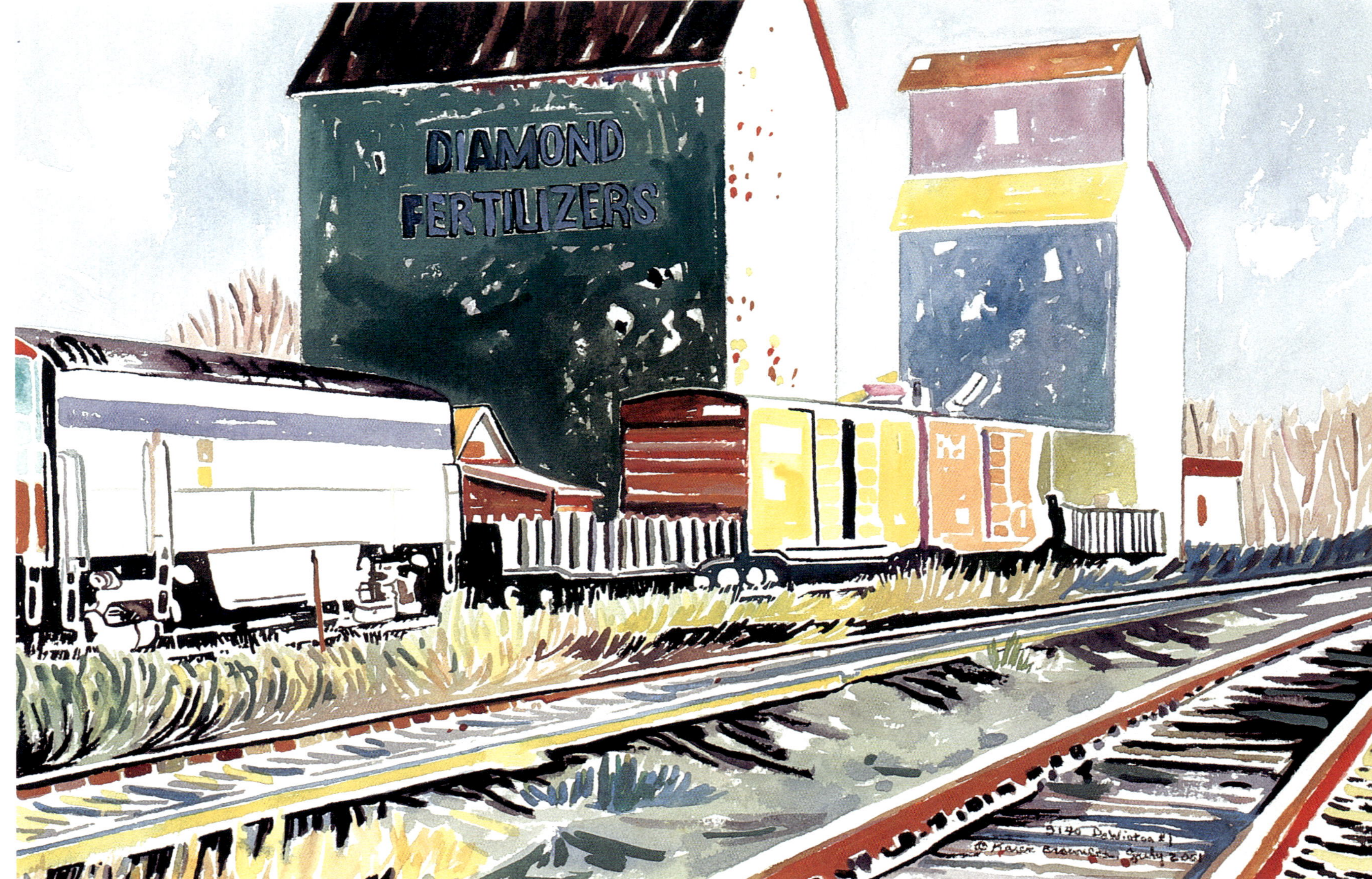

 DEWINTON #1, 2001, 18" X 12", CIRCA OCTOBER 1998.

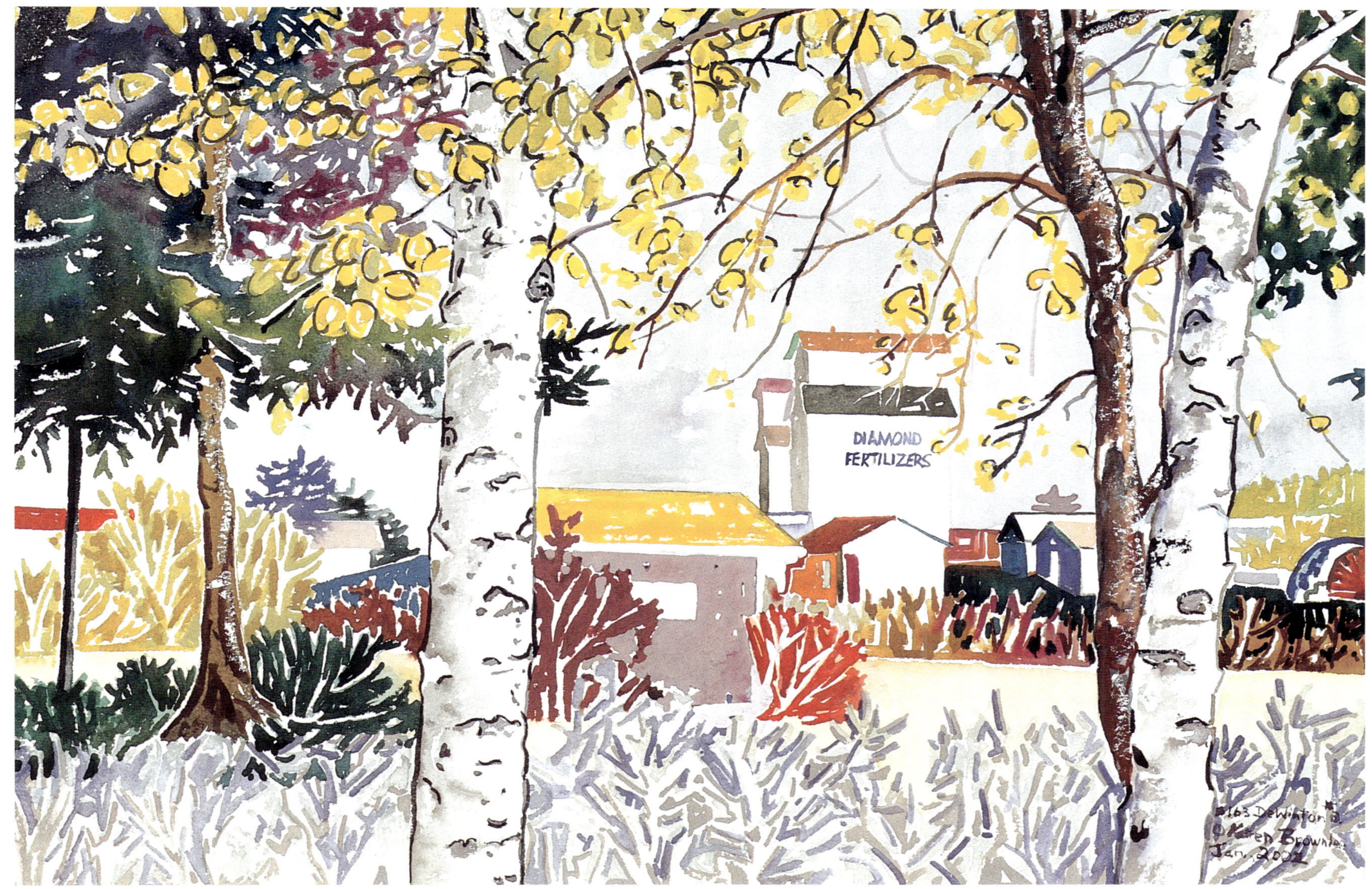

DeWinton was a productive grain area, prompting Midland and Pacific Grain Corporation to construct a 30,000-bushel elevator here in 1925. The Wheat Pool also operated an elevator here from 1929 to 1936 when it was torn down. In the true waste-not, want-not spirit of the time, a local barn was re-sided with some of the lumber, and the rest was used in an elevator at High River.

DeWinton #2, 2002, 18" x 12", circa October 1998.

Joseph Higginsbothan Saxon Moss passed through the Mossleigh area with the 1879 Dominion Government Survey. He subsequently freighted goods for the I.G. Baker Company of Fort Benton, Montana. When Moss settled in the area to farm, his name may have inspired the town's name. Railways and elevators, like the three Parrish & Heimbecker structures seen here, continued the early tradition of transporting grain to markets.

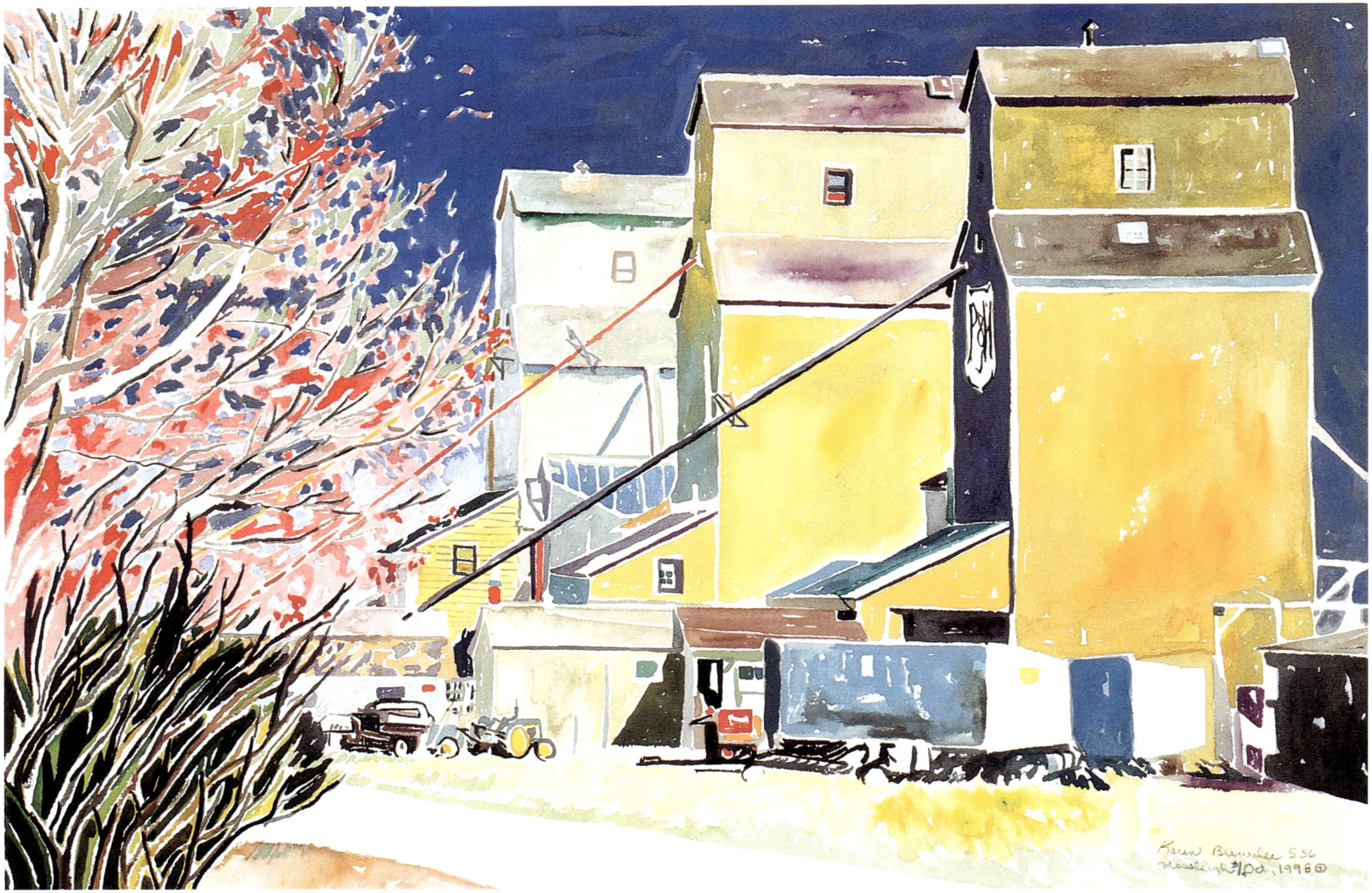

 MOSSLEIGH #1, 1998, 18" X 12", CIRCA MAY 1998.

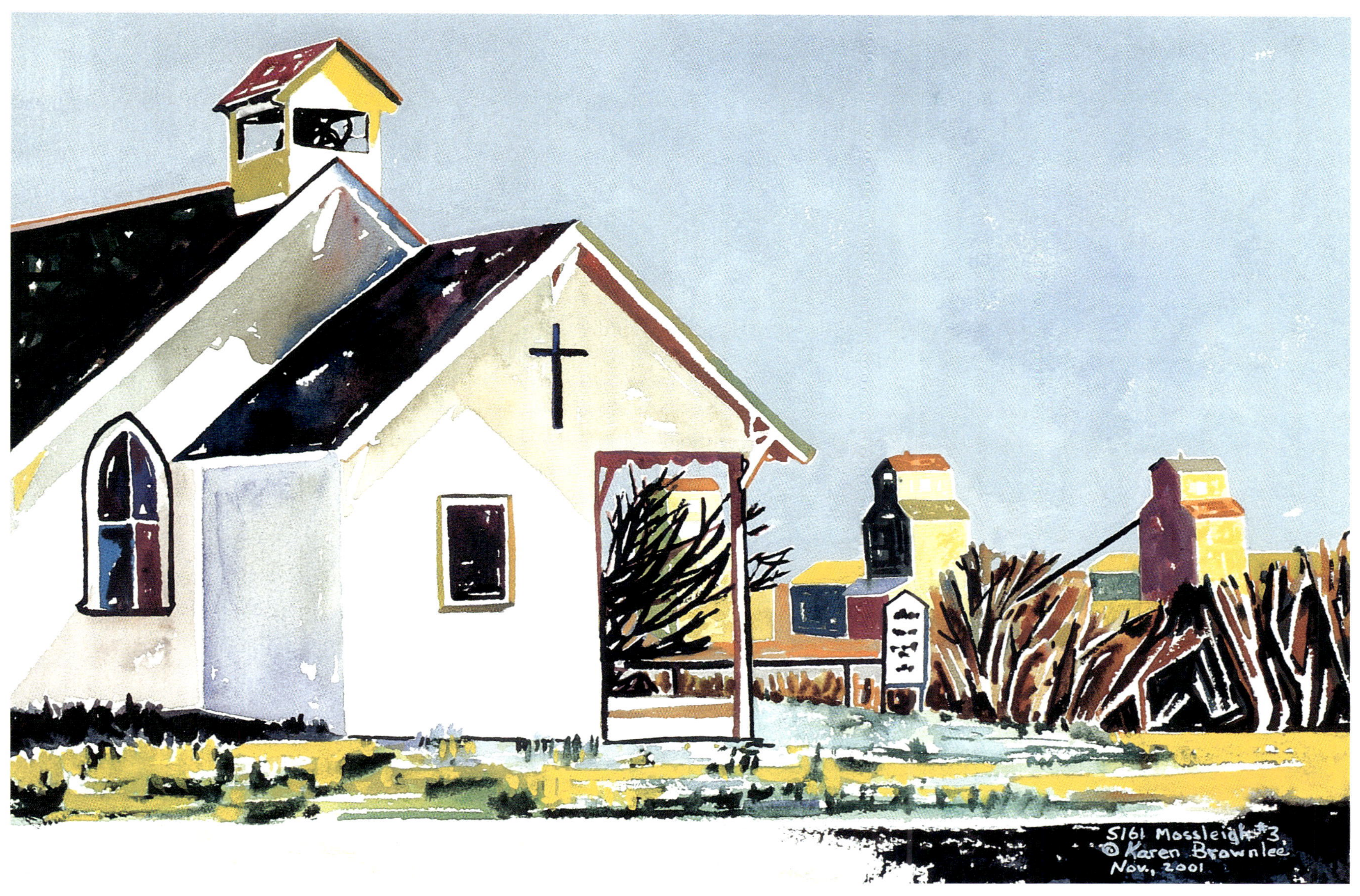

Before the railway came through Mossleigh, teams moved grain considerable distances to shipping points. Elevators eliminated the longest trips, but there was still a good deal of grain to deliver, and teamsters vied to move the most with one team. Mossleigh sent a 32-horse team, pulling eight wagons, to the 1925 Calgary Stampede to demonstrate the transporting of grain.

MOSSLEIGH #3, 2001, 18" x 12", circa May 1998.

High River, called The Crossing in the 1870s, was a very reliable ford on the Highwood River. Ranching was the primary early enterprise in the area, and High River was known predominantly as a "cow town" until the beginning of the 20th century.

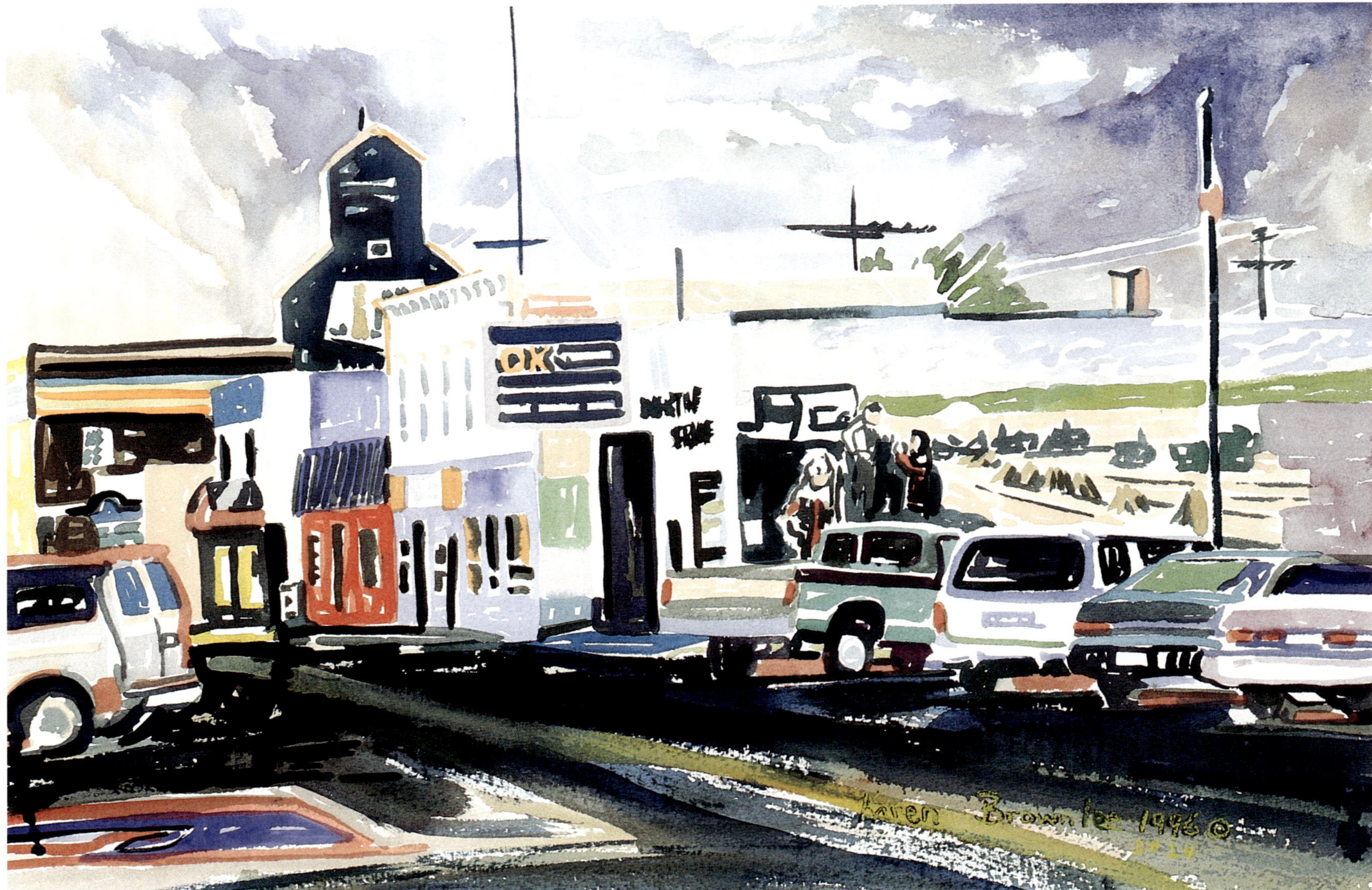

 High River #1, 1996, 18" x 12", circa August 1996.

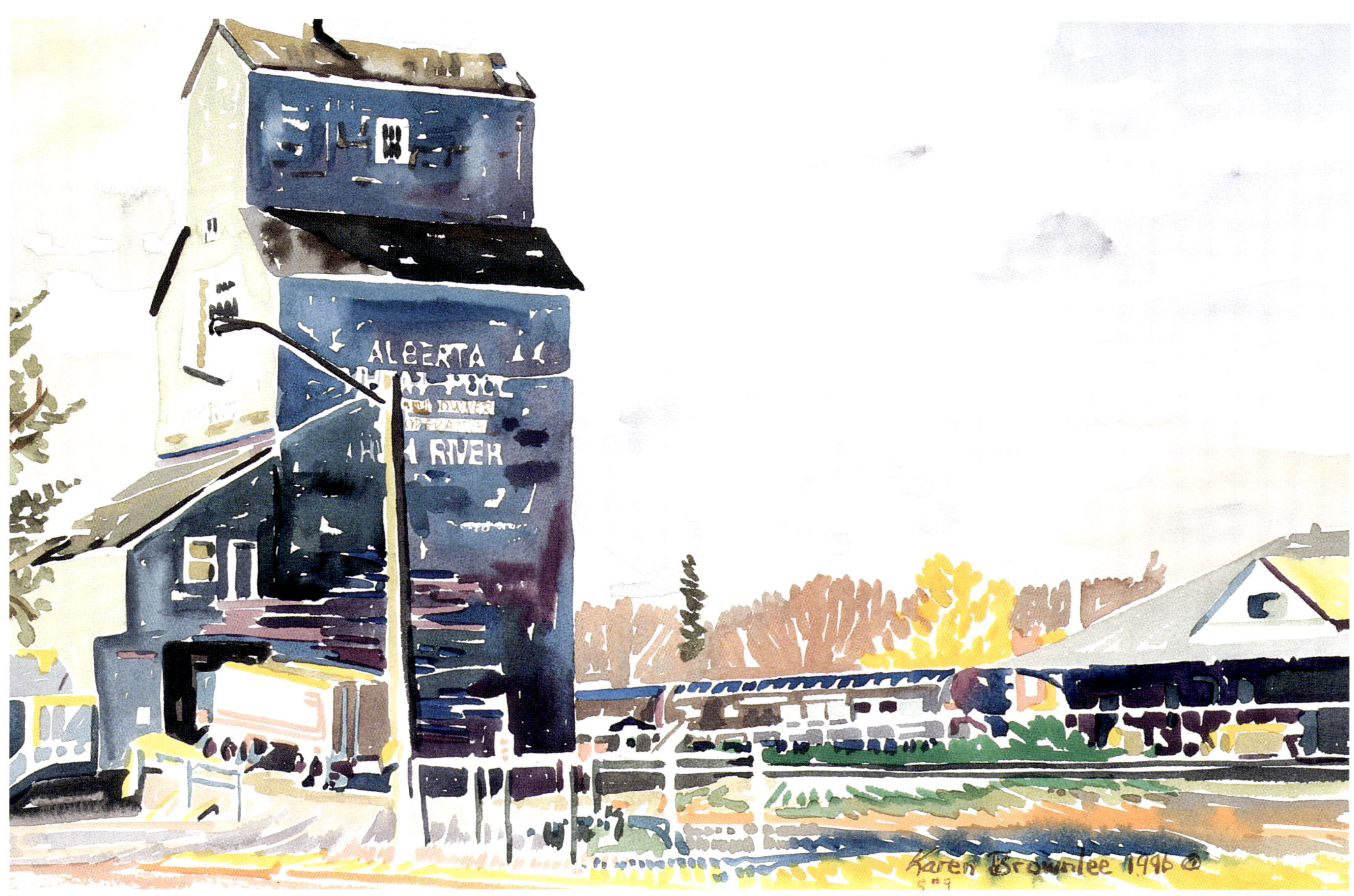

The Calgary and Edmonton Railway arrived in High River in 1892, a rare instance of the railway actually coming to the location of the settlement rather than settlement springing up along the railway. Original surveys showed the railway placed eight miles west of High River, following Cameron Coulee in order to avoid the marshy areas near Midnapore and the steep grade between High River and Azure Siding.

High River #3, 1996, 18" x 12", circa August 1996.

Wet years in 1901–1902, ended a drought and brought an influx of settlers to High River. The railway had not yet built to the east, so long lines of grain wagons came to High River. Business boomed with four hotels and four livery stables being constructed in 1901. The residents applied to change from hamlet to village status, and in April 1902 the first village meeting was held.

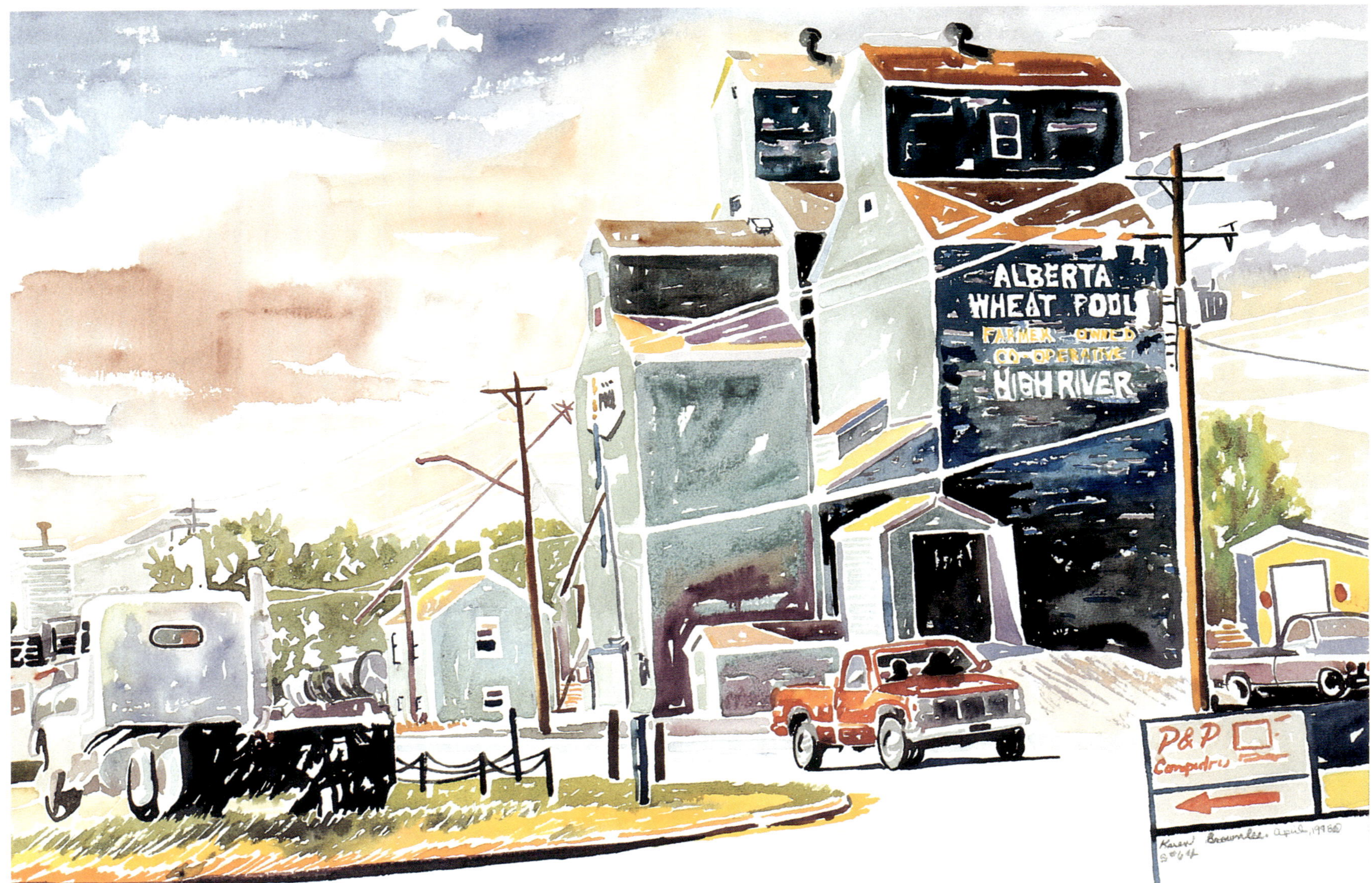

High River #4, 1998, 18" x 12", circa August 1996.

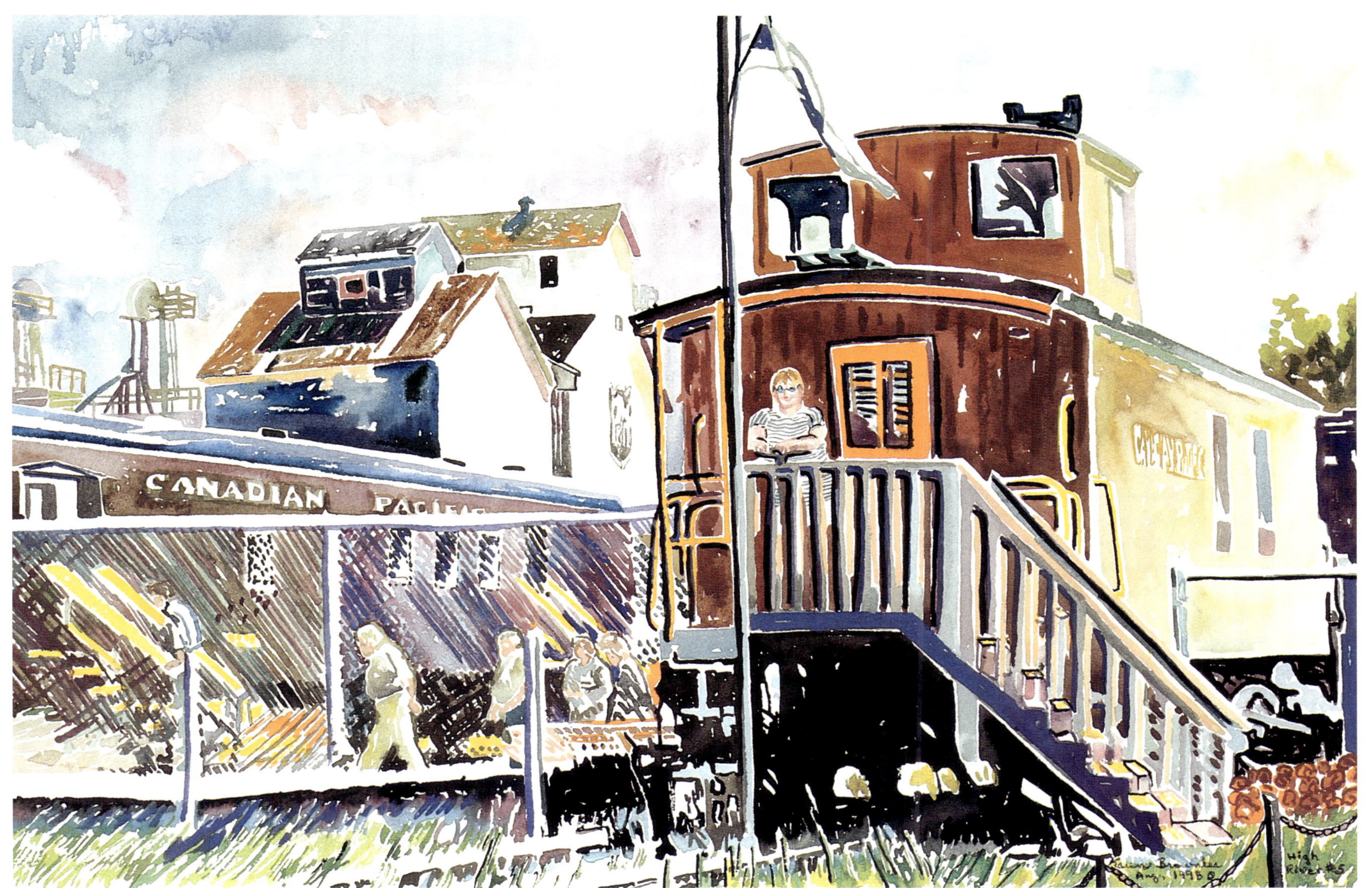

The Canadian Pacific Railway made four passenger stops a day in High River in 1900, but transporting cattle and grain was the mainstay of the railway. In the early years, grain was loaded directly from wagons to railcars. The first elevator, Alberta Pacific Elevator Company #14, was raised in 1905. In 1907 a second elevator was raised by the High River Elevator and Lumber Company.

High River #5, 1998, 18" x 12", circa July 1998.

In 1909 the largest volume of grain shipped in Canada originated in High River when 1,100,000 bushels were transported via Vancouver and the Panama Canal. Production grew, and by 1928 the town had seven elevators. With increased production, more storage was needed, and annexes and other emergency facilities were added to the main elevators. High River was the home of eight elevators with annexes into the 1980s.

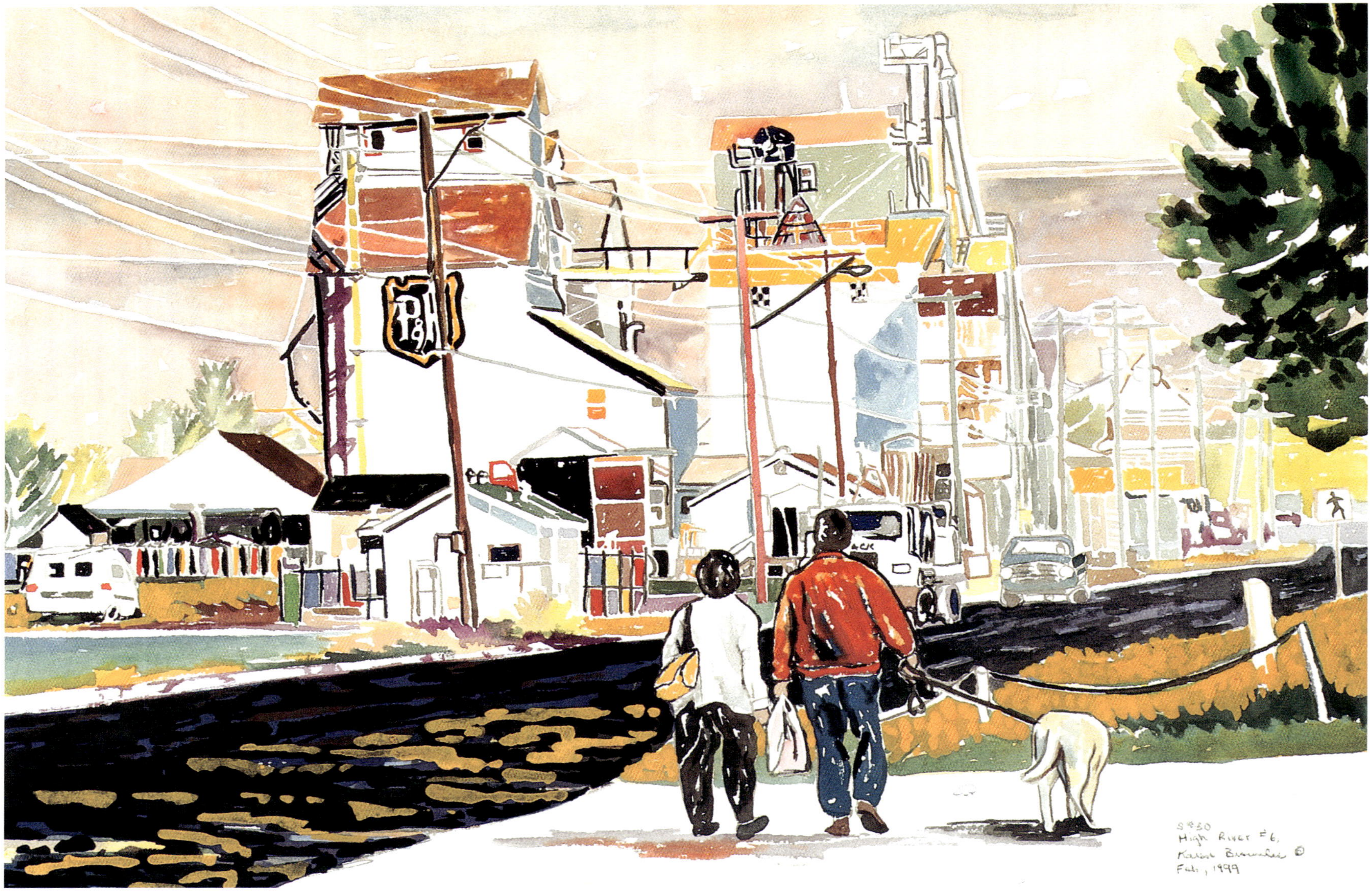

HIGH RIVER #6, 1999, 18" x 12", CIRCA SEPTEMBER 1998.

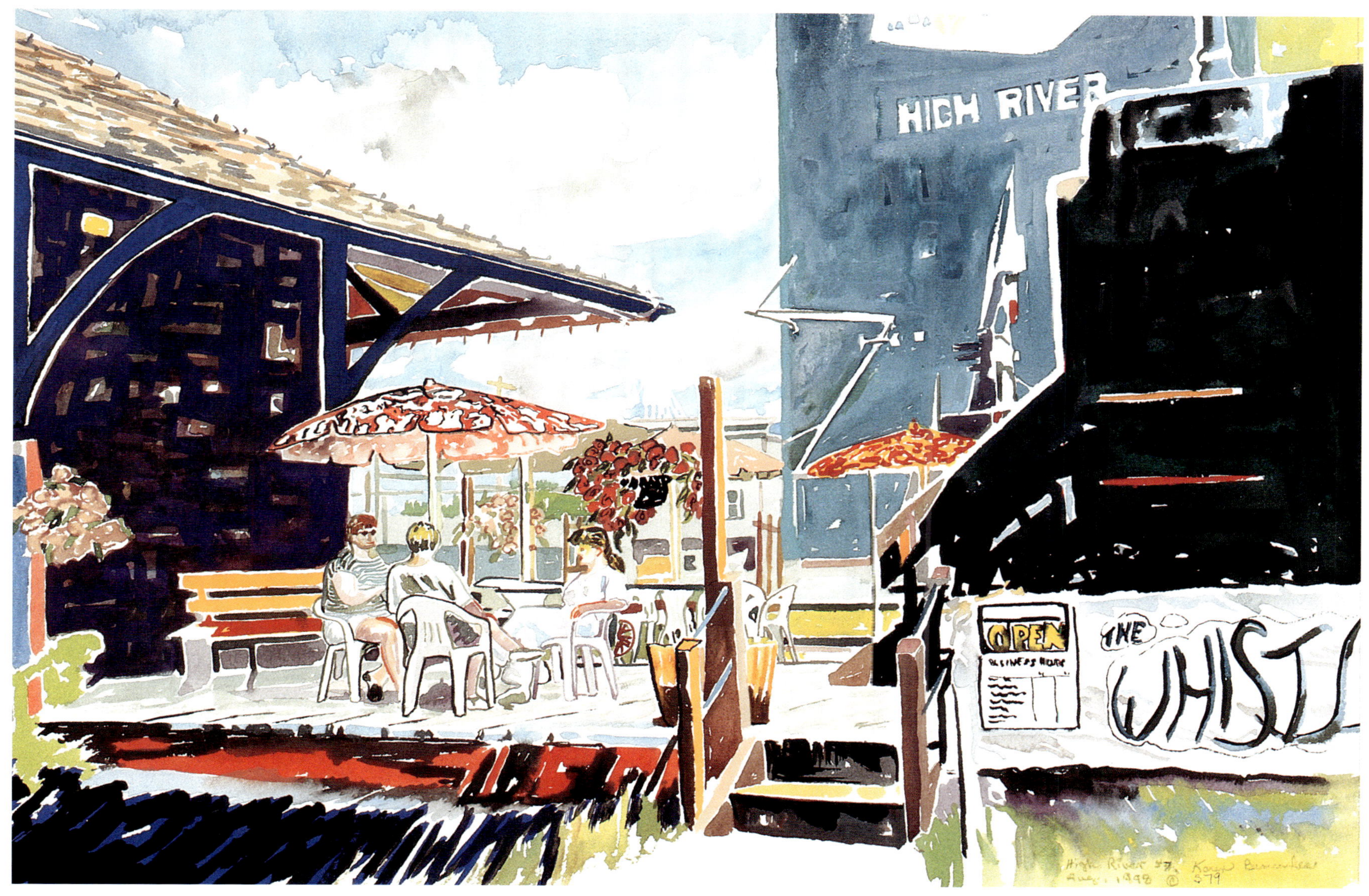

Elevators and railway stations, central to the prosperity of early communities, have disappeared. Once there were 1750 grain elevators in Alberta. Less than 200 remained in 2003. High River citizens planned to save their last elevator in conjunction with the station only to have it burn. The profile marking the town's skyline for nearly a century disappeared in an hour and a half on May 25, 2003.

HIGH RIVER #7, 1998, 18" x 12", CIRCA JULY 1998.

Vulcan was surveyed in 1910 and had its first elevator built in 1911. The town became famous for the "Nine-in-a-Line" grain elevators, which stretched along Vulcan's railway tracks and came to symbolize western agricultural potential during the 1920s. The storage capacity of this row of elevators, 750,000 bushels, was the largest in western Canada until a fire in 1971 destroyed many of the structures.

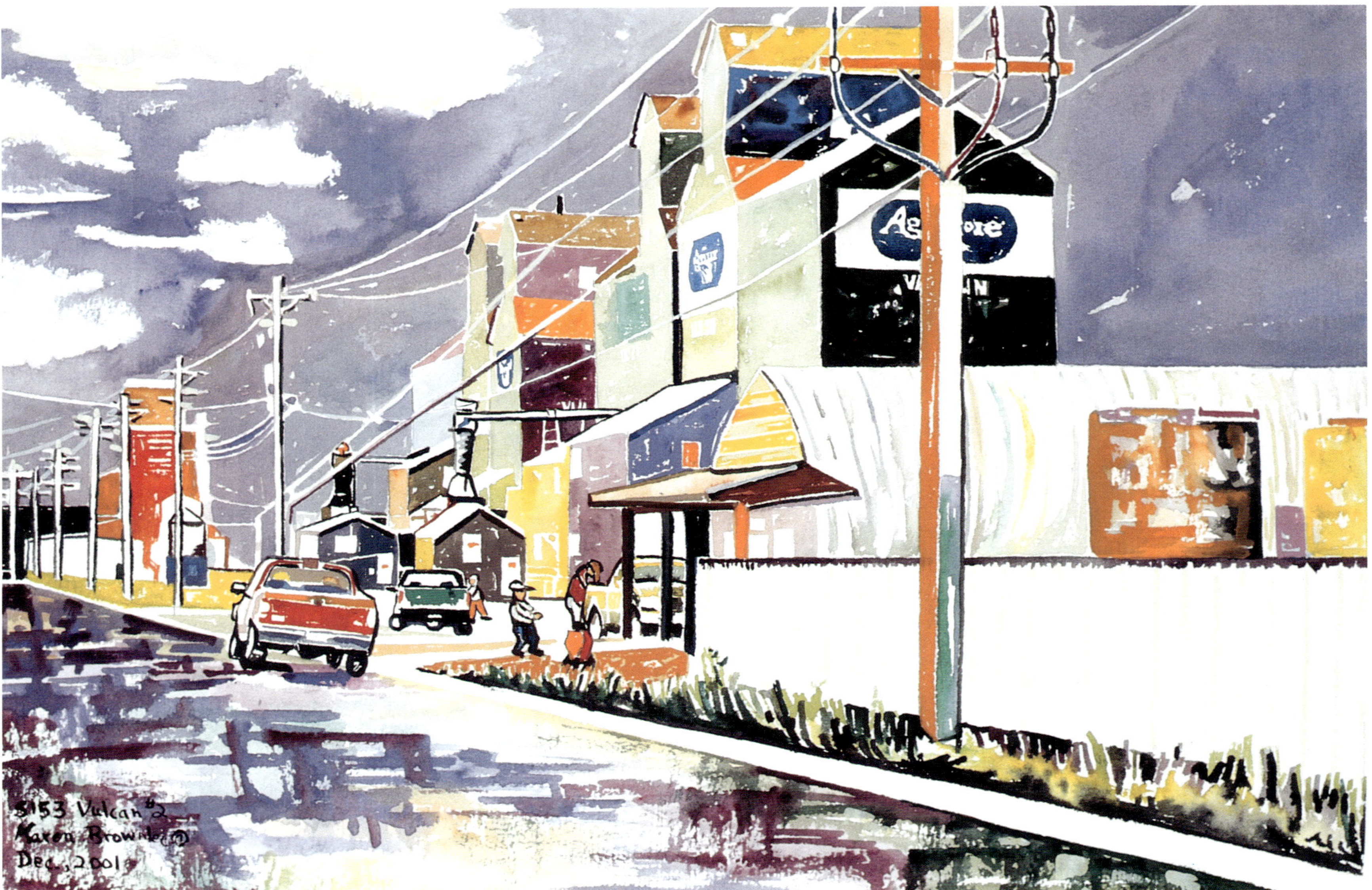

 VULCAN #2, 2001, 18" x 12", CIRCA AUGUST 1999.

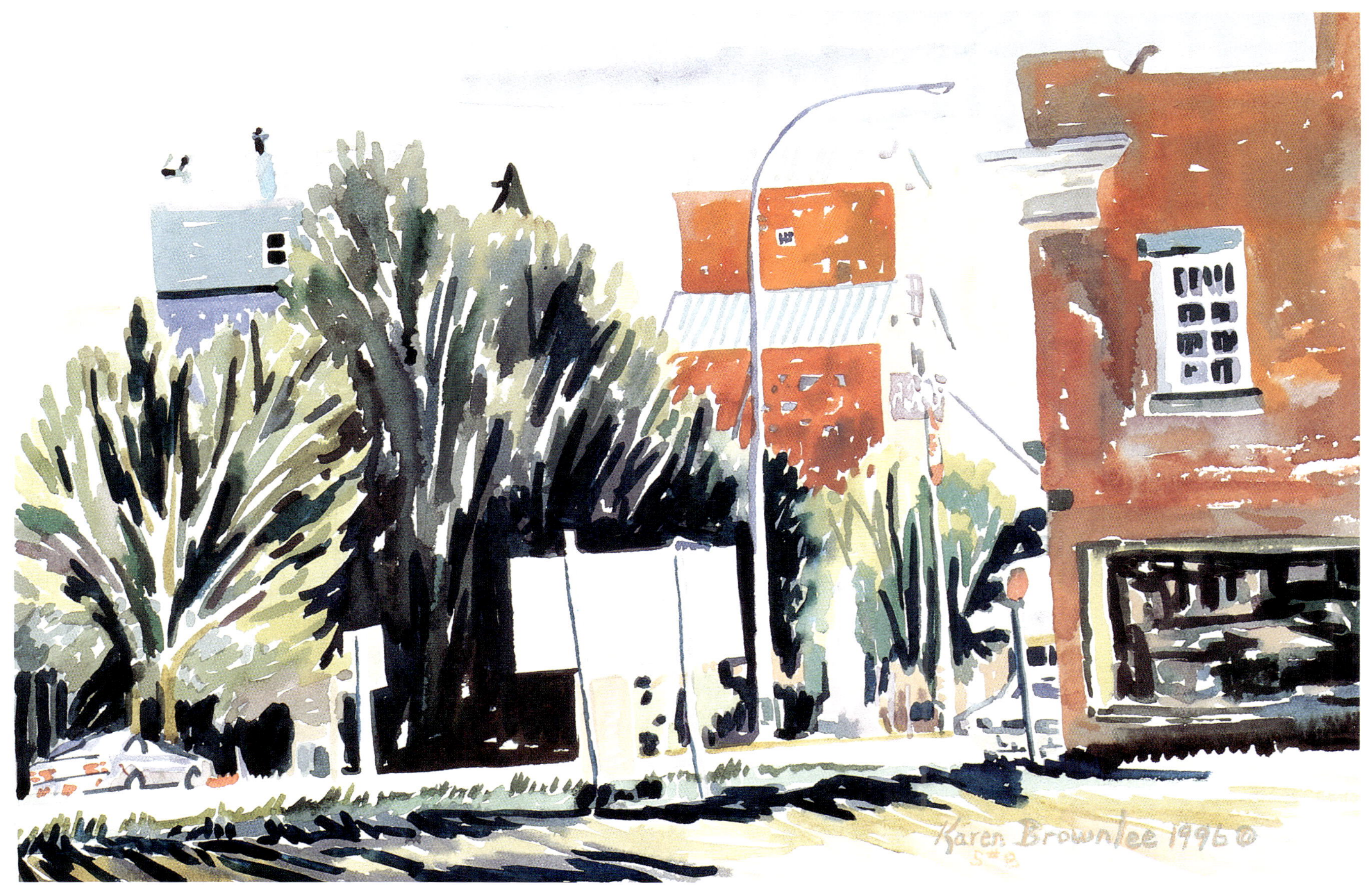

Nanton Lumber and Grain Company built Nanton's first elevator in 1906. By the 1940s seven elevators marked the town's skyline. By 2001 Nanton's elevators were under a 30-day demolition order. The community rallied, buying the land and elevators from CPR in 2003. Pioneer's 1929 "orange elevator" may yet operate again as a tribute to the agricultural history of Nanton.

Nanton #1, 1996, 18" x 12", circa August 1996.

The church and the grain elevator were both gathering places in prairie communities like Scandia. The Canadian Pacific Railway arrived in 1927, and the Alberta Wheat Pool erected the first elevator. As agricultural activity increased, a Federal Grain Company elevator came into service in 1937. Decline came with railway branch line closures. The Eastern Irrigation Historical Park in Scandia now maintains the single surviving elevator.

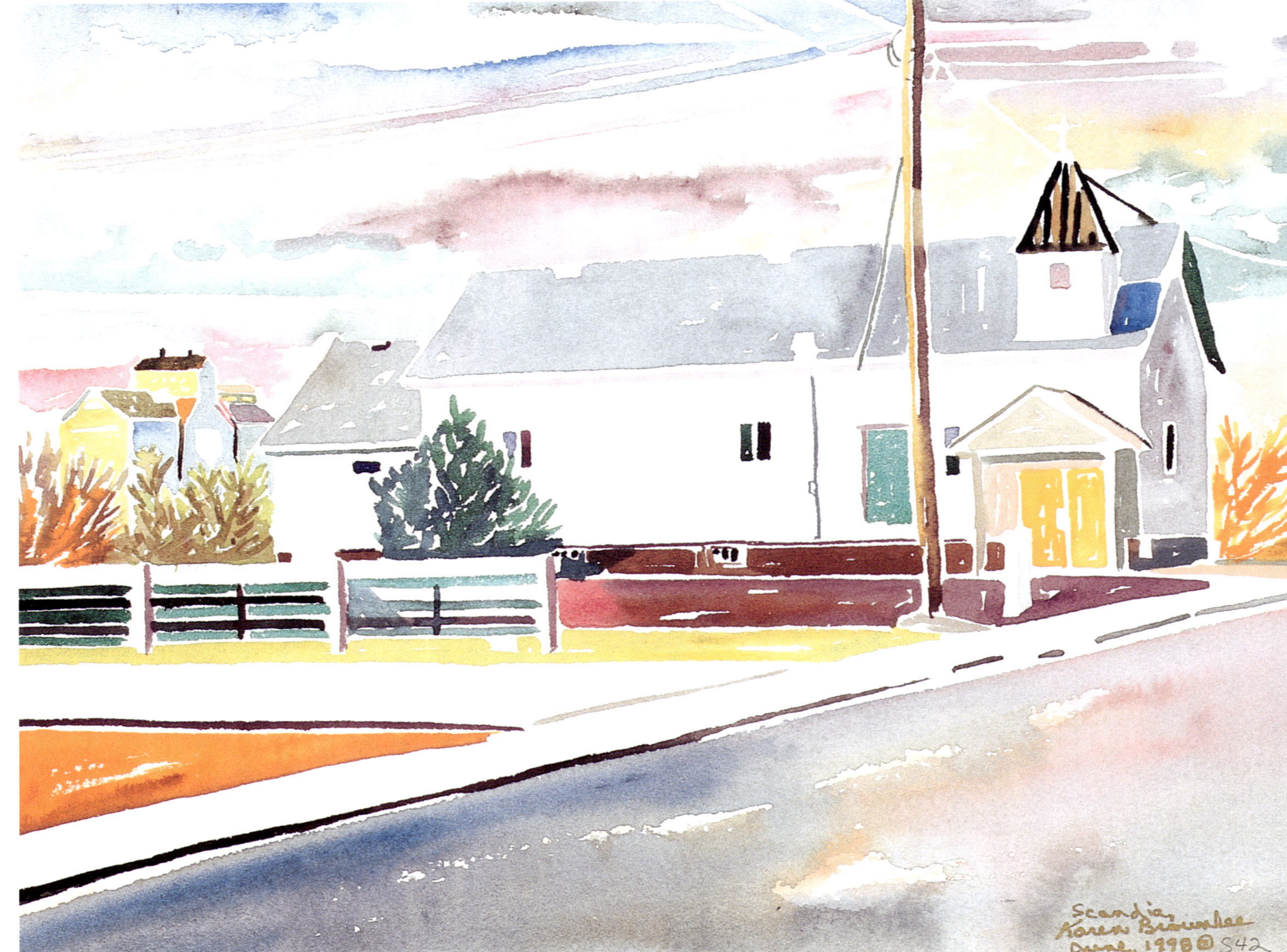

Scandia #1, 1998, 12" x 9", circa June 1997.

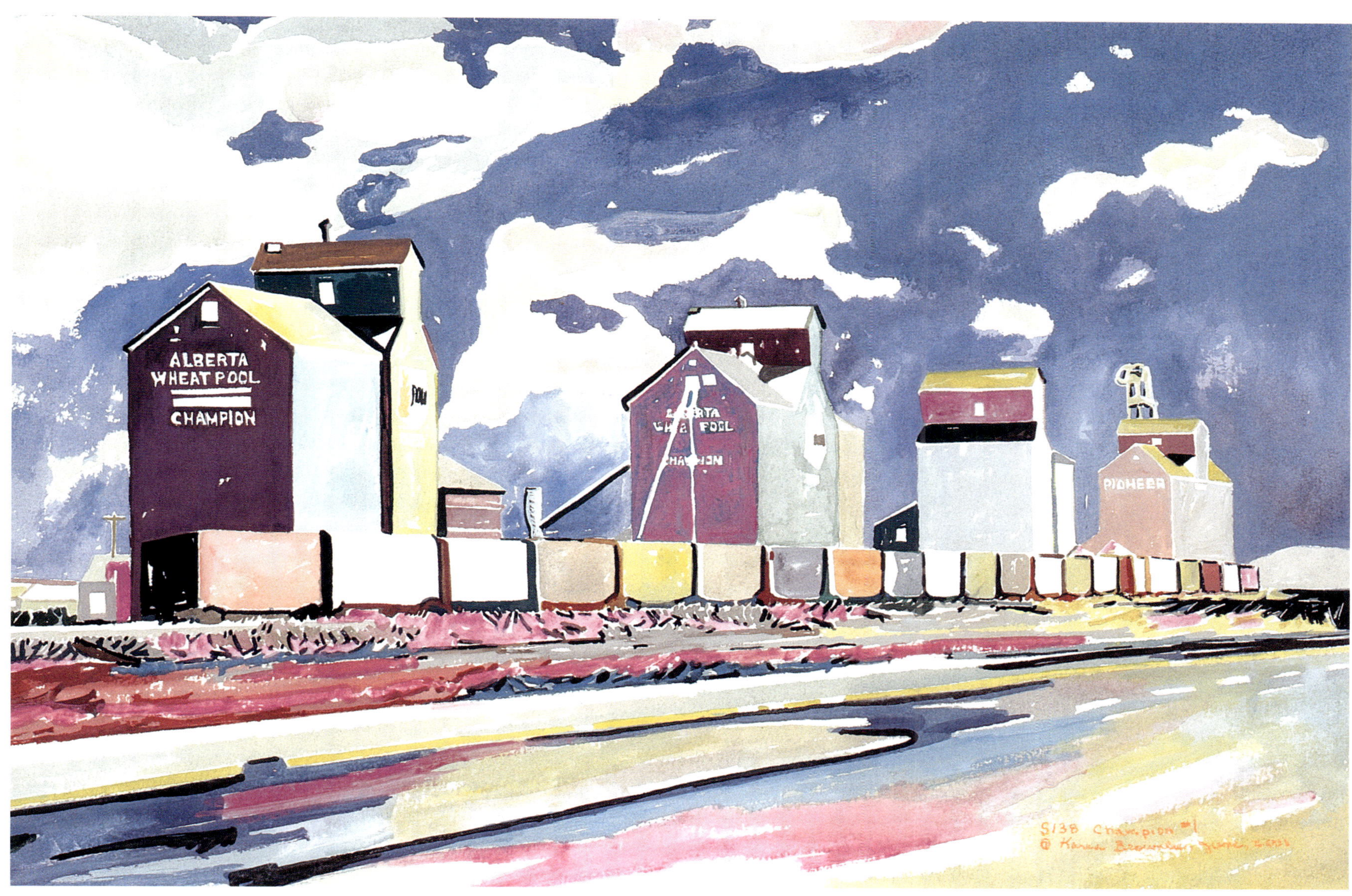

The Alberta Pacific Grain Company built the first elevator in Champion in 1912. Much of the local crop was hailed out that year, but in 1915 Champion was acclaimed as the "Million Bushel Town," when yields as high as 72 bushels per acre were reported. As in neighbouring Vulcan, these yields attracted numerous elevators.

Champion #1, 2001, 18" x 12", circa May 1998.

The Oxley Ranching Company dominated the Stavely area from 1880 to 1900. The company, established in 1882 by Alexander Staveley Hill, QC, MP and Judge Advocate of the Fleet, was named after Hill's residence, Oxley Manor, in Wolverhampton, England. Originally the settlement took the name Oxley, but the name was changed to Staveley to honour Hill. With incorporation in 1912, the second *e* was dropped, and the name became Stavely.

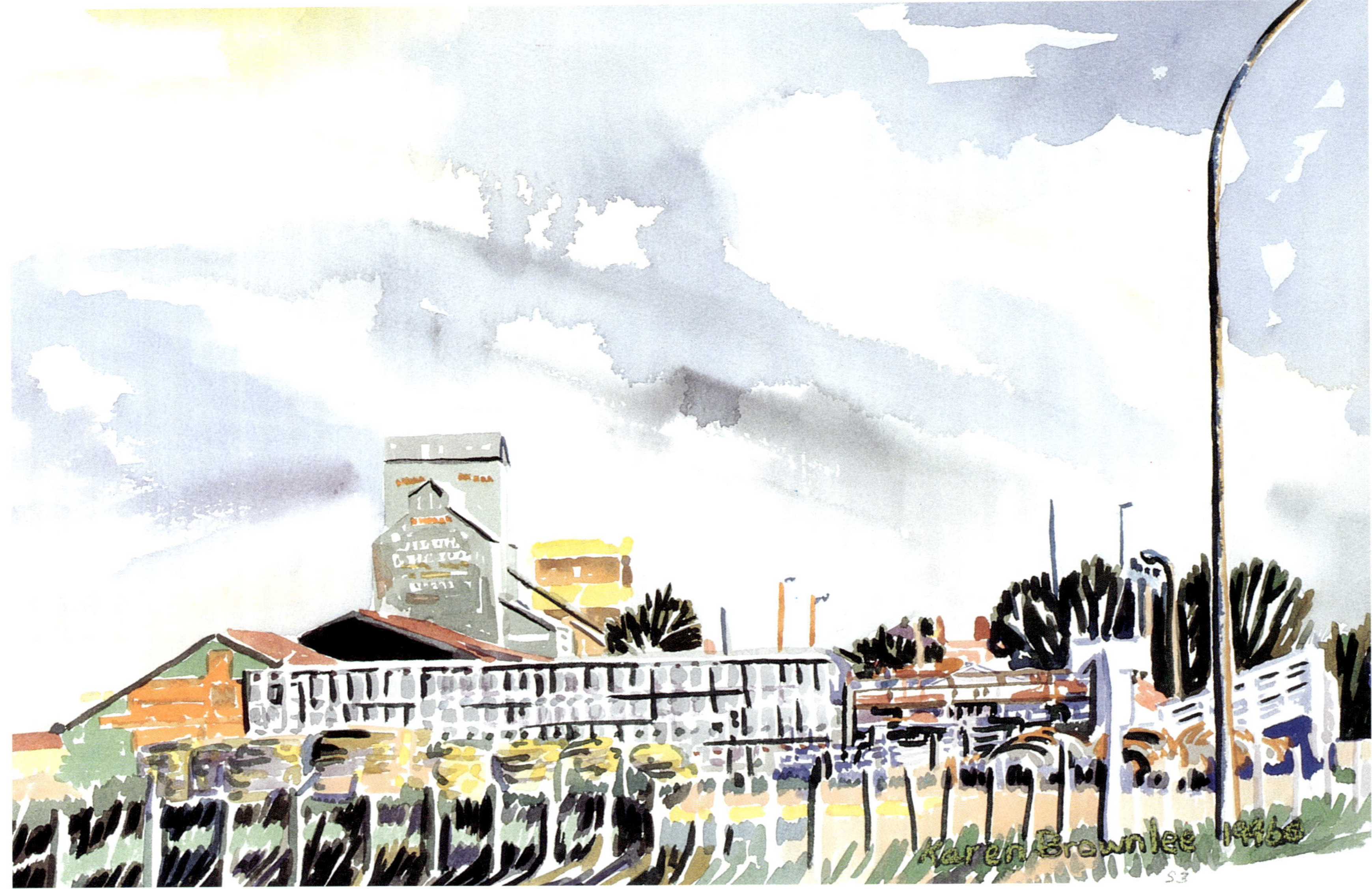

STAVELY #1, 1996, 18" x 12", CIRCA AUGUST 1996.

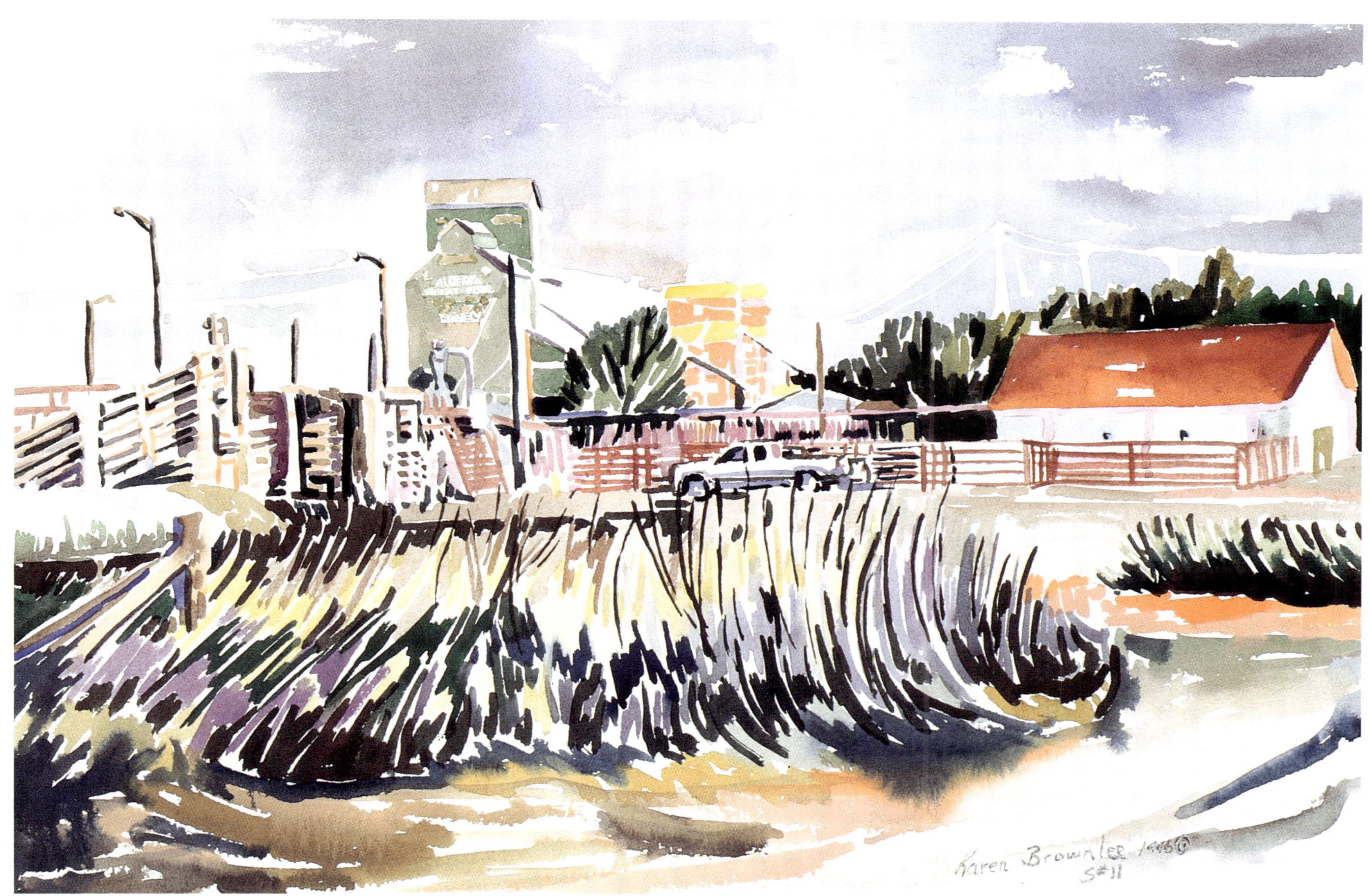

In keeping with its ranching beginnings, Stavely was home to many businesses, including an active auction mart. Like elevators, auction marts served as meeting places, and many generations converged here. The Stavely Auction Mart was owned at one time by friends and neighbours of the artist.

Stavely #2, 1996, 18" x 12", circa August 1996.

The Alberta Farmers' Association, formed in 1906 in Stavely, created a farmer-owned marketing system. In 1907 the association sold 40 shares and purchased Gabe Severson's Lumber and Grain Company elevator. Early pictures reveal an elevator with a pyramid-shaped cupola, similar to the structures on the smaller storage annexes in this painting. These pyramid cupolas were a design that preceded the gable-end cupolas that became more common later.

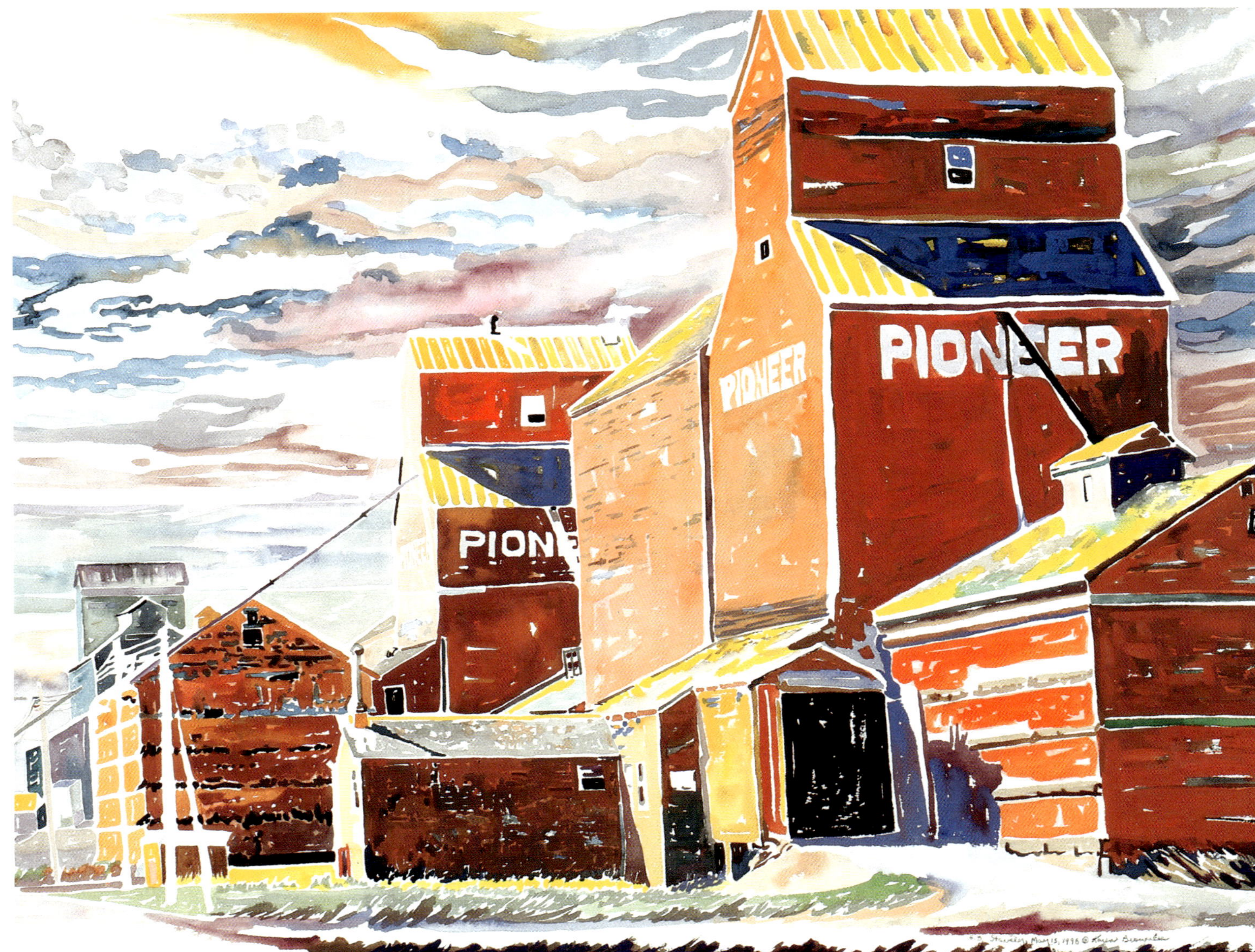

 Stavely #3, 1998, 28" x 21", circa August 1996.

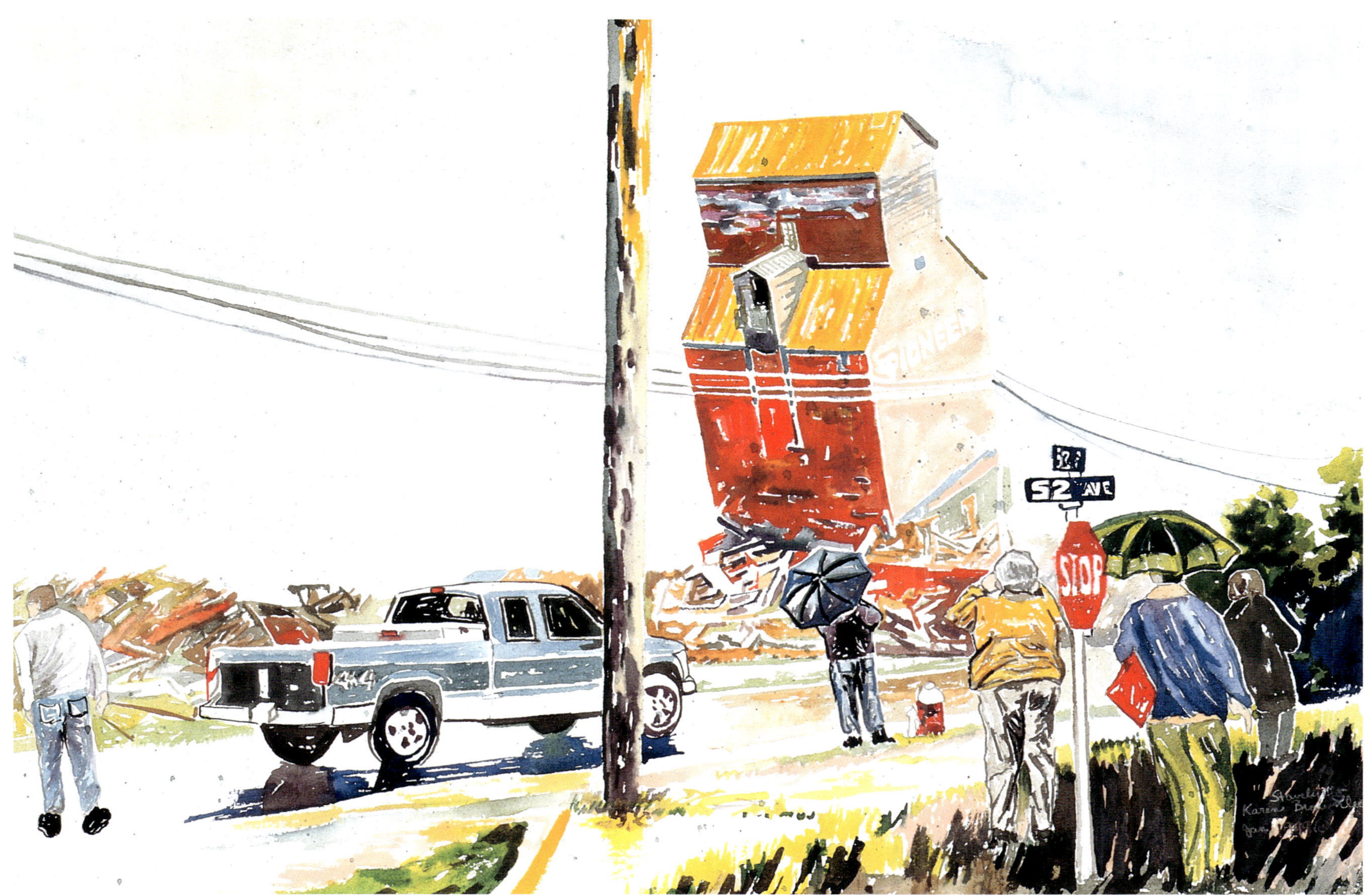

Fire was always the nemesis of the grain elevator. Under the title "A Passage of Old Friends," the *Edmonton Journal* of June 5, 1999, reprinted Karen's colour painting of the destruction of a Stavely landmark. More recently, bulldozers, wrecking balls and changing economic times have taken on the role that fire once played in destroying elevators.

STAVELY #5, 1999, 18" x 12", CIRCA OCTOBER 1998.

In 1920 Stavely boasted Alberta's largest rural elevator, operated by United Grain Growers, a company that first built here in 1913. Historical photographs show a high count of five elevators along the Canadian Pacific Railway track in Staveley. Now the highway bypasses the town entirely. A landmark sign informs travellers of the significance of both ranching and grain farming to the locality.

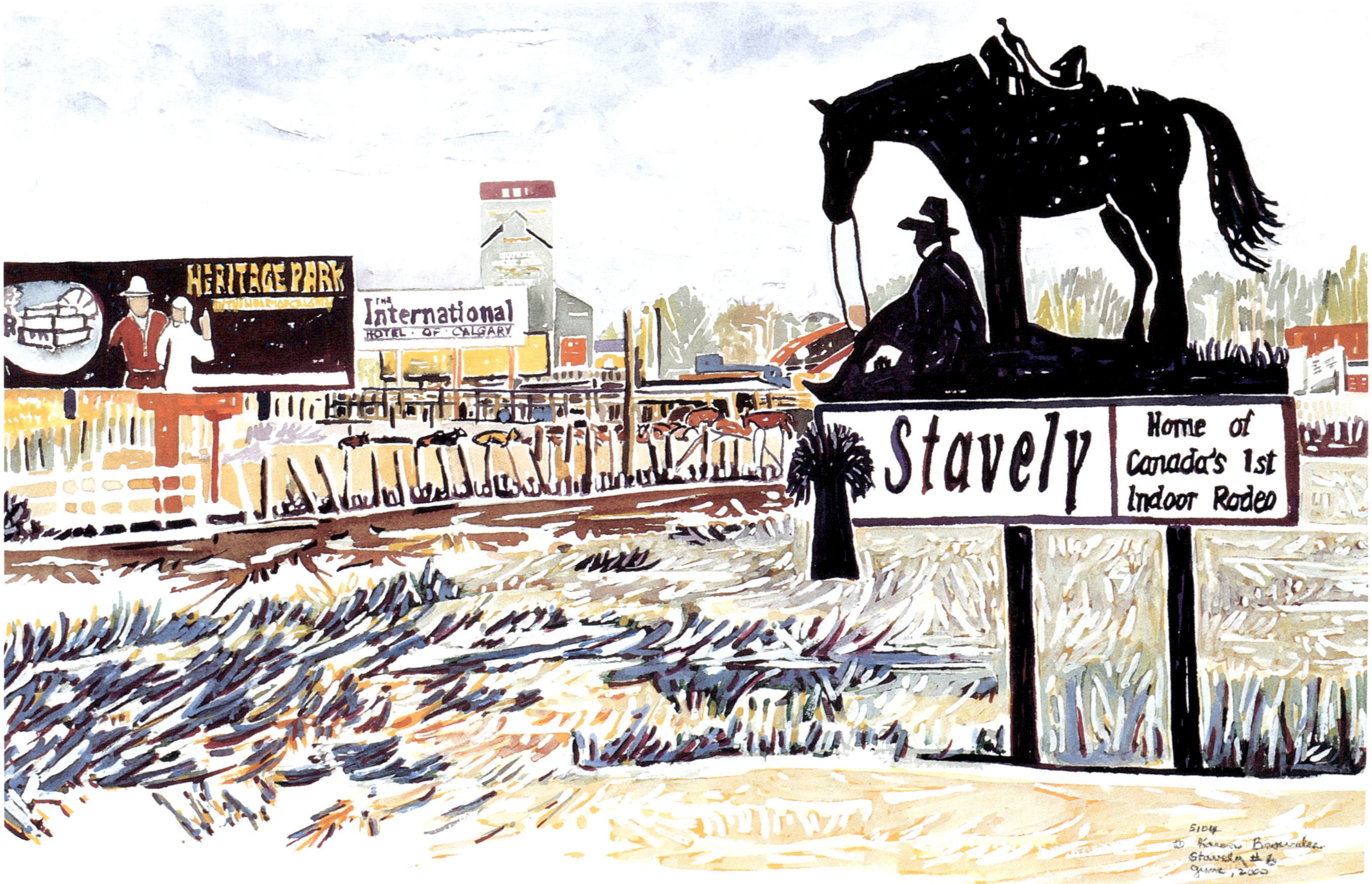

 STAVELY #6, 2000, 18" x 12", circa September 1998.

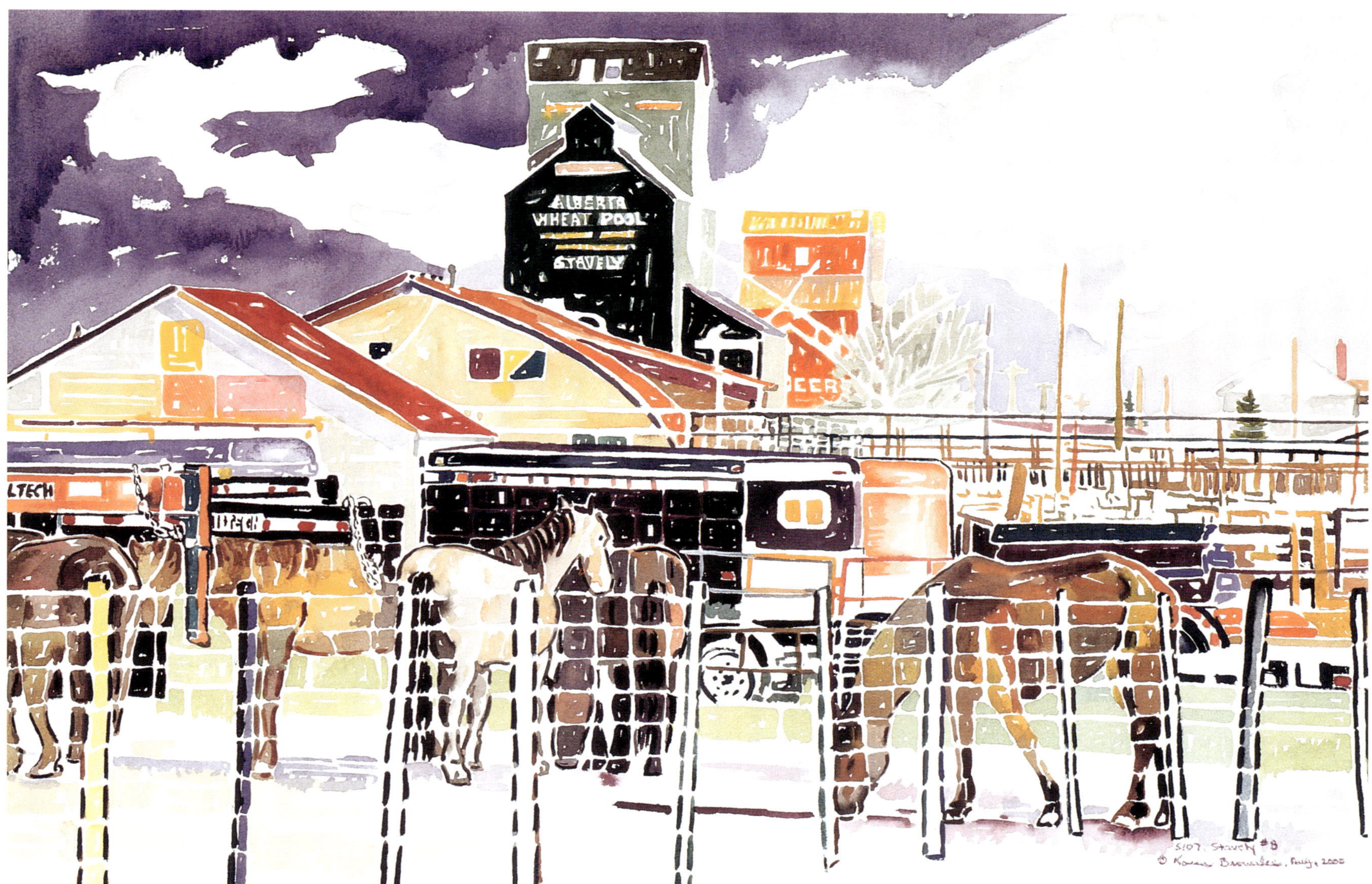

In 1920 CPR grain cars holding 700 bushels were loaded by hand before being moved, 17 cars at a time, to Cayley for shipping. Grain handling capacity at Stavely expanded from the 65,000 bushels in 1911 to over 325,000 bushels in 1928. More development was to come.

Stavely #8, 2000, 18" x 12", circa May 1998.

Stavely boomed as an elevator town through the 1940s. Even though fire destroyed the Searle and United Grain Growers facilities in 1941, capacity increased with the building of annexes. Wooden or metal storage facilities attached directly to the main elevator, or free standing units connected by moveable delivery spouts and augers, were constructed. Both types can be seen in this watercolour.

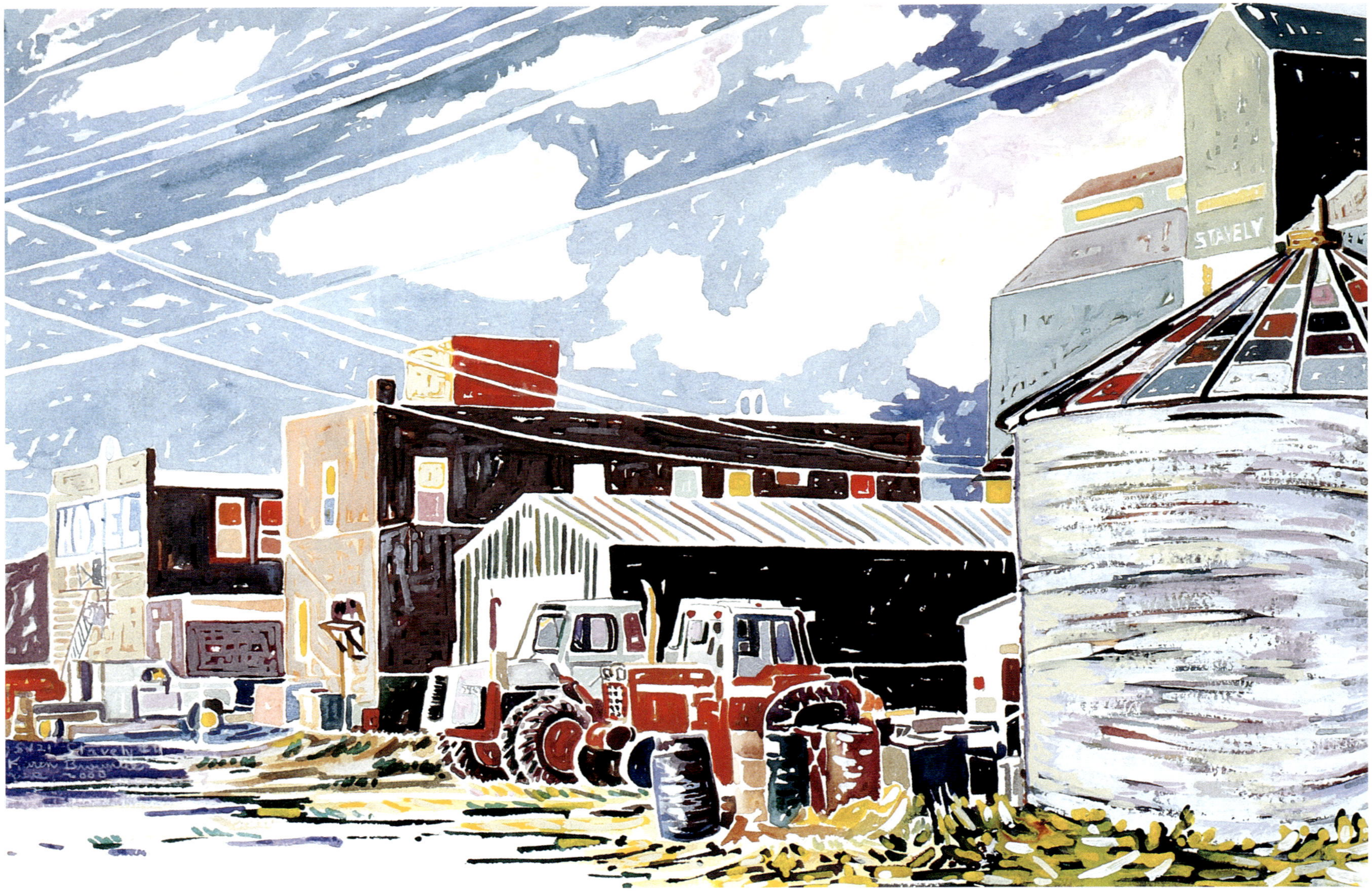

 Stavely #9, 2000, 18" x 12", circa May 1998.

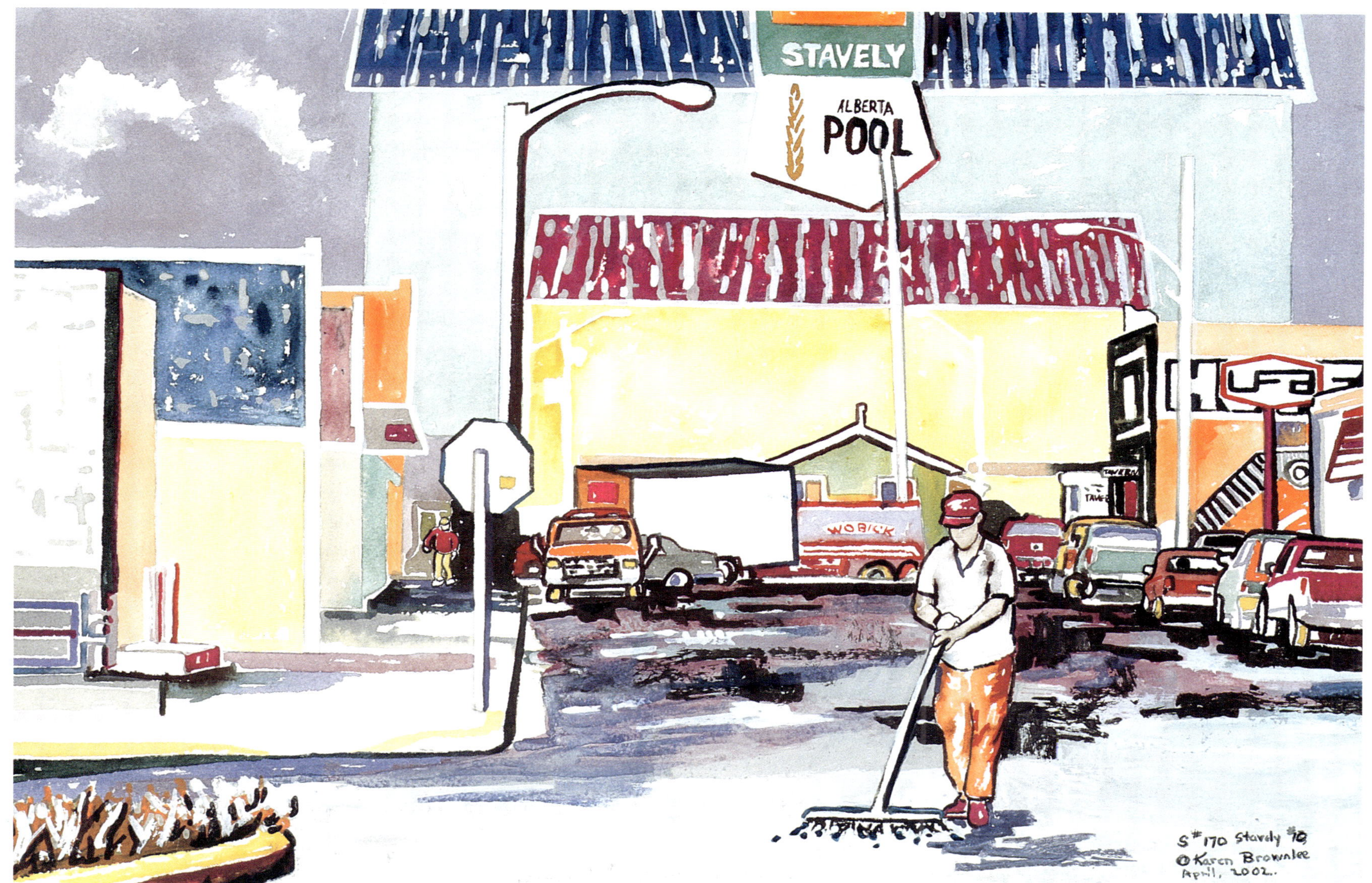

The Alberta Wheat Pool elevator still looms over the daily activities of Stavely. Storage needs increased with slower grain movement, and by the mid-1970s, the Wheat Pool, United Grain Growers and Pioneer operated elevators with a capacity of just over 700,000 bushels. The decline of rail service reduced the need for this kind of capacity in small communities across the prairies.

Stavely #10, 2002, 18" x 12", circa September 1998.

Three colour schemes were common among elevators: white and deep reddish-brown (not depicted here) were early colours. Bright orange, the signature of Pioneer, and the muted blue-green of United Grain Growers, Alberta Wheat Pool and Agricore are newer. The drive shed attached to the elevator, adjacent engine shed and ancillary storage facilities also demonstrate a typical configuration of buildings.

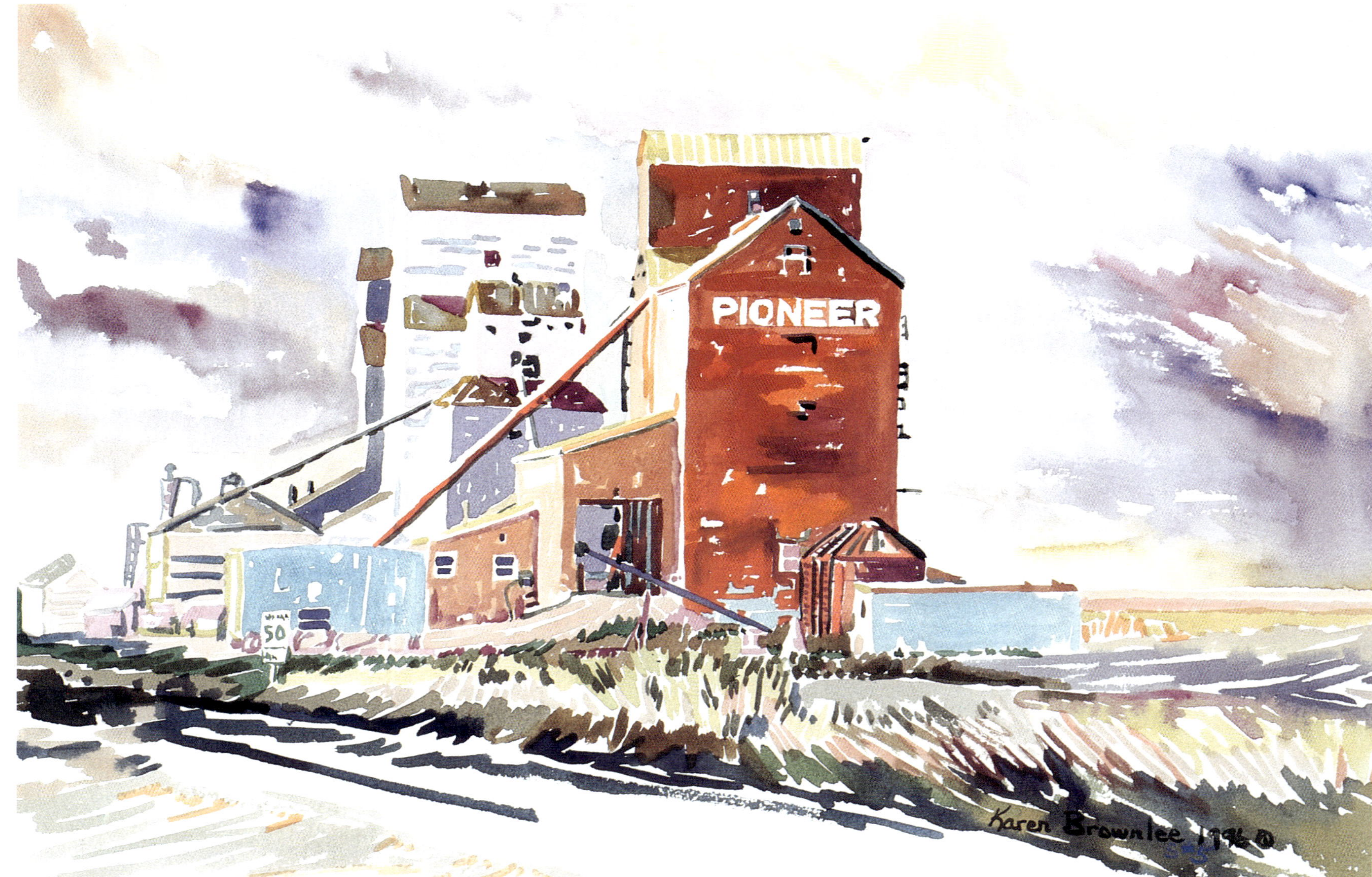

 SOUTHERN ALBERTA GRAIN ELEVATORS #1, 1996, 18" x 12", CIRCA 1995.

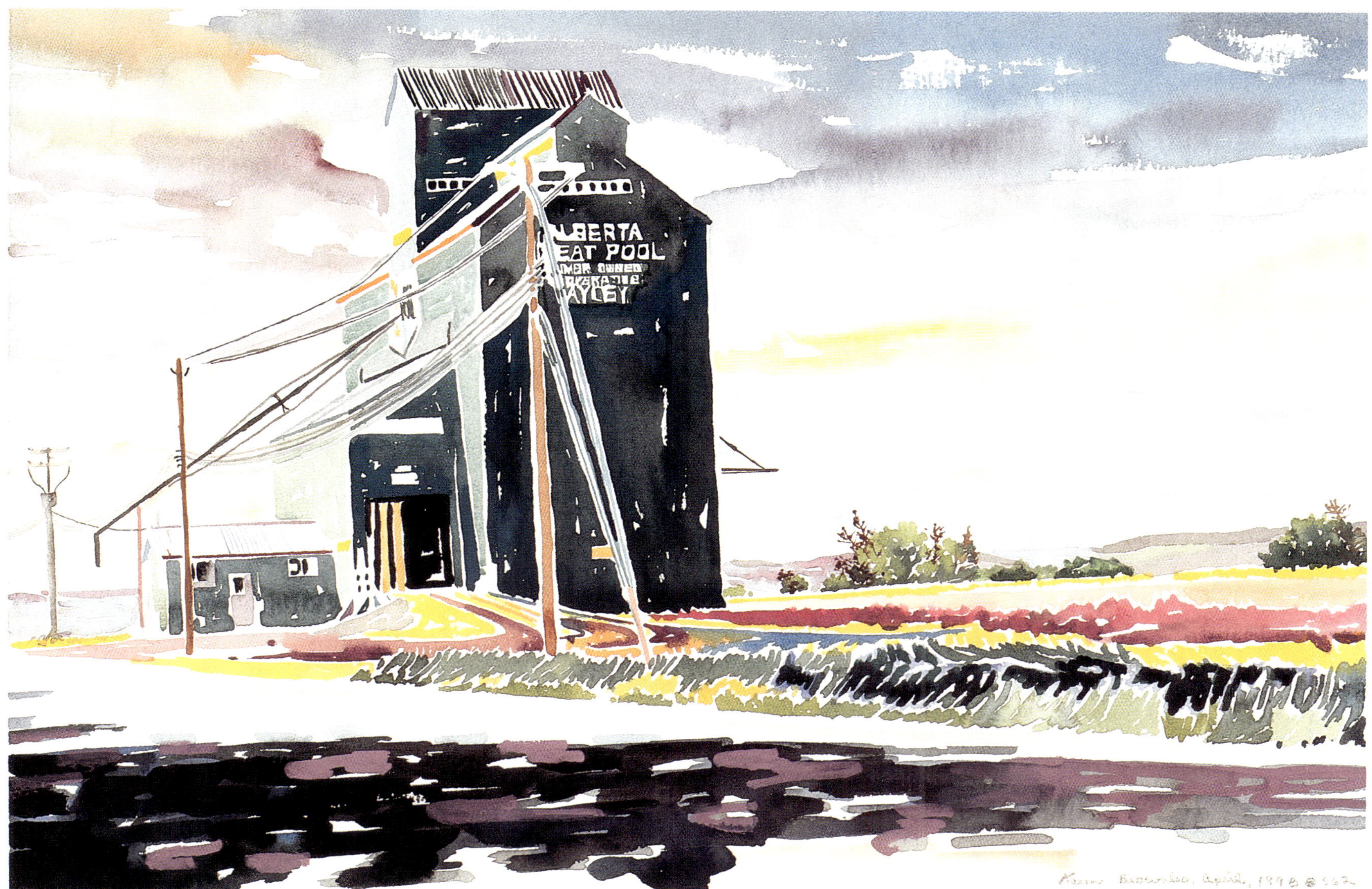

Cayley's first elevator was built in 1906 by the Cayley Union of the Society of Equity. Farmers often banded together to construct an elevator, thus ensuring fair returns for their grain. Communities planted trees in these gathering places, and the foreground shade recalls this fact. The artist recalls replanting the 100-year-old poplars that were dying out on the family farm in the 1990s.

Cayley #1, 1998, 18" x 12", circa October 1998.

The name *Enchant*, bestowed in 1915, says it all. Like most prairie towns, Enchant was born in hope. Hope meant elevators to market the bounty hard work would bring. The first elevator opened in Enchant in 1915, an through the years, six served the community. Though drought was always a threat, irrigation, implemented more fully in 1954 under the Prairie Farm Rehabilitation Act, provided a boost to local agriculture.

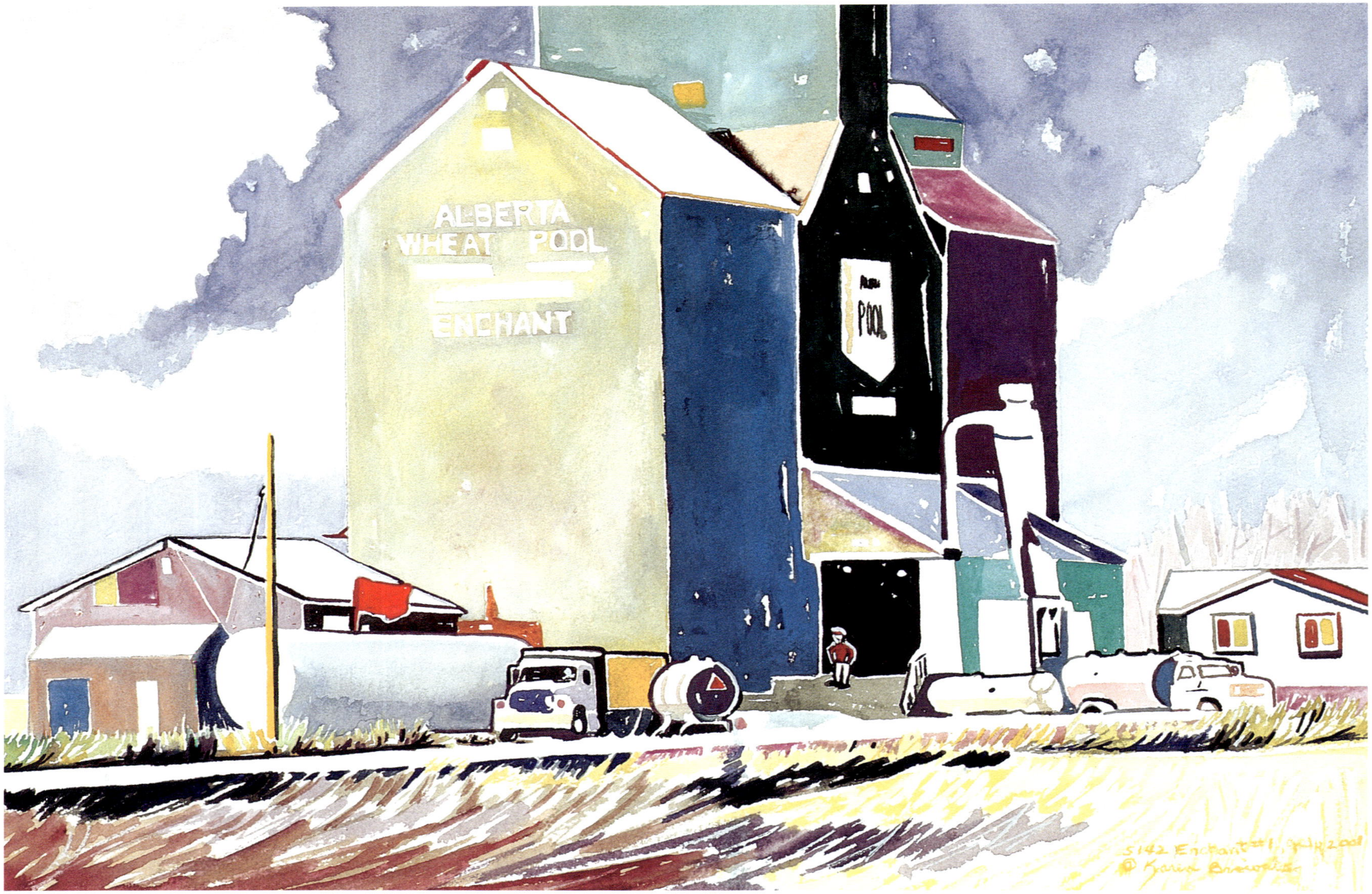

 Enchant #1, 2001, 18" x 12", circa June 1997.

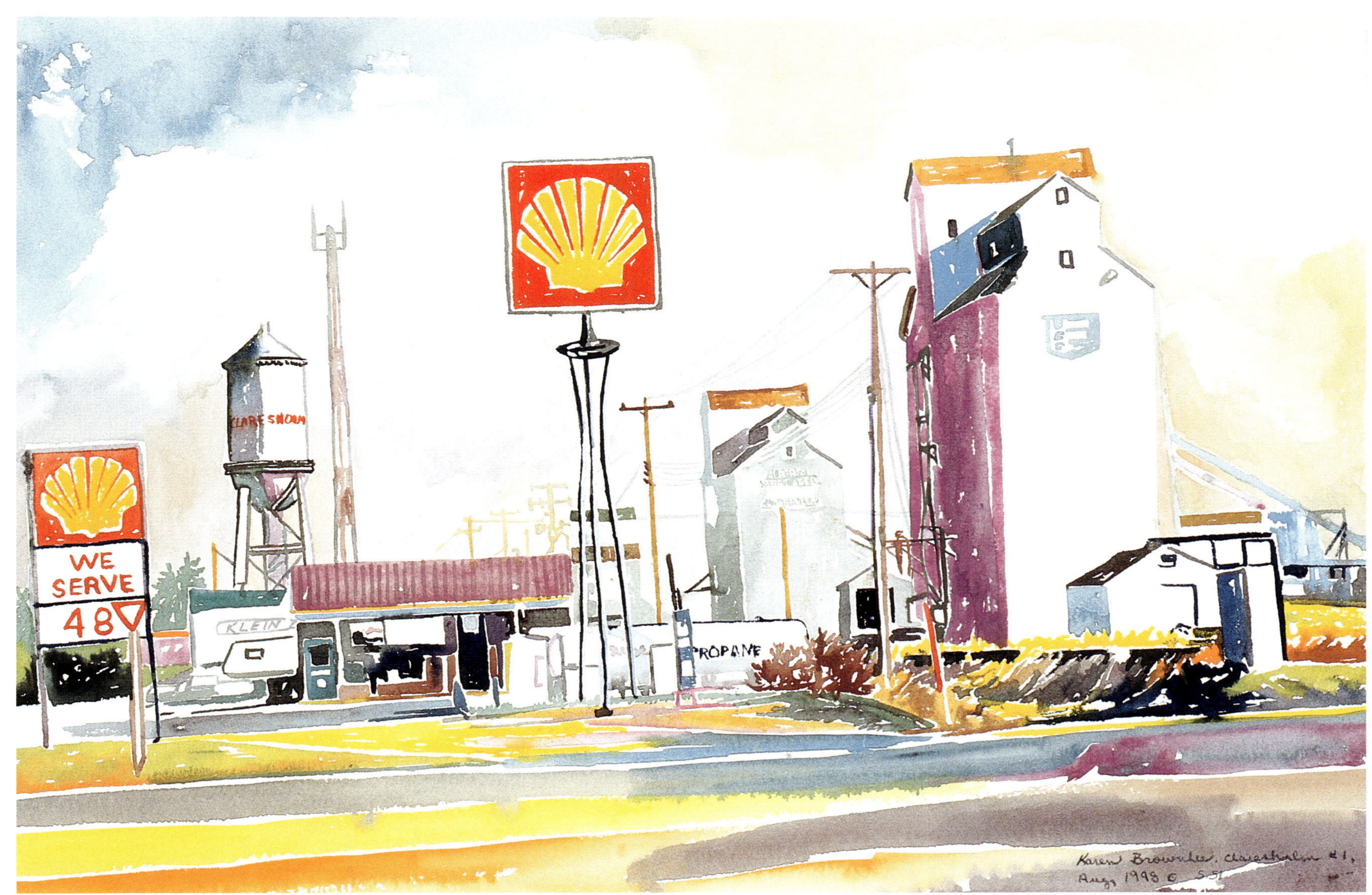

Claresholm was chosen as a railway station and siding in 1891 because a slough provided ample water for the steam engines. It was also in a hollow, thus preventing boxcar run-aways. The first elevator, constructed on the west side of the track, was later dismantled and moved to the east side. At its height, Claresholm boasted six elevators.

CLARESHOLM #1. 1998, 18" x 12", CIRCA MAY 1998.

Named for a well-known Winnipeg wholesale merchant, Whitla had four elevators over the years. Only two were standing by 1960, both owned by the Alberta Wheat Pool. This image shows the one remaining, with the operator's house and its planting of trees. The artist observes that the land, apart from this evidence of human habitation, "appears as a sea of flowing, sweeping grass."

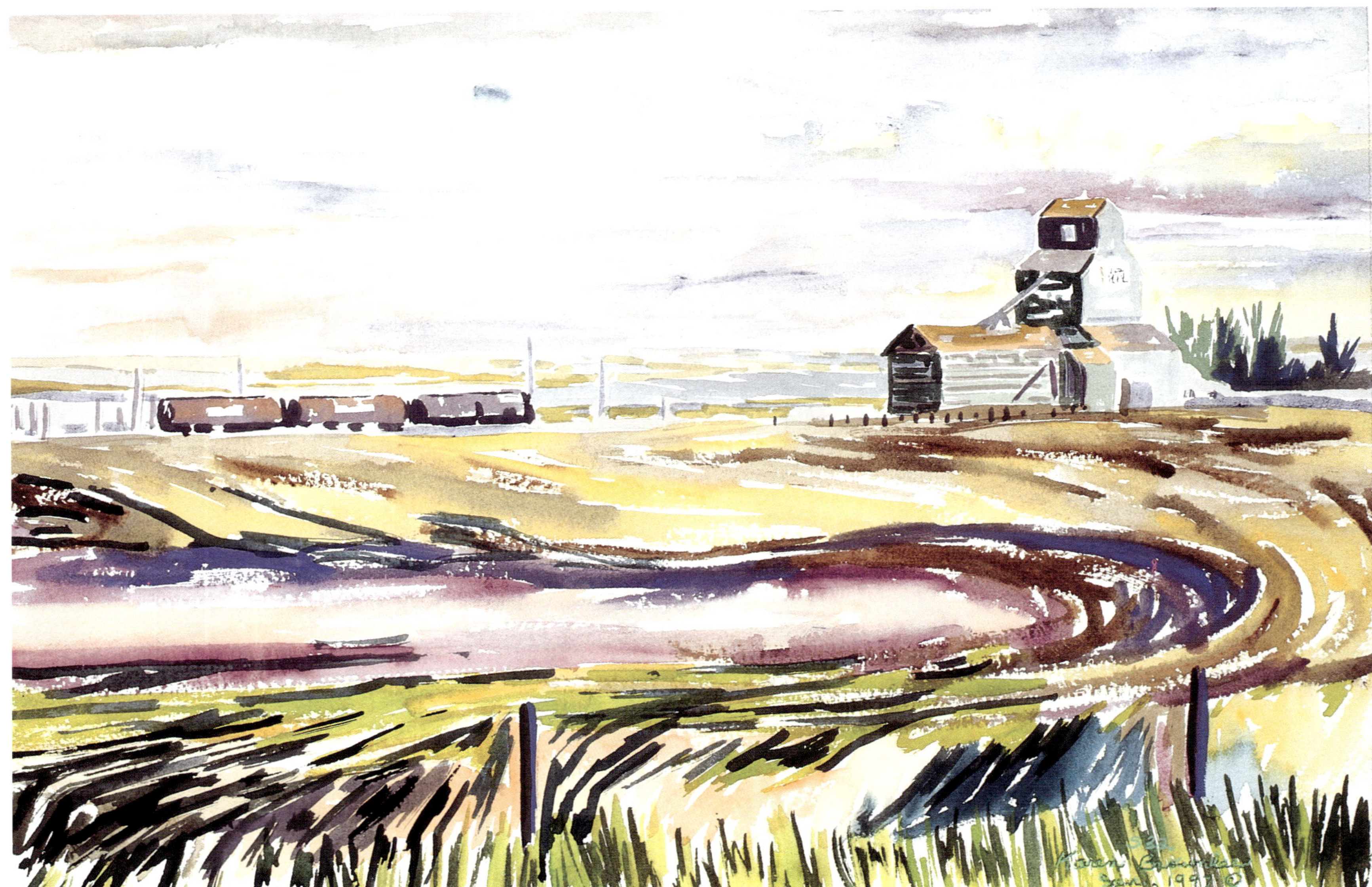

 Whitla #1, 1997, 18" x 12", circa June 1996.

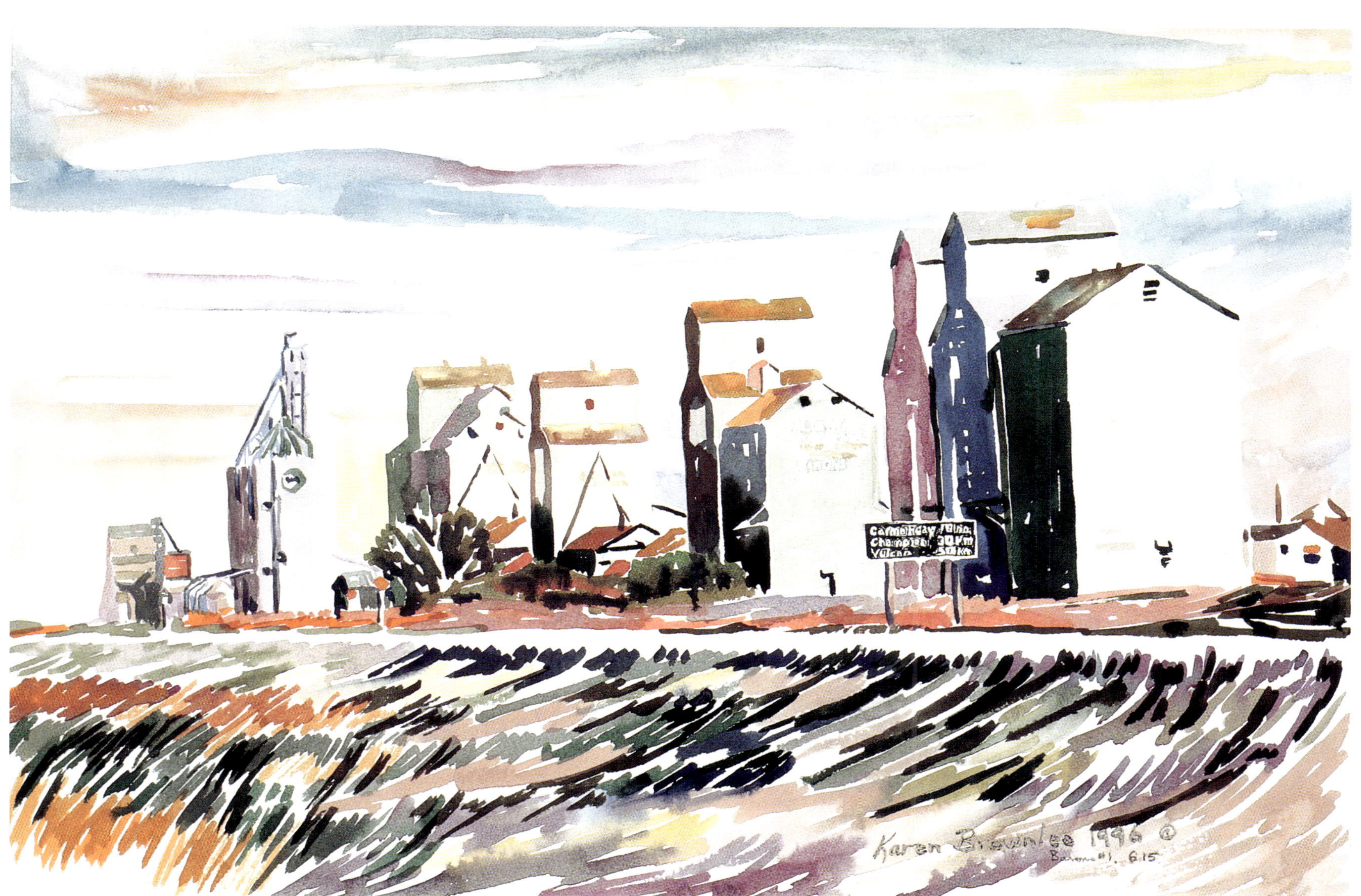

Until 1909 shipping grain from Barons meant two days of travel to Lethbridge or Claresholm. Between 1910 and 1912, five companies—the H.E. Norris Elevator Company, Alberta Pacific, Independent, National Grain Company, and Vancouver Milling Company—had facilities here. Barons' long-time slogan, "The Wheat Heart of the West," was still valid in the mid-1970s, when the town's nine elevators had a capacity of over 1,125,000 bushels.

BARONS #1, 1996, 18" x 12", CIRCA JUNE 1995.

The first post office at this site was named Blayney. When the land was purchased by the Canadian Pacific Railway in 1909, a new settlement was established just across the track, and Blayney disappeared. The CPR named the new settlement Baron to honour a company official. Local usage changed the name to Barons.

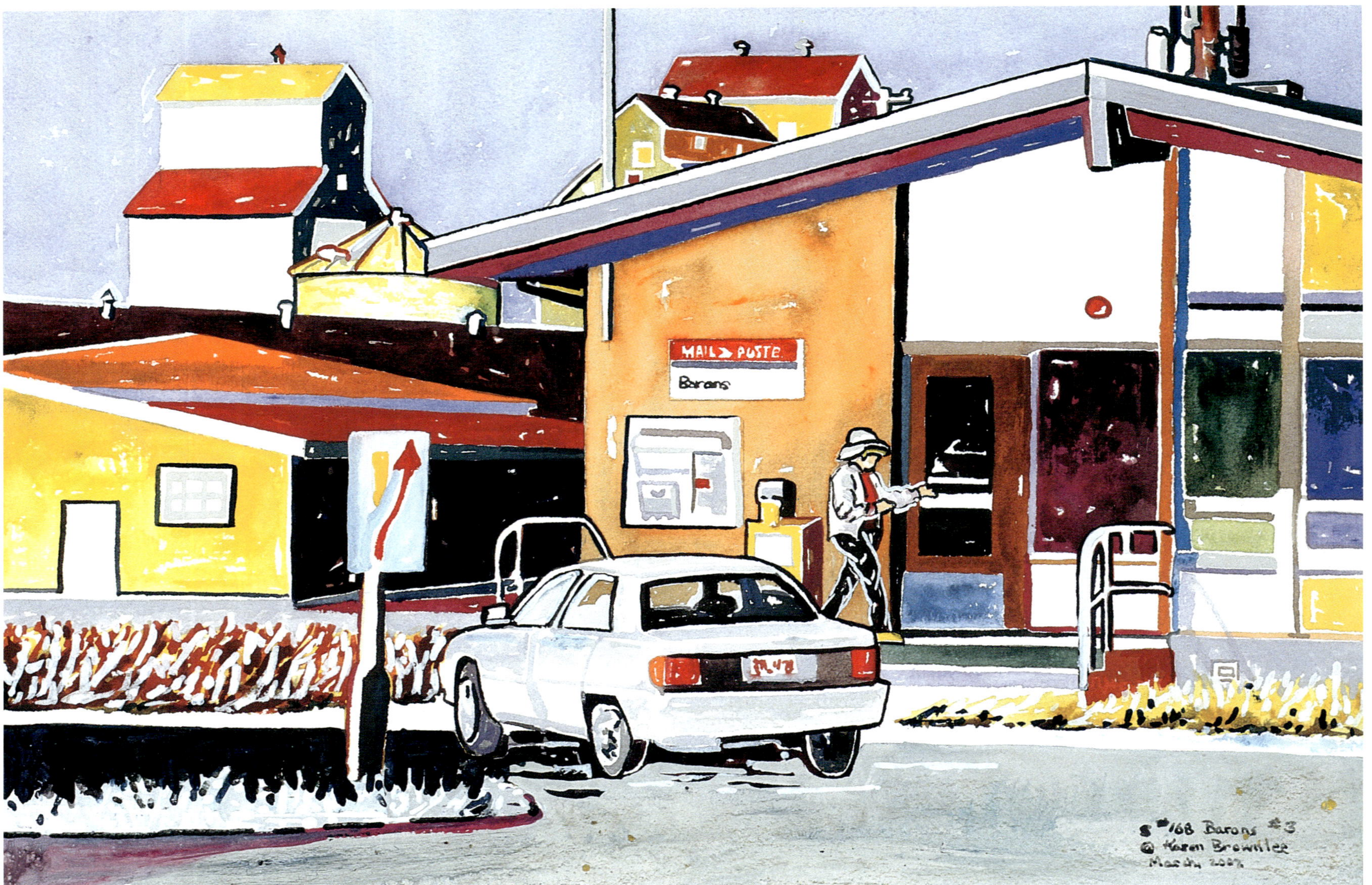

 Barons #3, 2002, 18" x 12", circa May 1998.

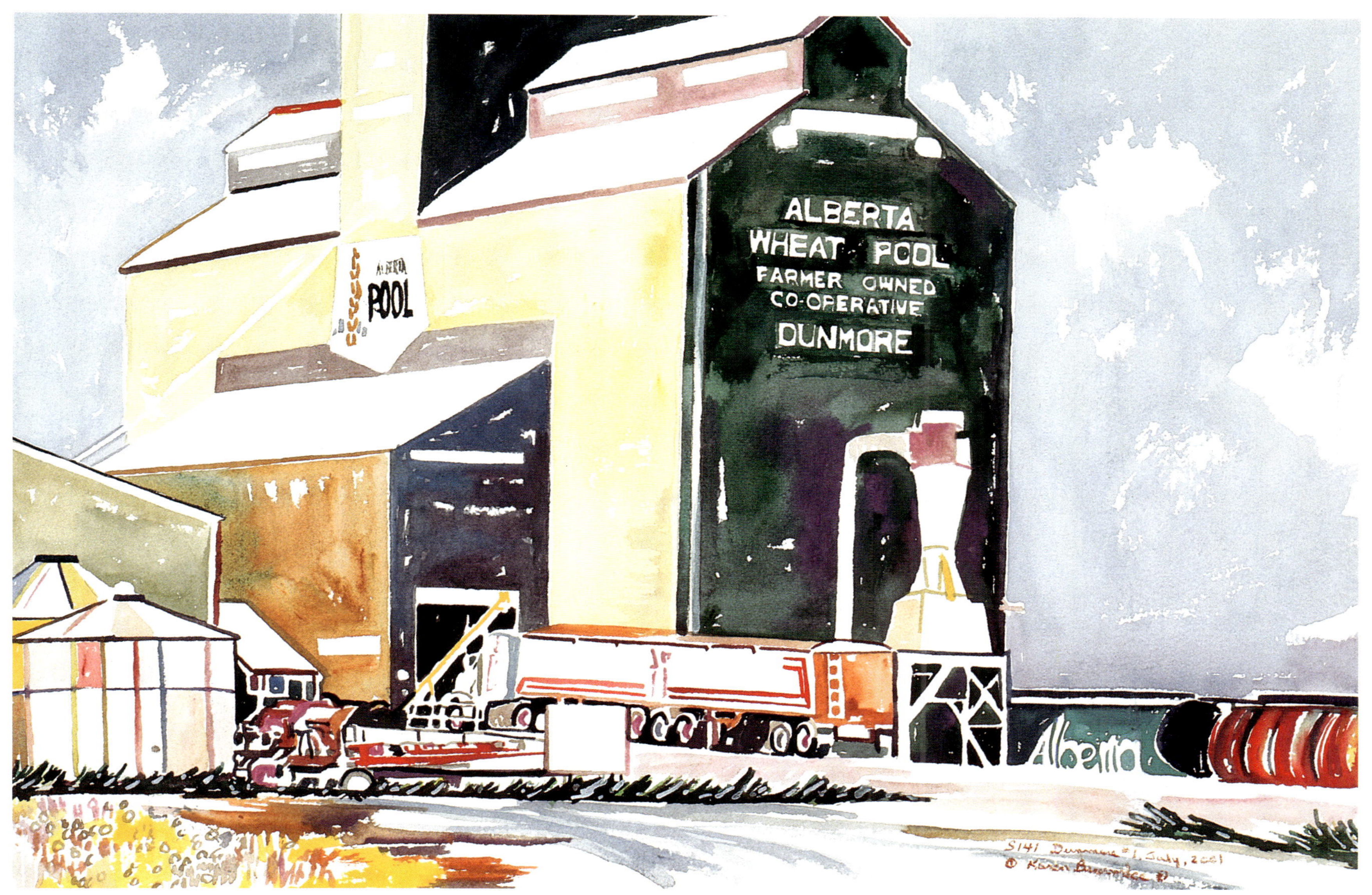

The railway came to Dunmore to access coal, but from 1883 onward the area was most noted as a coal-shipping centre. Lord Dunmore, a member of the Canadian Agricultural Coal and Colonization Company gave his name to the settlement. In 1911, Dunmore was the eastern terminus of the Crowsnest section of the Canadian Pacific Railway.

DUNMORE #1, 2001, 18" X 12", CIRCA JUNE 1996.

First known as Twenty Mile Post, Irvine was renamed to commemorate Colonel A. G. Irvine, a North-West Mounted Police commissioner during the Riel Rebellion of 1885. The CPR built a depot in the area in 1882. Local histories variously credit the first elevator to Five Roses in 1895 or the Irvine Elevator Company, which built an elevator in 1907.

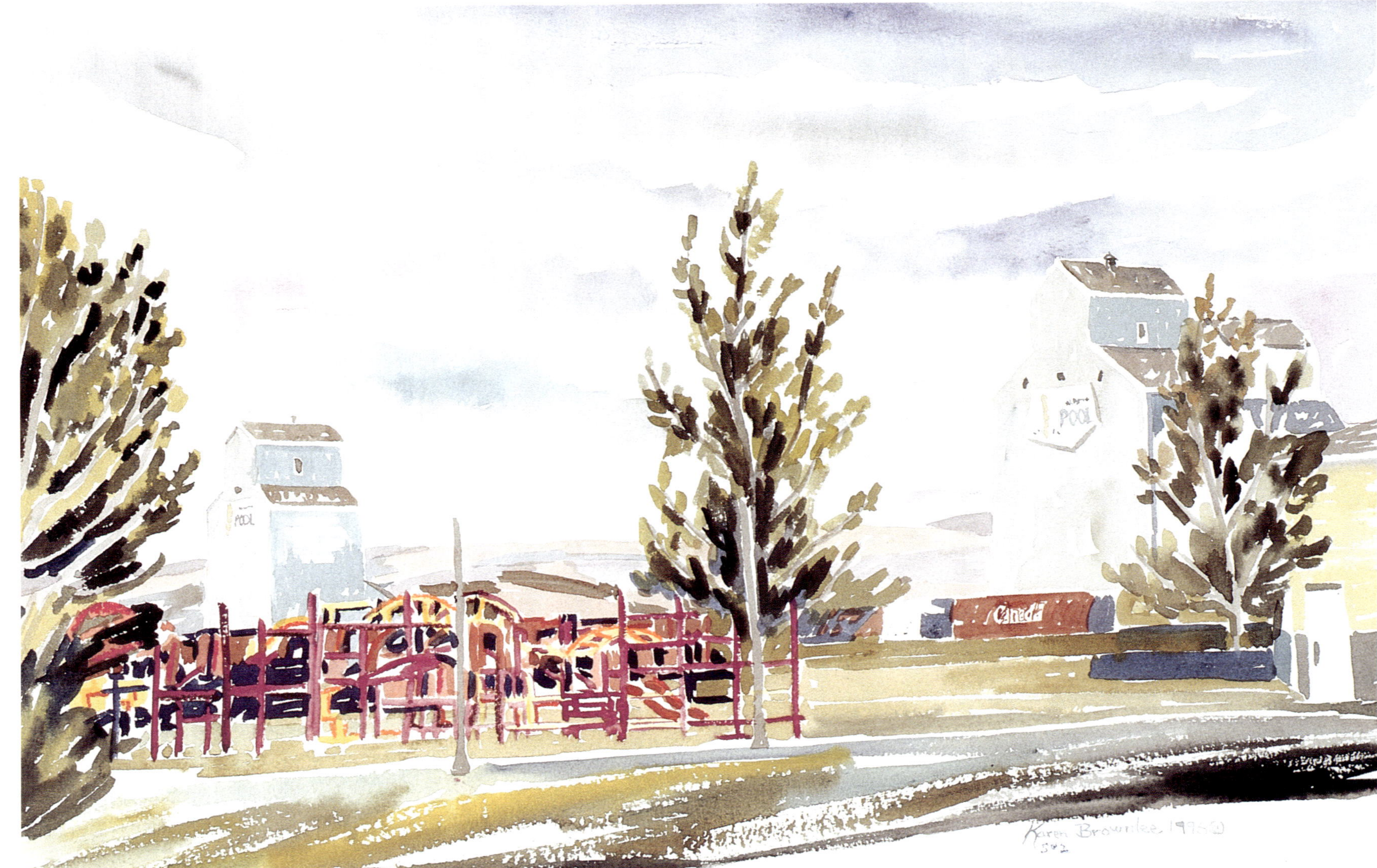

 IRVINE #1, 1996, 18" X 12", CIRCA JUNE 1996.

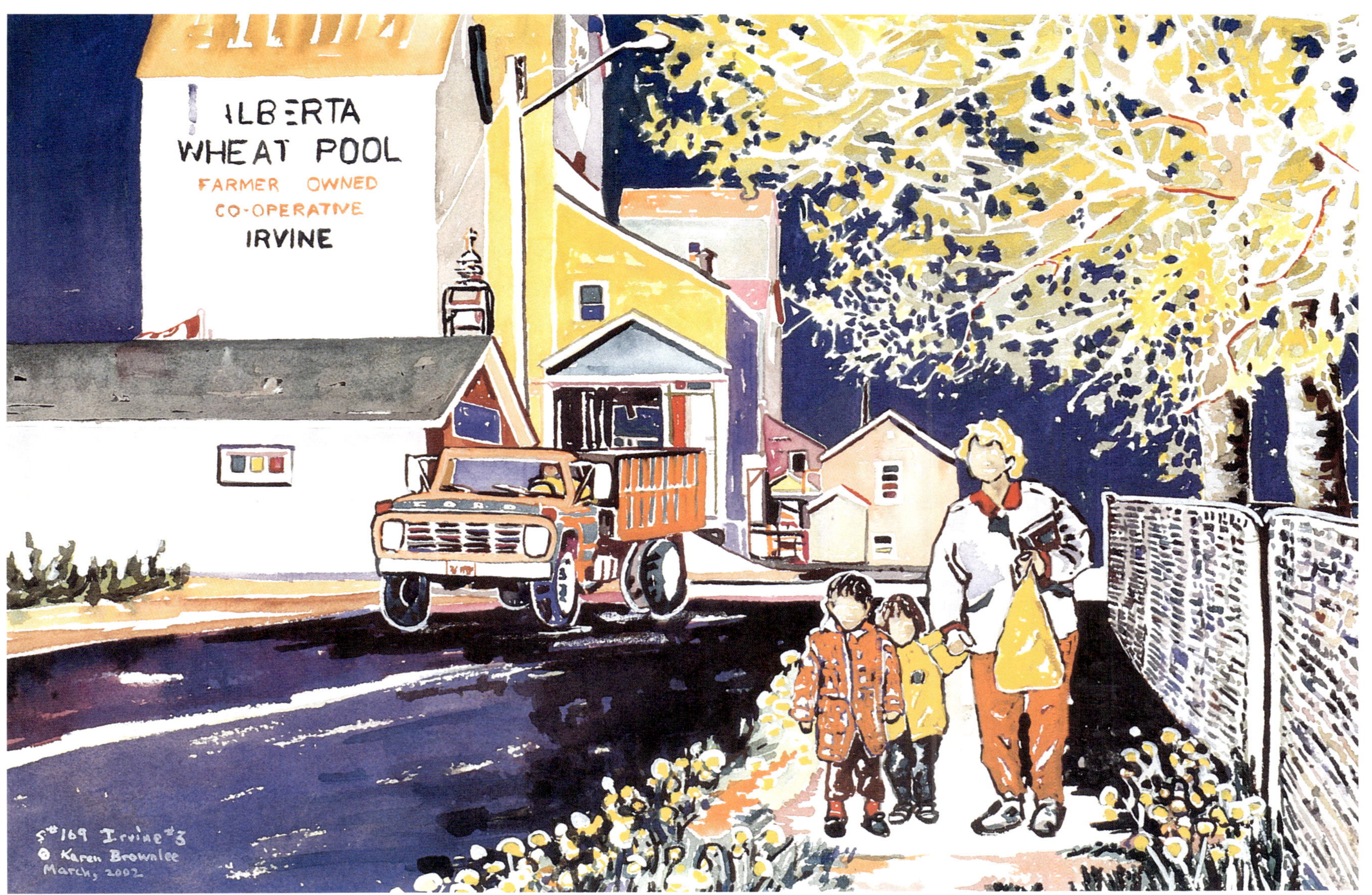

From 1907 to 1929, the Irvine Elevator Company, Alberta Pacific Grain Elevator Company, Ogilvie, Maple Leaf and Lake of the Woods all operated in Irvine. The Alberta Wheat Pool constructed an elevator here in 1929 and became an important presence over the years, adding a balloon annex in 1941, purchasing the Ogilvie Flour Mill in 1960 and building another 70,000 bushel structure in 1970.

IRVINE #3, 2002, 18" X 12", CIRCA JUNE 1996.

Turin became a name on the map with the opening of the post office on November 1, 1910. The name was taken from an imported Percheron stallion owned by a syndicate of local farmers. Percherons represented 70 percent of the draft horses in North America in a 1930 census. Such strong draft animals were needed well into the century to transport grain from field to elevator.

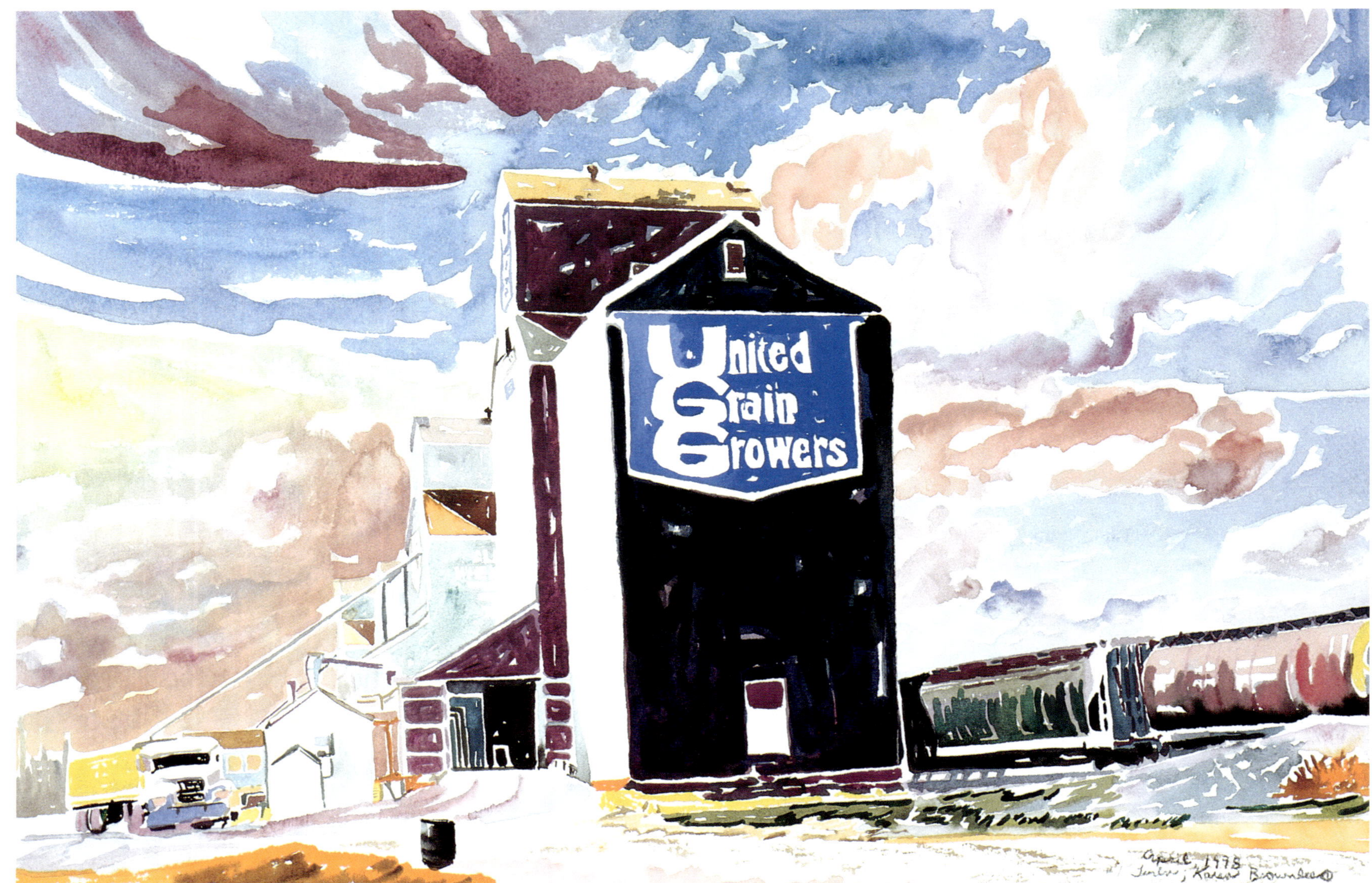

 TURIN #1, 1998, 18" x 12", CIRCA JUNE 1997.

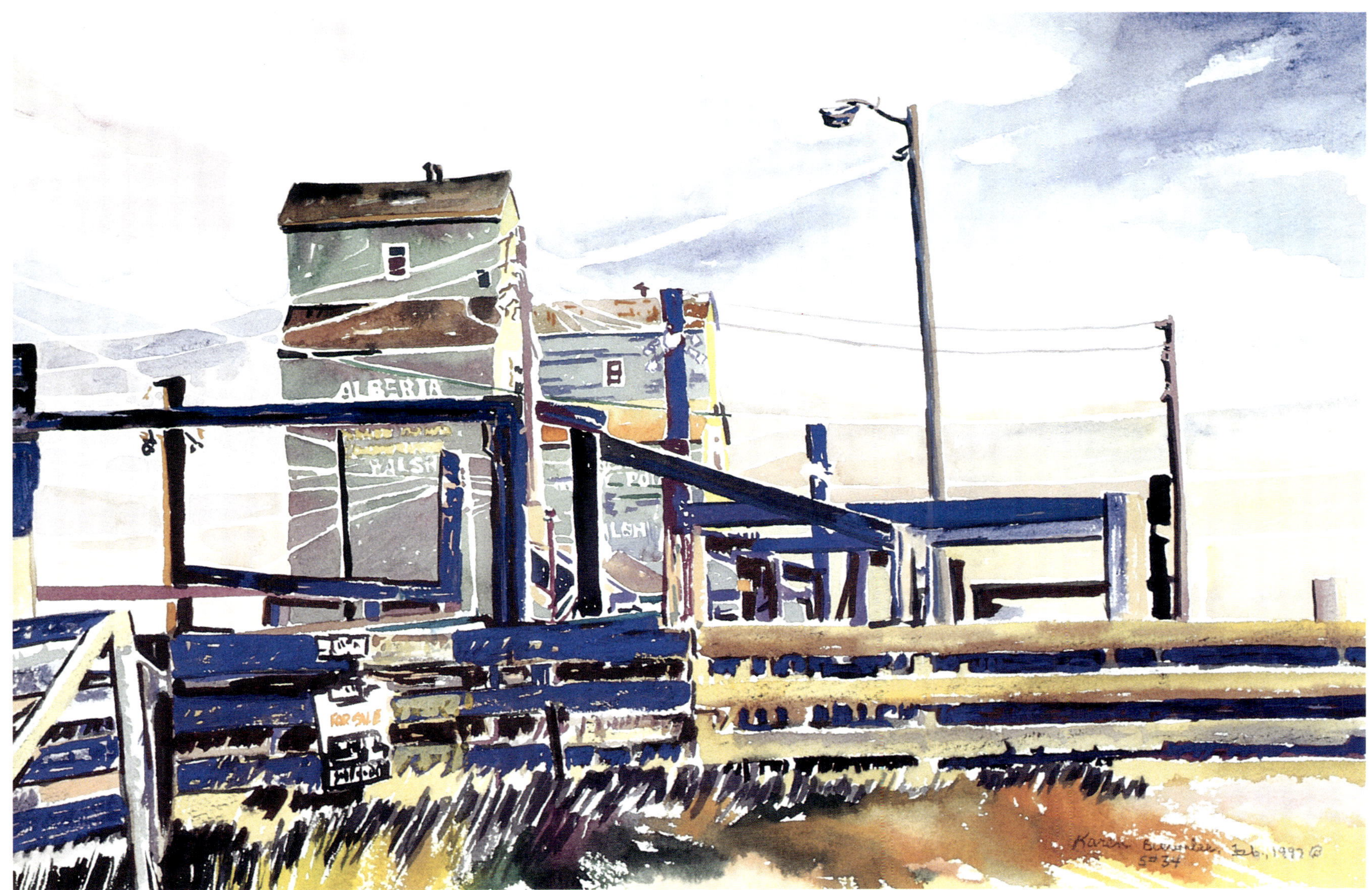

The town of Walsh, just inside Alberta's boundary with Saskatchewan, was named for James Morrow Walsh, superintendent of the North-West Mounted Police, who established Fort Walsh on the Saskatchewan side of the nearby Cypress Hills in 1875. The FOR SALE sign in the foreground is an indication of recent hard times for elevators and the small Alberta communities they serve.

WALSH #1, 1997, 18" x 12", CIRCA JUNE 1996.

Elevators, beginning as independent buildings, became the centre of groups of structures used to store and move grain. Some were attached, but others were deliberately separated from the main structure. Here, the agent's office is set well away from other buildings. Offices were often lined with tin to prevent any sparks from igniting a fire that could spread rapidly through the grain dust of the site.

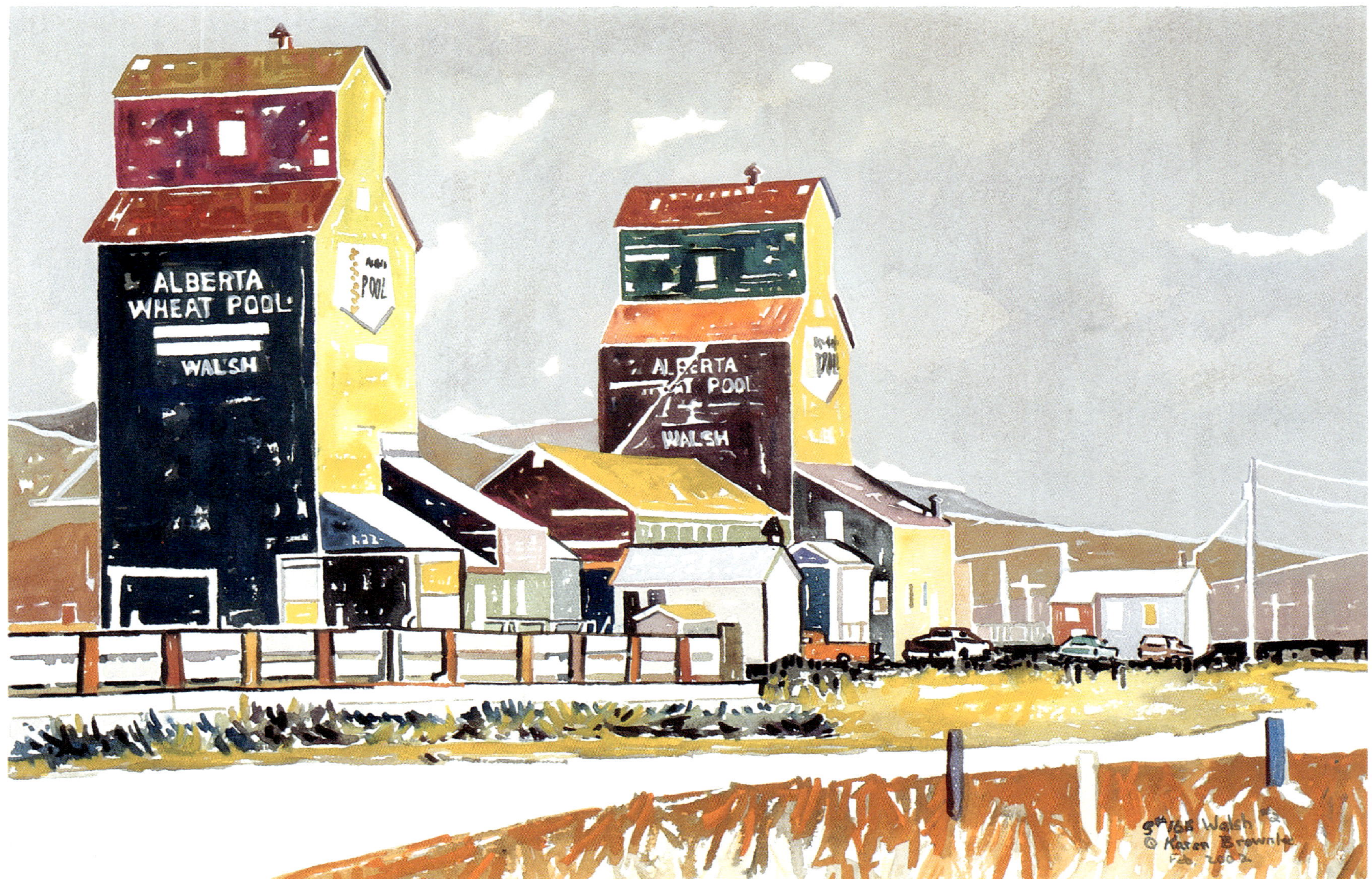

WALSH #2, 2002, 18" x 12", CIRCA JUNE 1996.

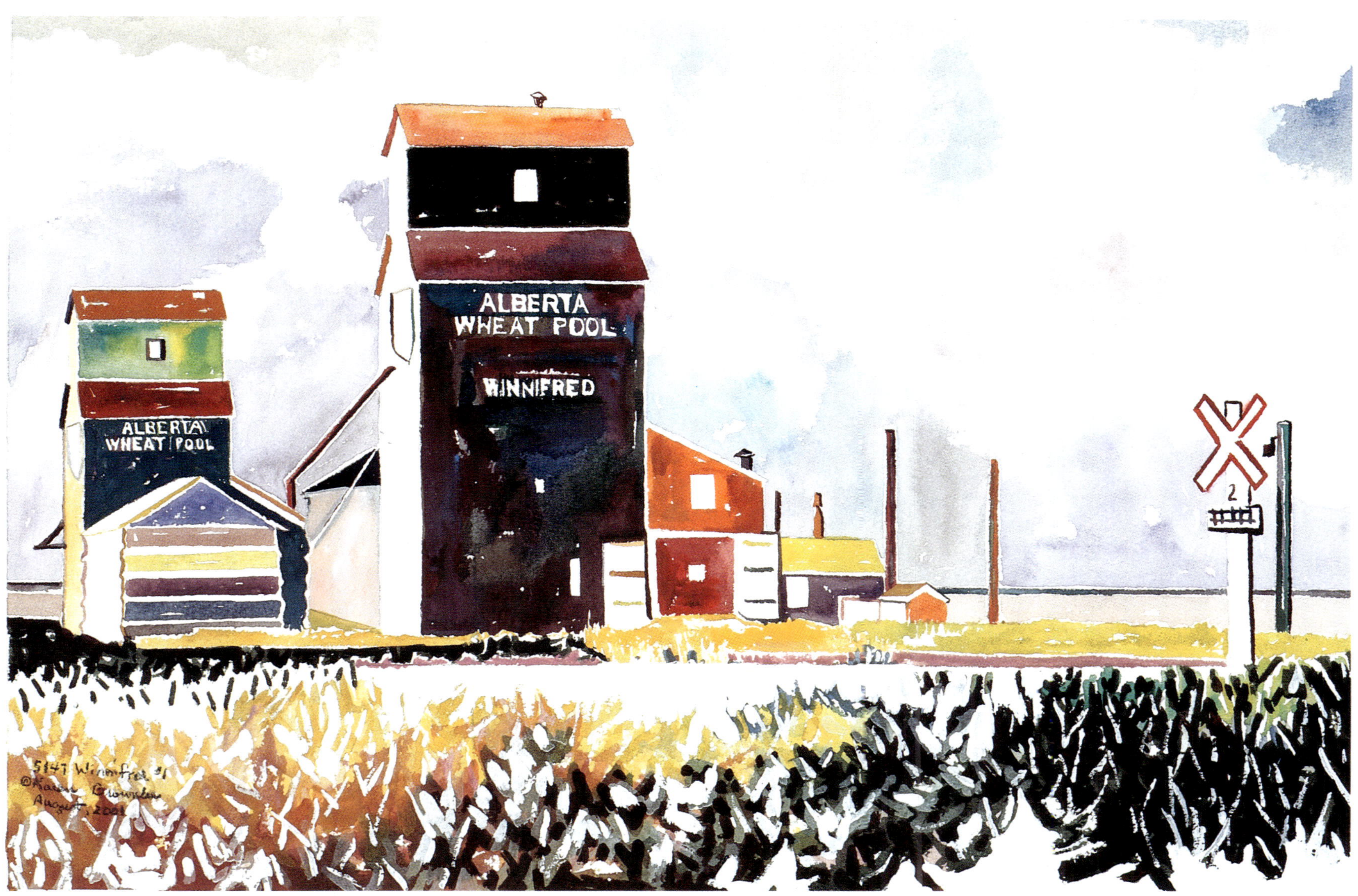

Winnifred was a town on the Alberta Railway and Irrigation Company "Turkey Track Railway." One of the owners of this narrow gauge line, which ran into the United States, was R.J. Whitla, namesake of Whitla, Alberta. The name of his daughter Winnifred was chosen for this settlement. The town's growth, prompted by the railway's 1913 arrival, lasted only until 1916. By 1960 elevators were all that remained in Winnifred.

WINNIFRED #1, 2001, 18" x 12", CIRCA JUNE 1996.

Despite the hard work of agents who tried to ensure that grain got shipped when cash was tight for farmers, the Winnifred area declined. With this decline, even the elevator fell. When the artist visited in the 1990s, she noted that "the elevator marked a place on the prairie; now the prairie can be seen through her."

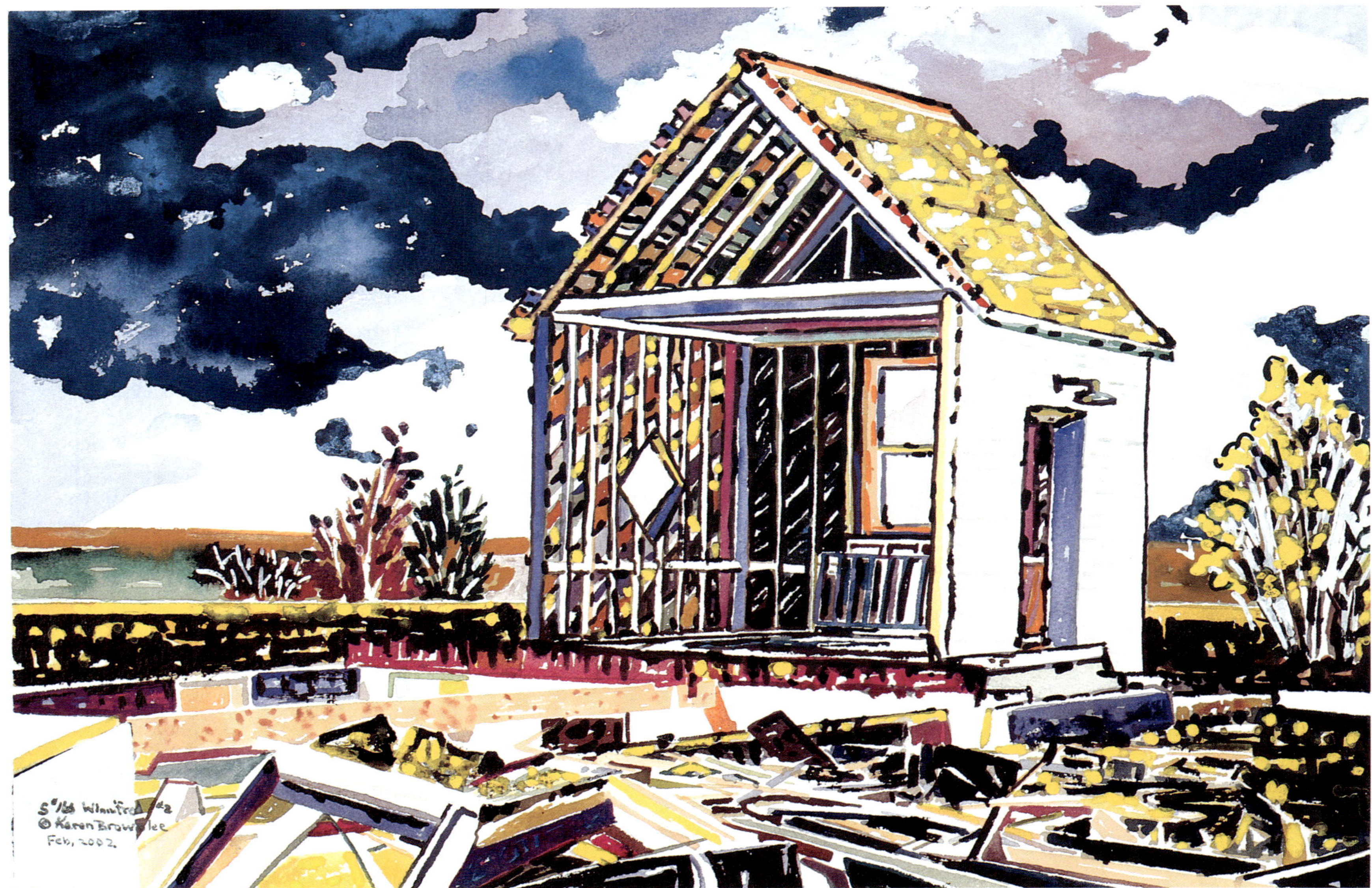

 WINNIFRED #2, 2002, 18" X 12", CIRCA MAY 1998.

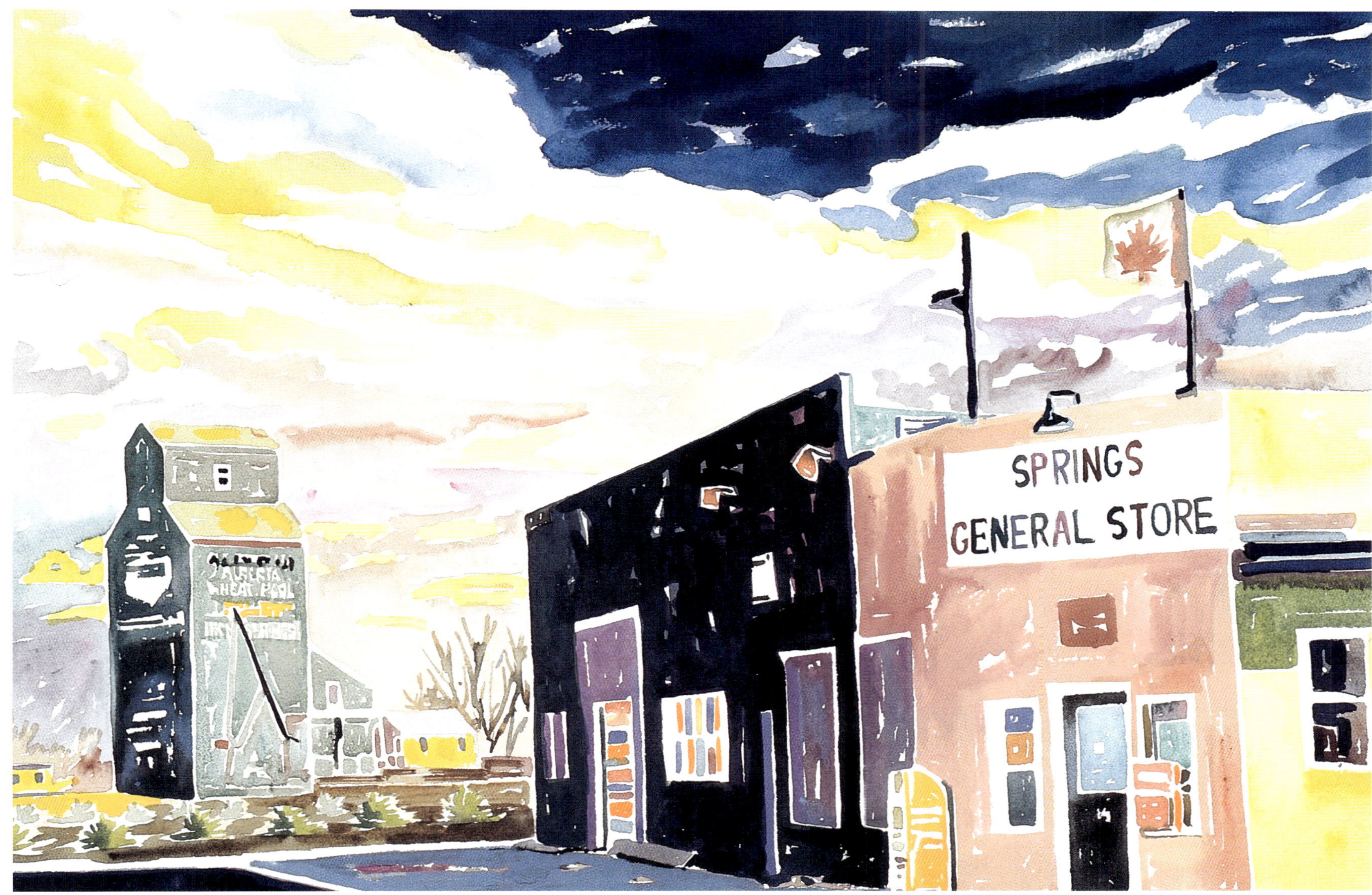

With the opening of the Lethbridge Northern Irrigation District in 1921 and the arrival of the railway in 1925, Iron Springs grew into a diverse community. Many new settlers emigrated from Europe and farmed or established businesses beside existing ones, including Iron Spring's very first business, a general store and Chinese restaurant owned by Sam Sing.

Iron Springs #1, 1998, 18" x 12", circa June 1997.

Businesses that opened and flourished in Iron Springs in the early years were in serious decline by the mid-1970s, with the elevator structures reflecting this growing impermanence. Instead of traditional annexes, a cluster of steel bins provides additional storage. The structures can be moved and sold off, unlike the wood crib annexes of earlier times.

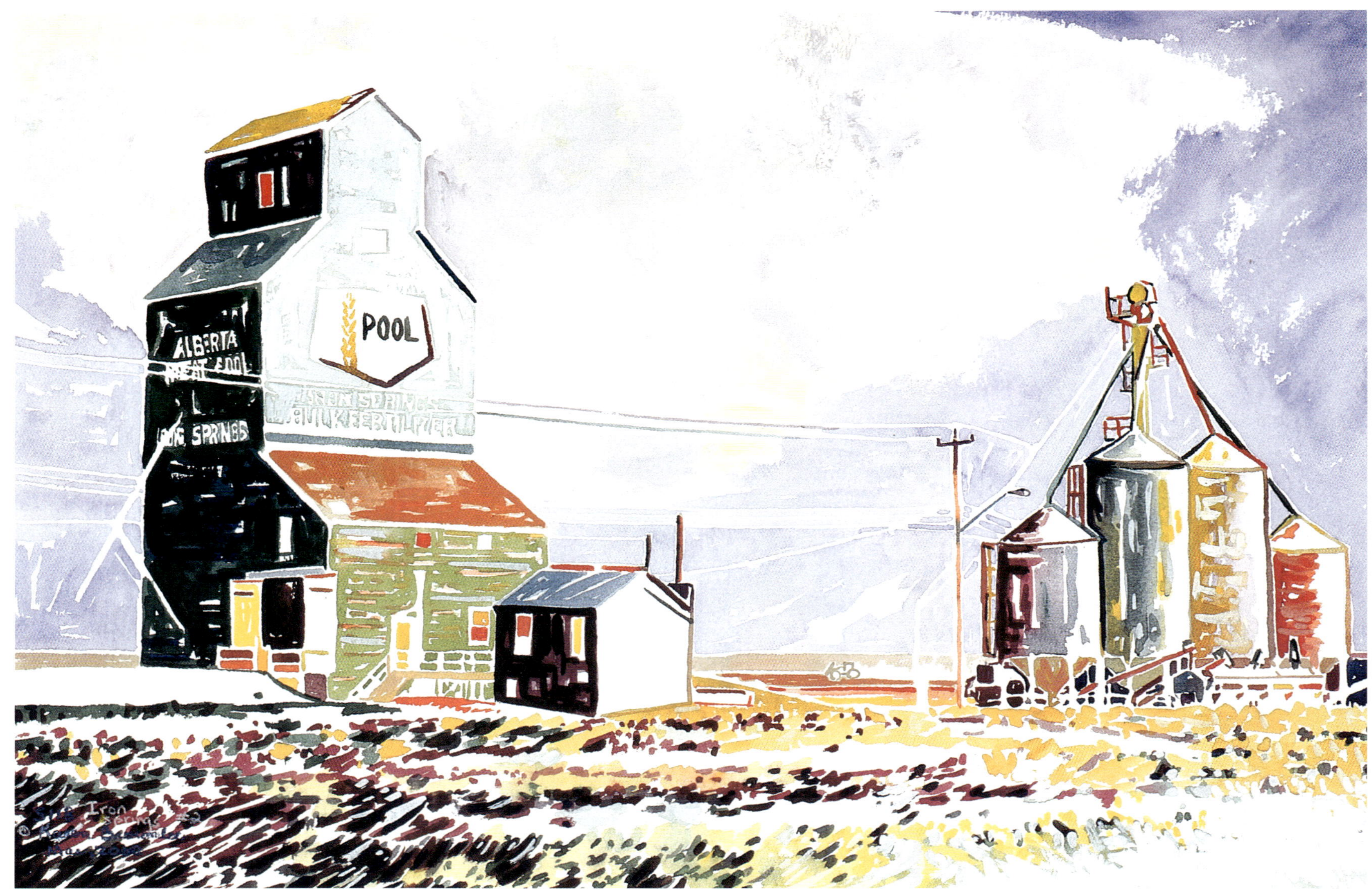

 Iron Springs #2, 2000, 18" x 12", circa May 1998.

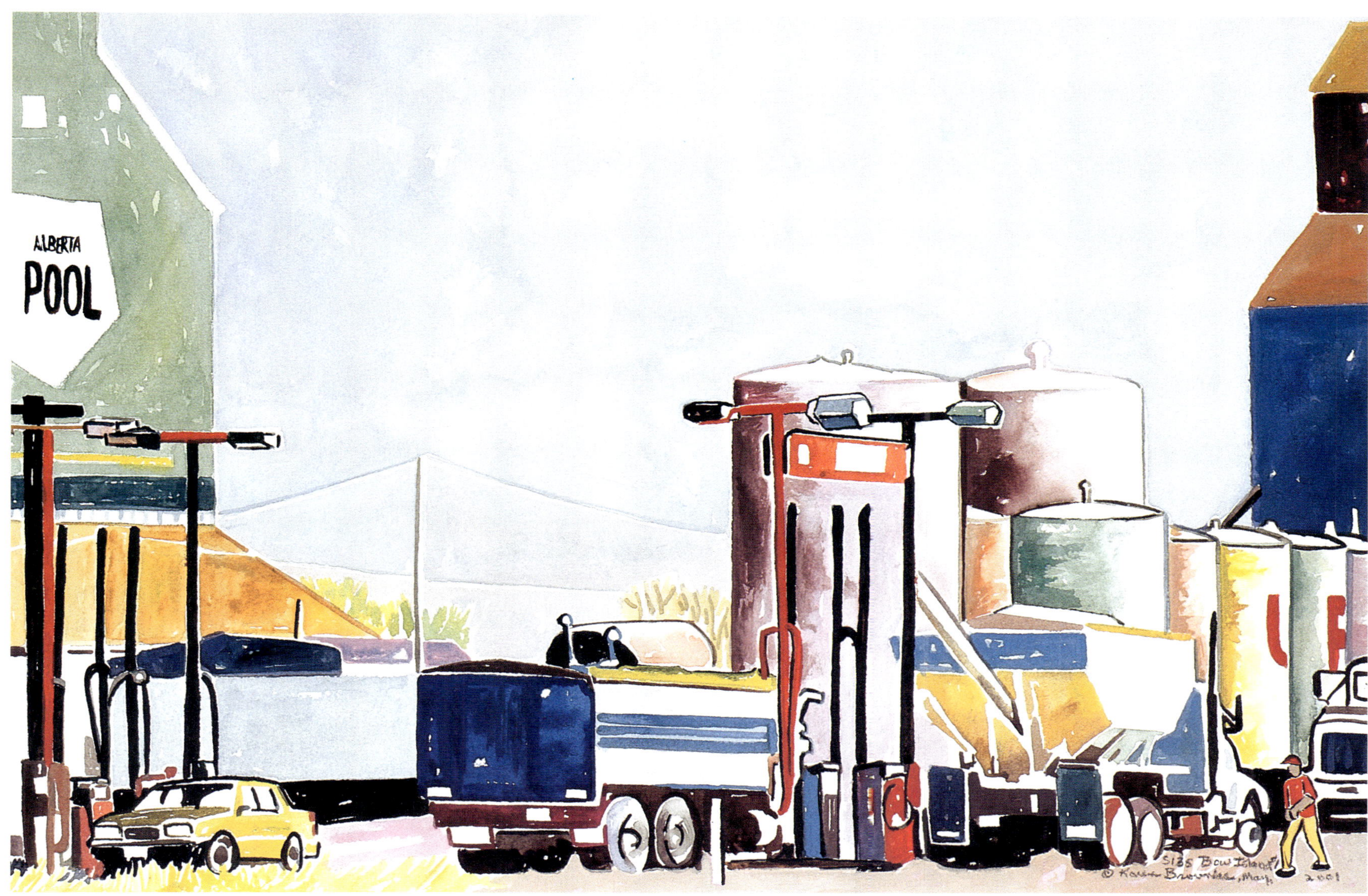

Bow Island #1, 2001, 18" x 12", circa May 1998.

Bow Island was a major grain shipping point. In 1911 the Alberta Pacific Elevator and Taylor Milling Company of Lethbridge erected elevators here. Five more elevators were constructed: the Empire Elevator and the Farmer's Elevator companies in 1913, the Home Grain and National Elevator companies in 1917 and the Searle Elevator Company in 1928. The Alberta Wheat Pool purchased the Taylor Milling Company structure in 1969.

Early in Seven Persons' history, five elevators anchored the settlement. Record-breaking yields gave way to drought, however, and the elevators were closed, torn down or moved to other locations. The Alberta Wheat Pool, organized in 1923, purchased one of the existing elevators. The Pool maintained the last elevator in the town in 1982.

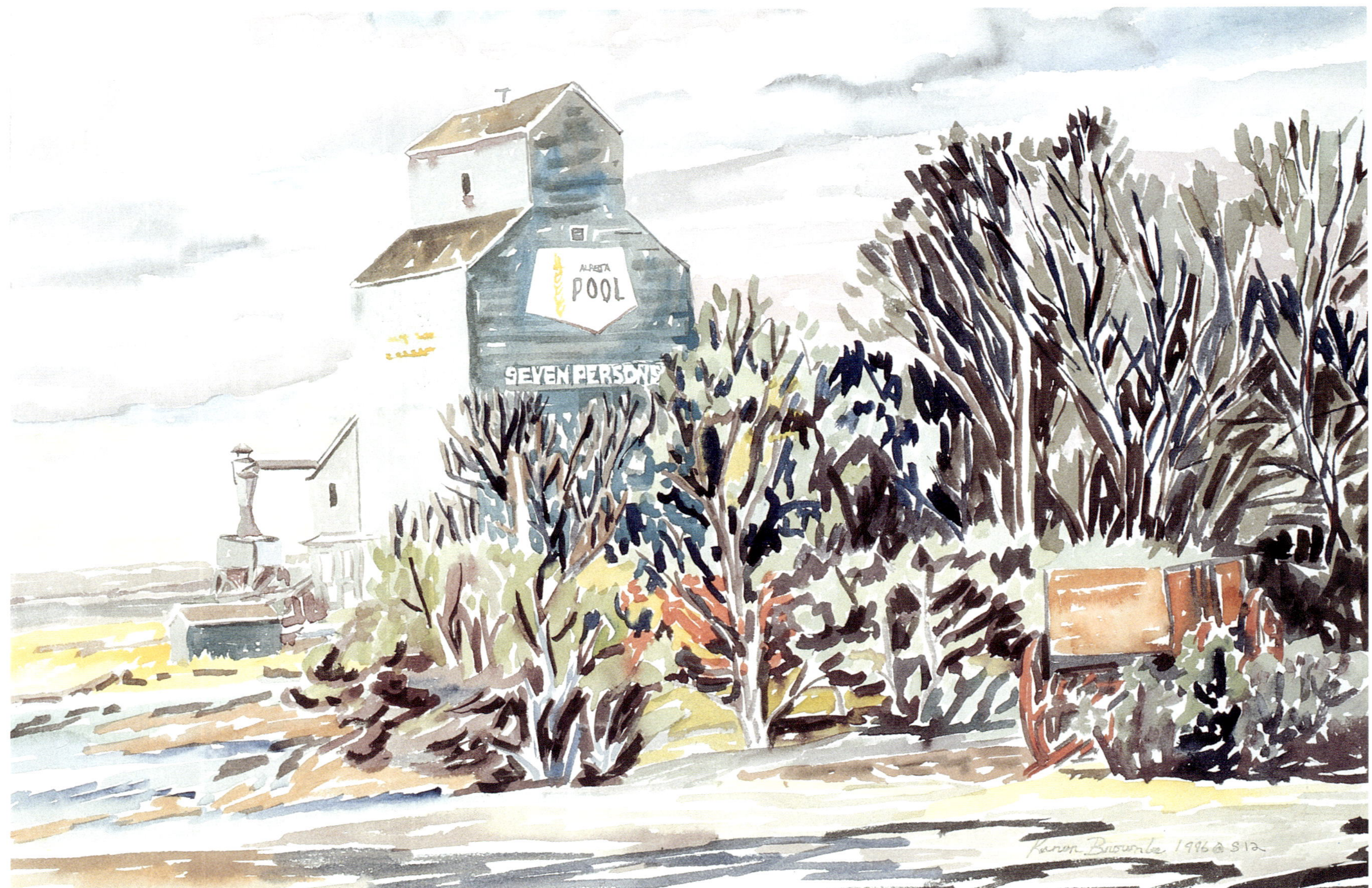

 Seven Persons #1, 1996, 18" x 12", circa June 1996.

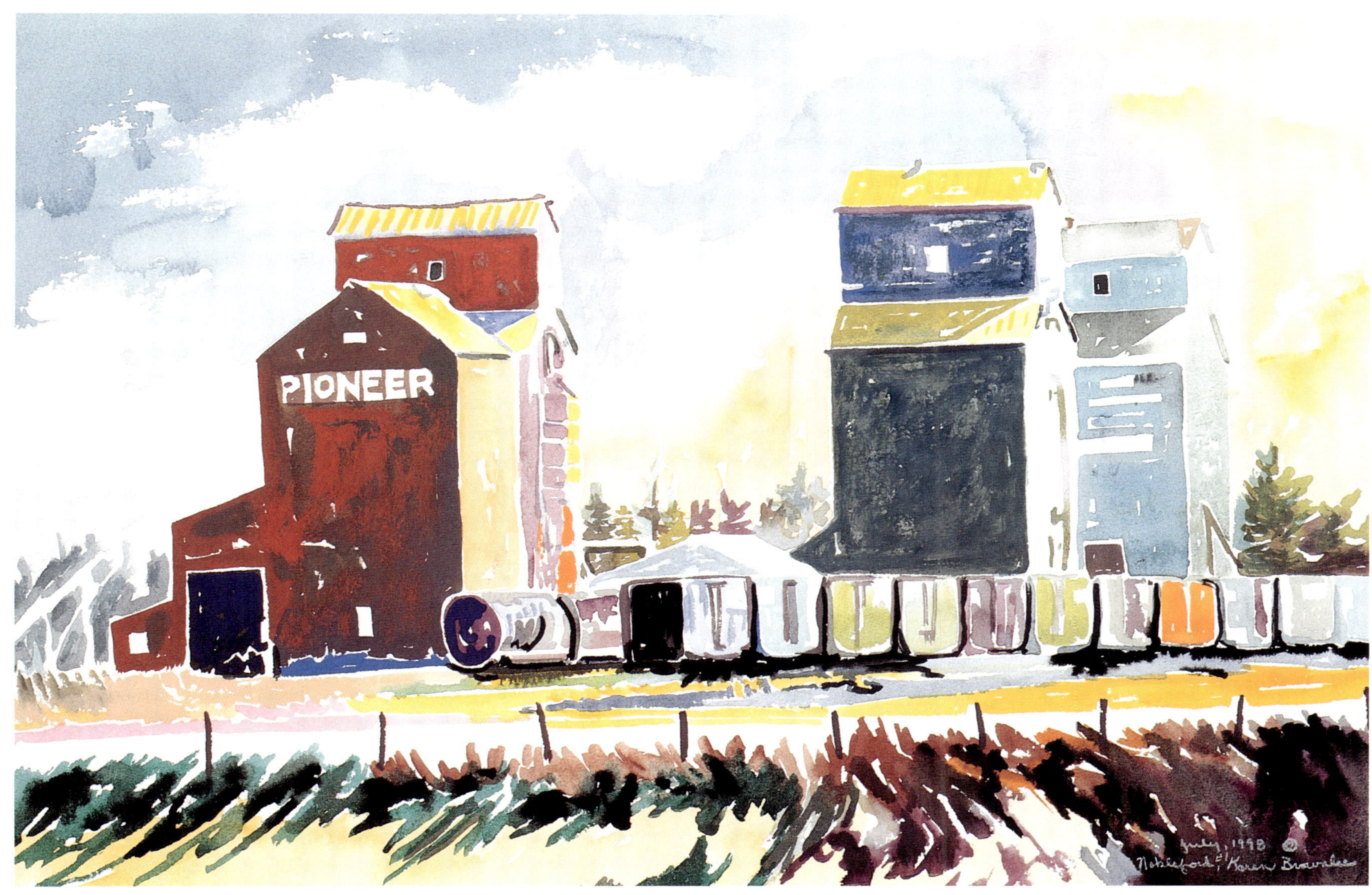

Starting in 1909, Nobleford became home to many elevators. In 1954 the Pioneer Grain Company purchased one of the earliest, the 1910 Independent Grain Company building. Pioneer added two temporary annexes to its facilities during the Second World War and a crib annex in 1956, bringing the overall capacity of this elevator to 158,000 bushels.

NOBLEFORD #1, 1998, 18" x 12", CIRCA MAY 1998.

Charles Sherwood Noble, a famous agricultural pioneer, settled in Nobleford in 1909 with his wife and two children. Originally called Noble, the hamlet's name was changed to Nobleford in 1913 to prevent confusion with Noble, Ontario. Charles Noble was created a Member of the Order of the British Empire in 1943 for his valuable service to agriculture.

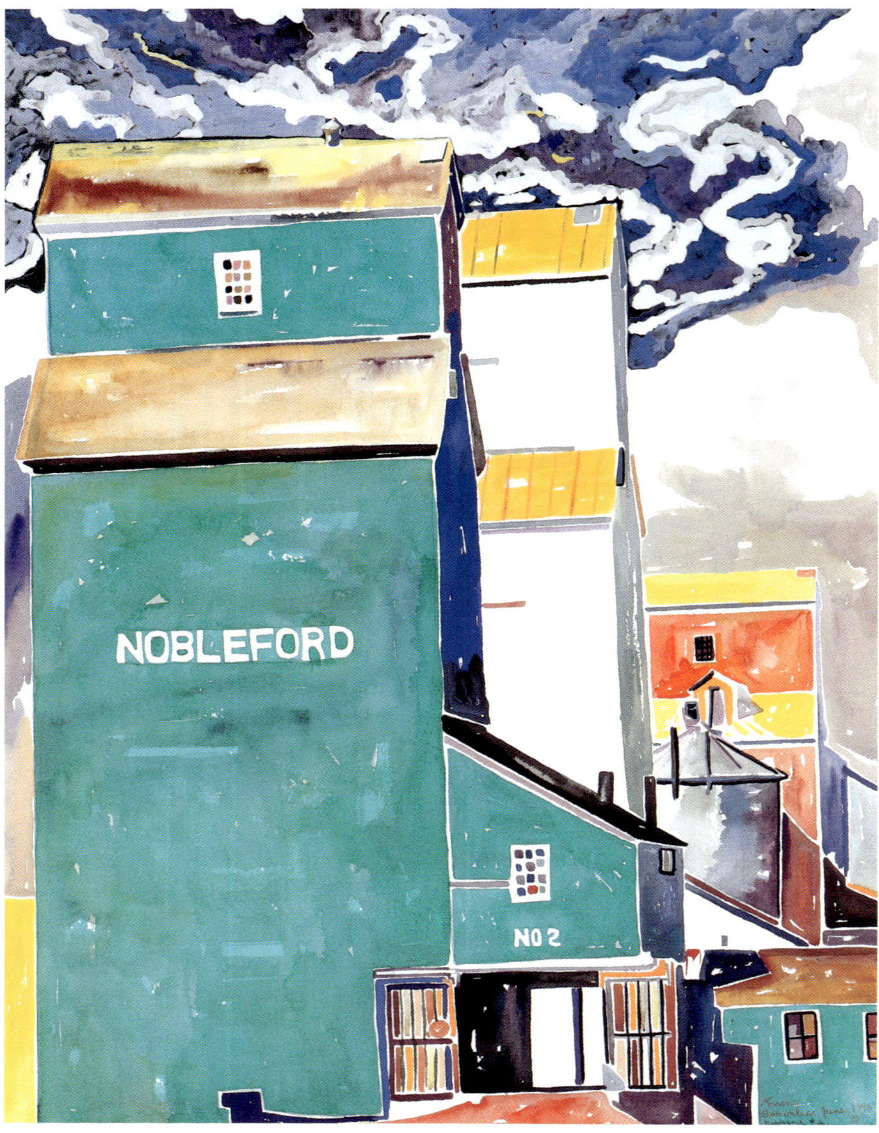

 NOBLEFORD #2, 1998, 21" x 28", CIRCA MAY 1998.

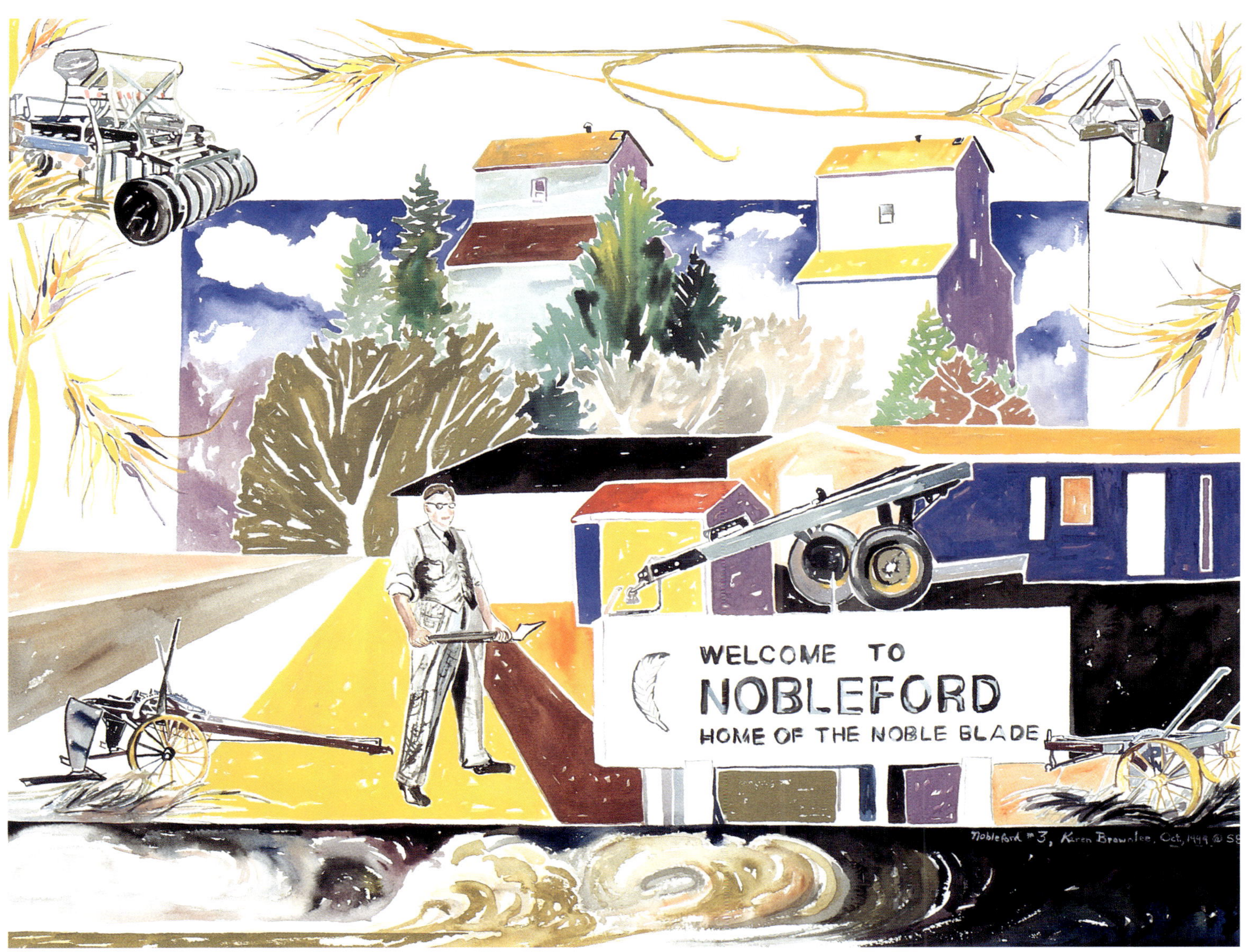

Noble received an honorary degree from the University of Alberta in 1943. Agriculture Dean A.G. McCalla commented: "It can seldom be said of any man that he has changed the face of the land, and have it taken literally. It can be so said of Mr. Noble." Planting winter rye to stabilize topsoil and inventing the Noble Blade that cultivated the sub-surface were among his innovations.

NOBLEFORD #3, 1999, 28" x 21", CIRCA MAY 1998.

Noble lost his holdings in 1922 to declining markets. He fought back, doubling his land by 1936, and inventing the Noble Blade, which cut weed roots below the surface, leaving the soil undisturbed and less vulnerable to erosion. Noble's first 1941 factory was superceded by a larger facility in 1951. The first building, beyond and to the right of the Pioneer elevator, is now a Provincial Historic Resource.

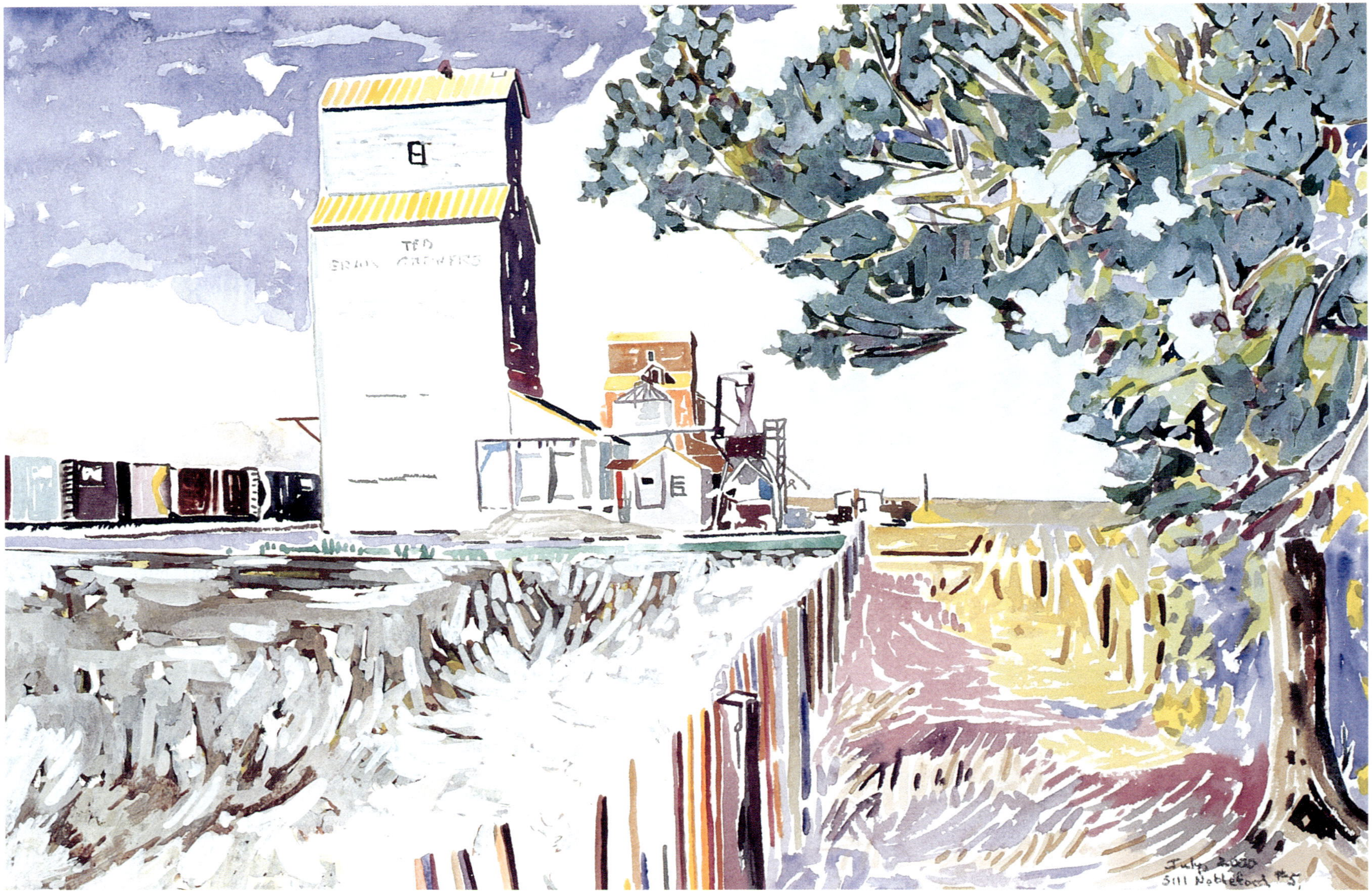

 Nobleford #5, 2000, 18" x 12", circa May 1998.

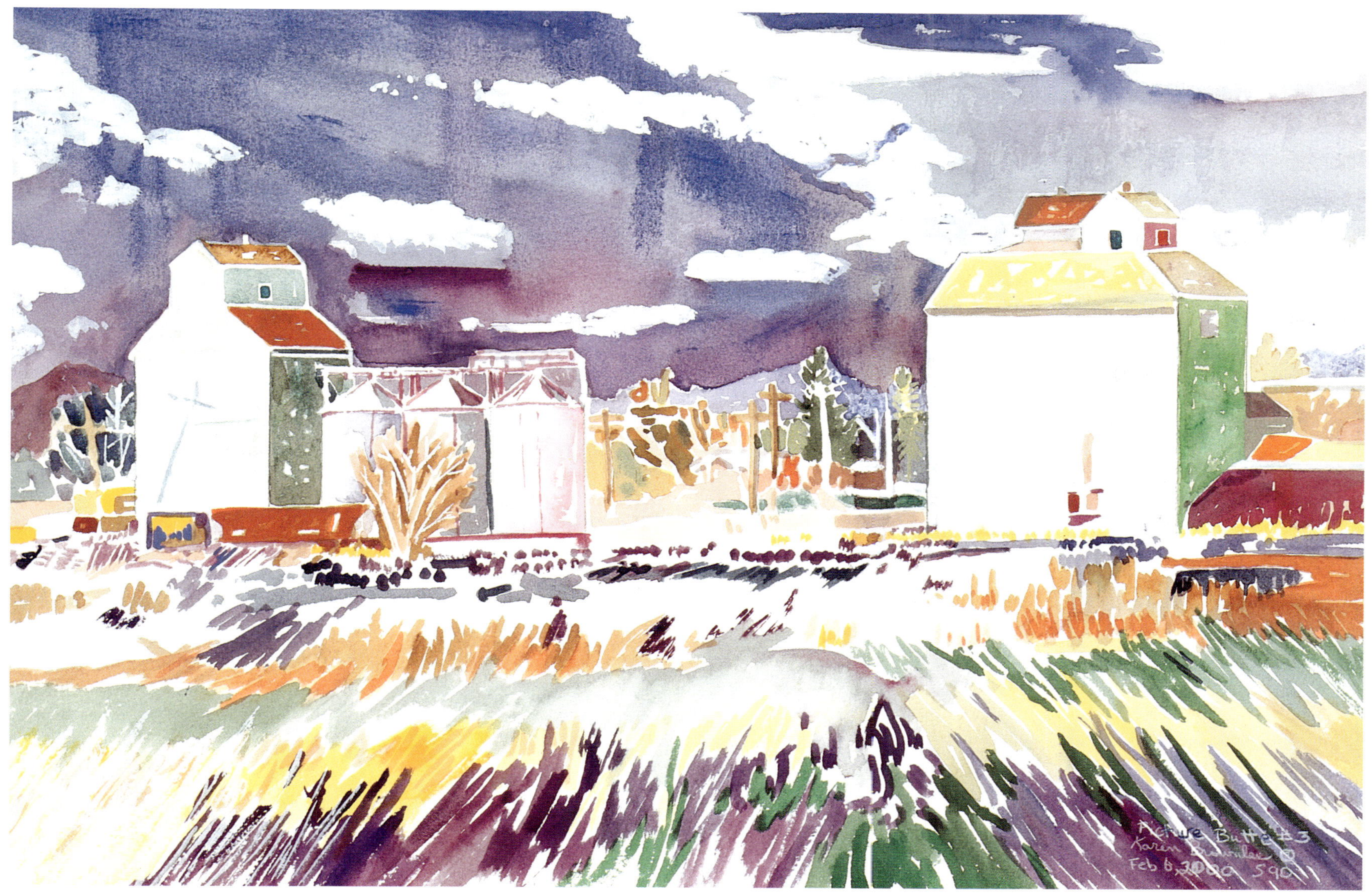

Picture Butte began as a post office and two dwellings in 1926. Times were ripe for change, however, as irrigation had come to the area in 1923, and the Canadian Pacific Railway had arrived from Diamond City in 1925. In short order, Ellison Milling and Elevator, the Alberta Pacific Grain Company and the Alberta Wheat Pool constructed elevators to serve the community.

PICTURE BUTTE #3, 2000, 18" X 12", CIRCA JUNE 1995.

Burdett and Coutts are named for Georgina Baroness Burdett-Coutts. She was a major shareholder in the North Western Coal and Navigation Company, later part of the Alberta Railway and Irrigation Company, which brought a railway to the area in 1885 and irrigation in 1899. Both elevators and increasingly large and efficient tillage equipment followed from these initiatives.

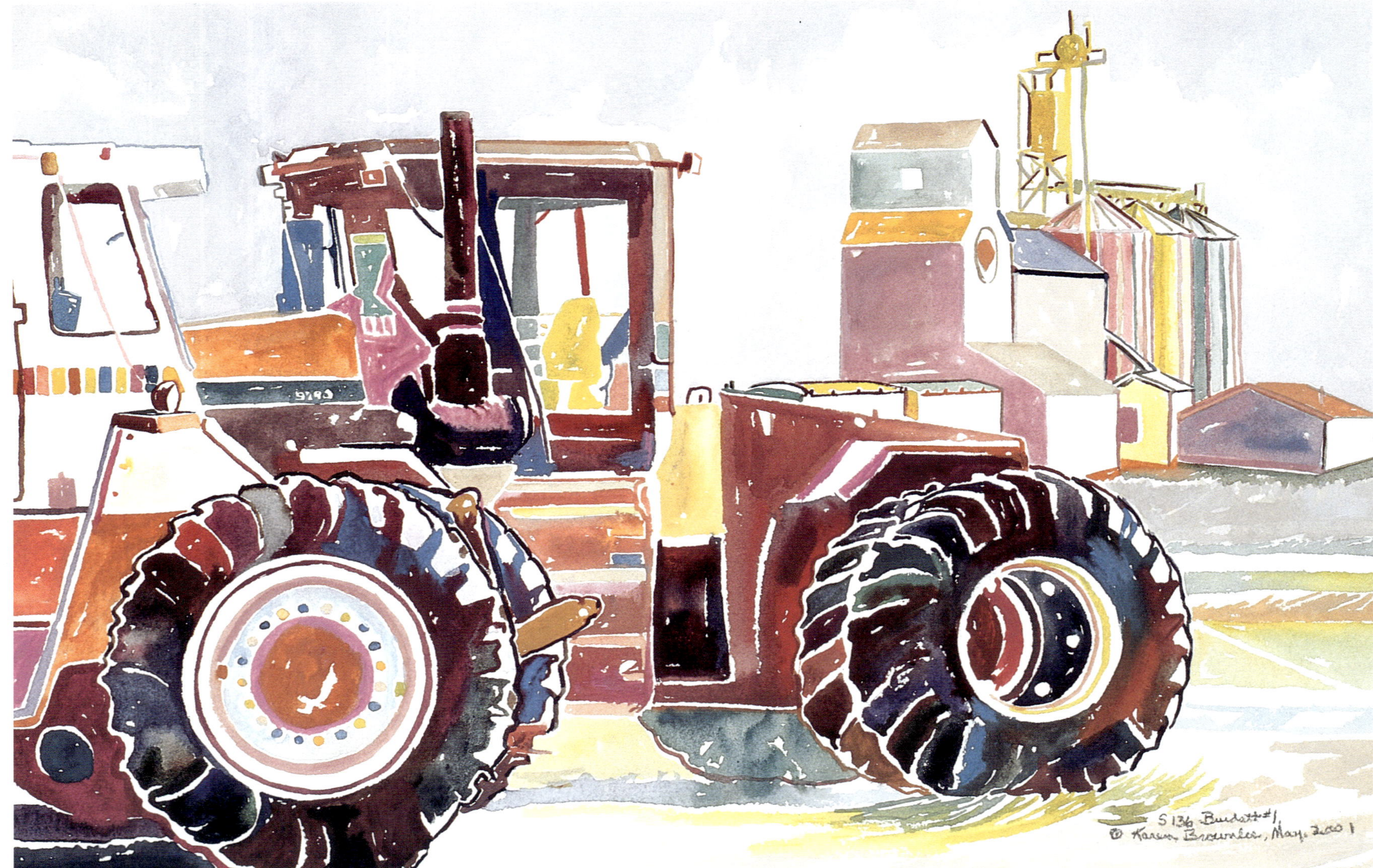

 BURDETT #1, 2001, 18" X 12", CIRCA MAY 1998.

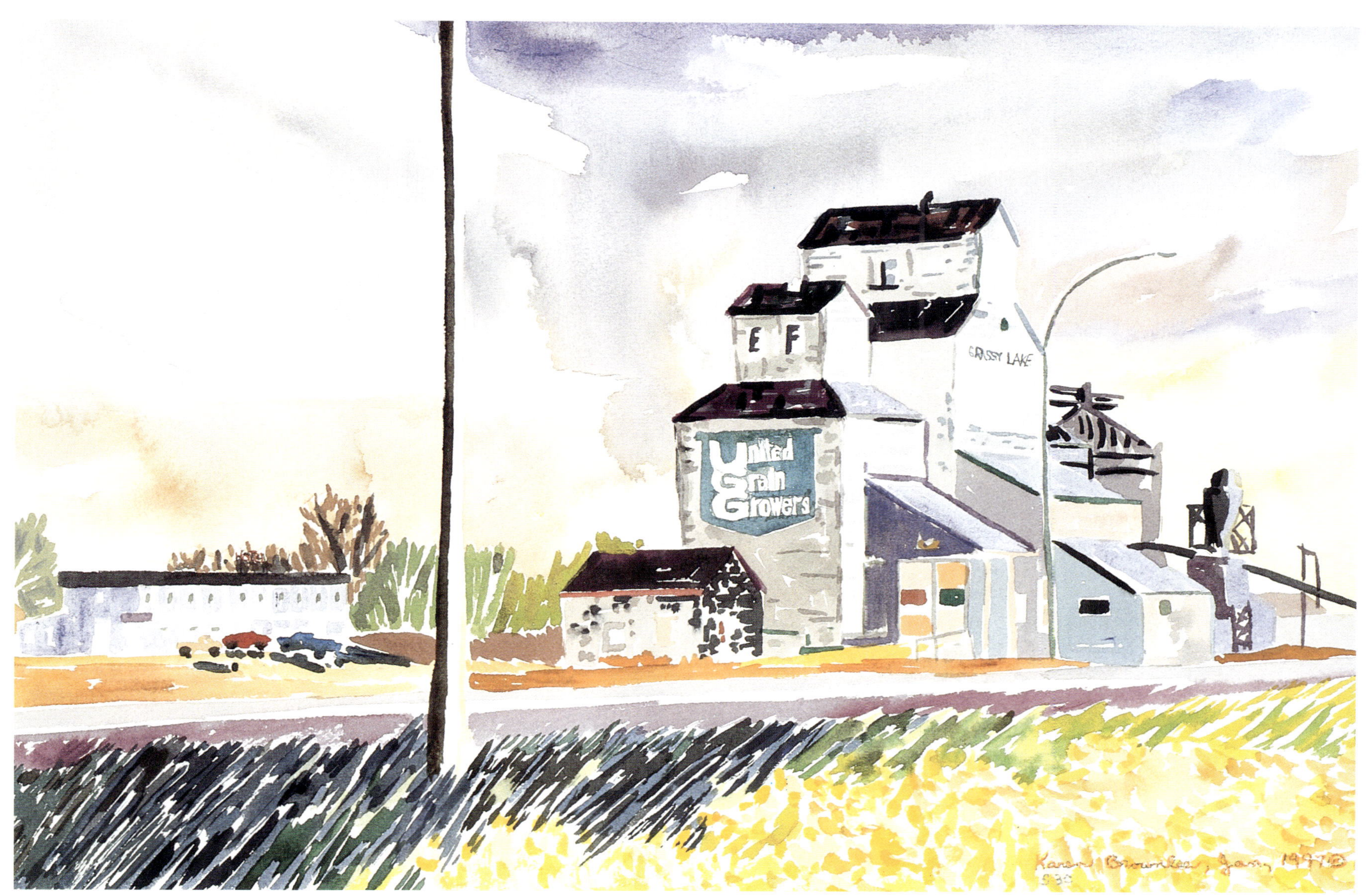

Over the years eight elevator companies have operated in Grassy Lake. The first, owned by the Medicine Hat Milling Company, opened in 1911 but burned in 1912. The 10,000 bushels it held at the time were insured, however, and rebuilding was swift. The Taylor Milling Company also opened in 1911, and in 1913 both the Ogilvie Milling Company and the Alberta Farmers' Co-operative Elevator Company Limited began operations.

GRASSY LAKE #1, 1997, 18" x 12", CIRCA JUNE 1996.

Natural disaster struck in 1915 when a cyclone swept away the top of the National Elevator. It was not rebuilt. Despite this, Grassy Lake's elevator capacity grew. Lake of the Woods operated a facility in the 1920s, and the Alberta Wheat Pool built in 1928 and bought the Ogilvie operation in 1960. United Grain Growers, last in the locality, bought the Farmers' Co-operative Elevator in 1952.

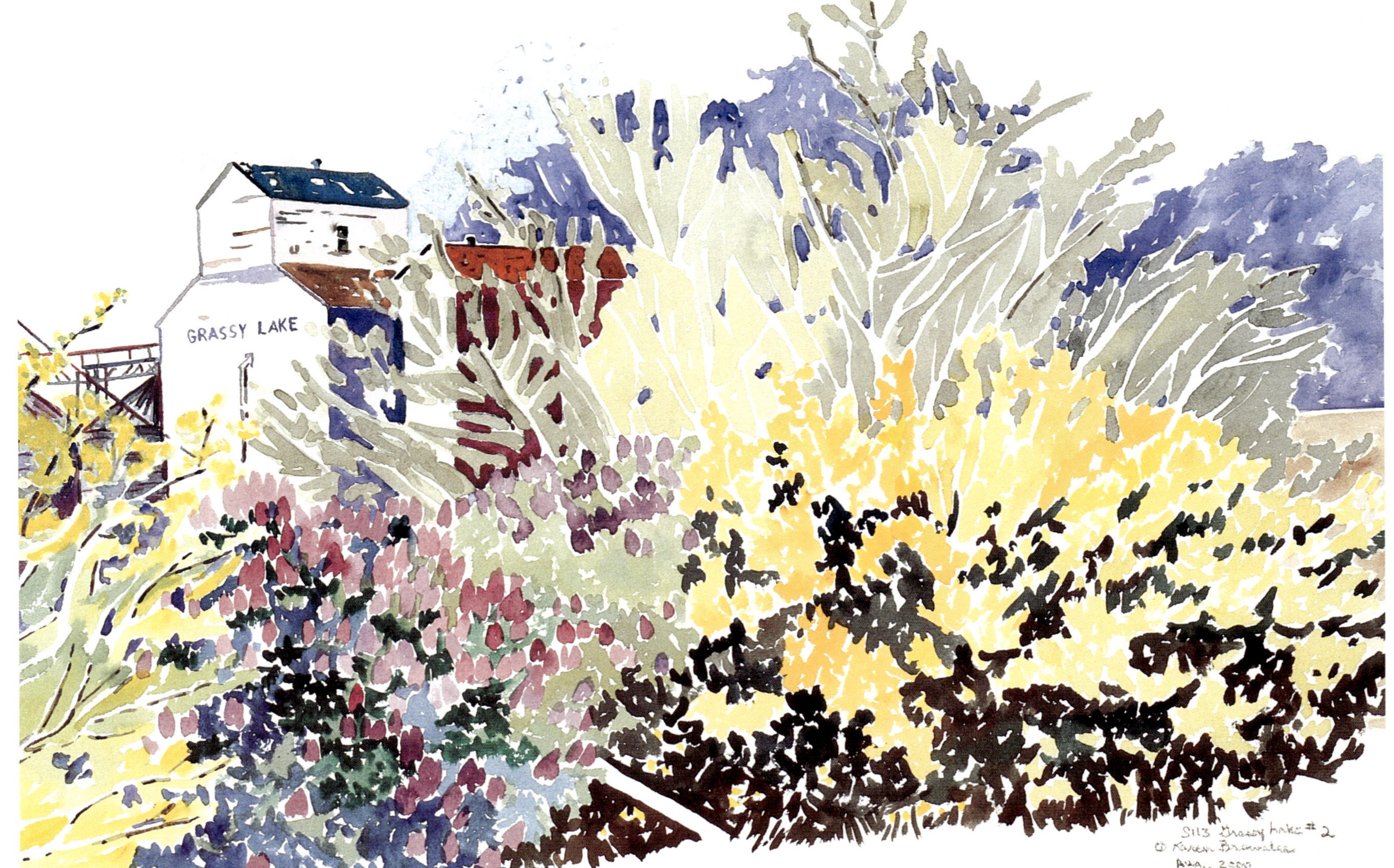

 Grassy Lake #2, 2000, 18" x 12", circa May 1998.

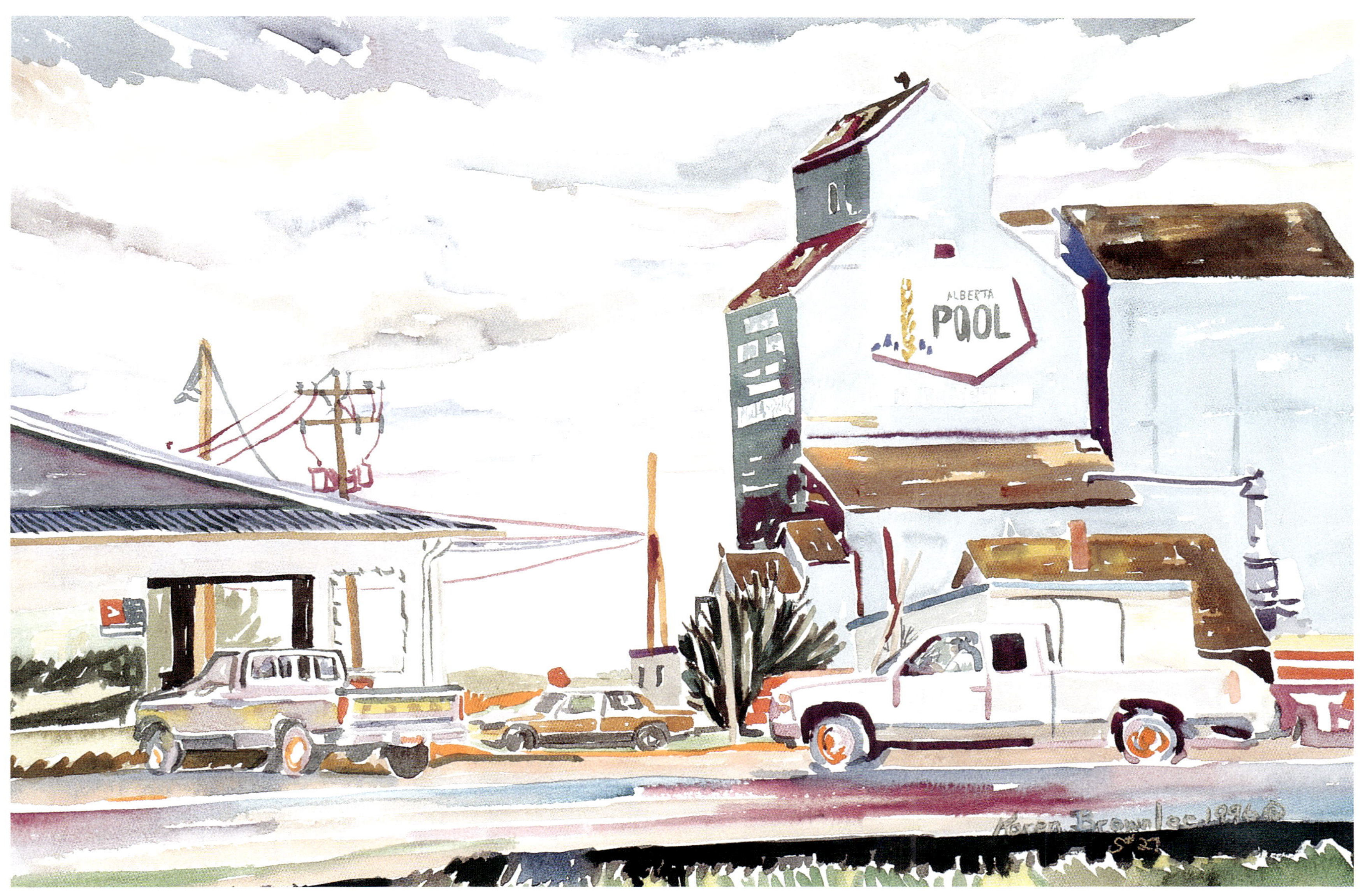

Narrow-leaf purple vetch grew in profusion by a spring in a coulee near here, hence the name Purple Springs. Early on, delivering grain from the north meant fording the Oldman River. Teams were unhitched, and wagons were pulled up the bank one at a time. The return trip was also tricky. Empty wagon boxes that weren't well lashed down could float off down stream.

Purple Springs #1, 1996, 18" x 12", circa June 1996.

Chin is named for a hill resembling a chin. The Blackfoot name, *mistoamo,* meaning "beard," was also descriptive. Archaeological evidence shows human activity dating back at least 6,000 years, with bison kills in Chin Coulee to the southeast. The Canadian Pacific Railway made early use of the area, with four sections of land used for a hay farm in 1913.

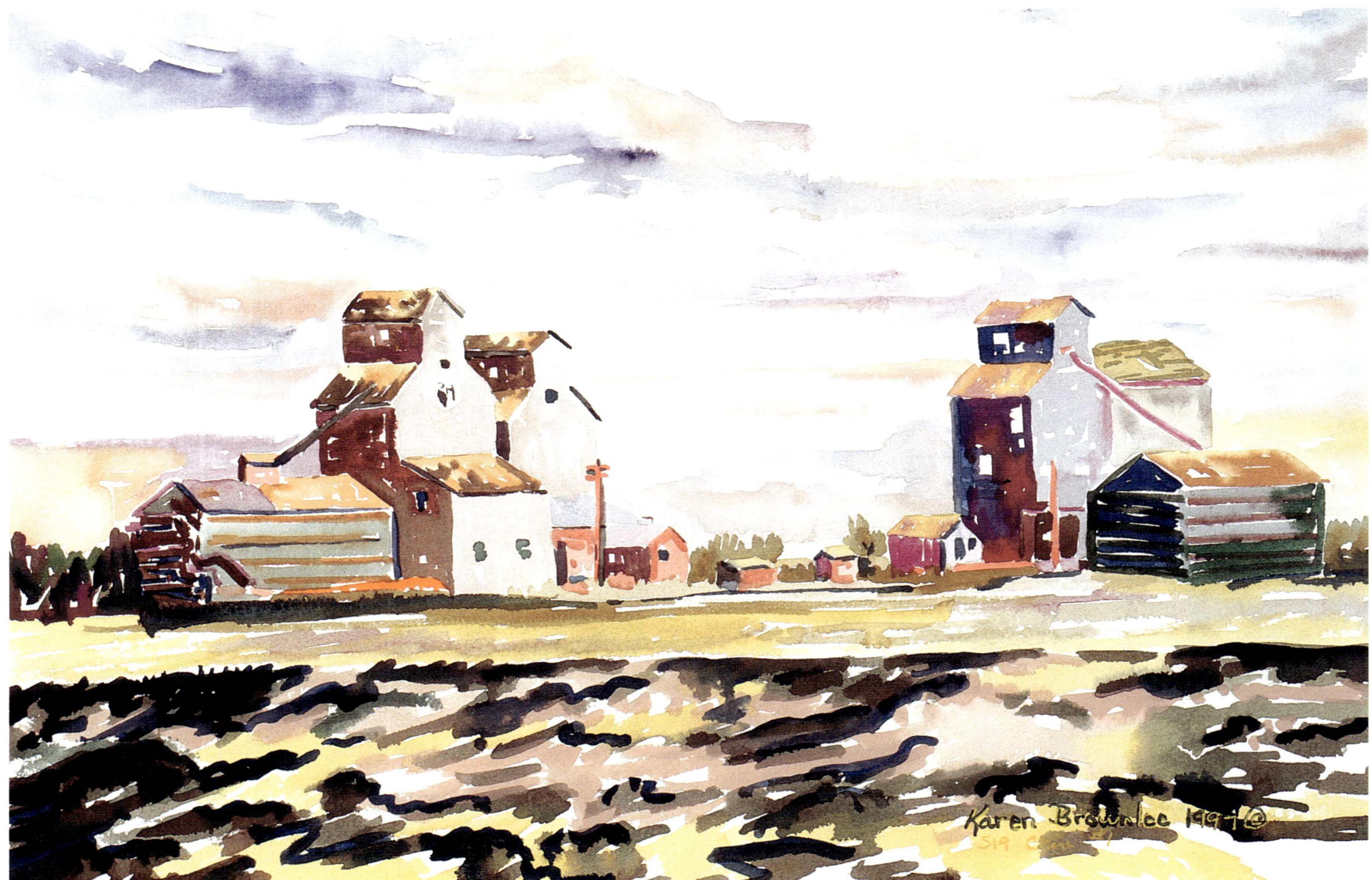

CHIN #1, 1996, 18" x 12", CIRCA JUNE 1996.

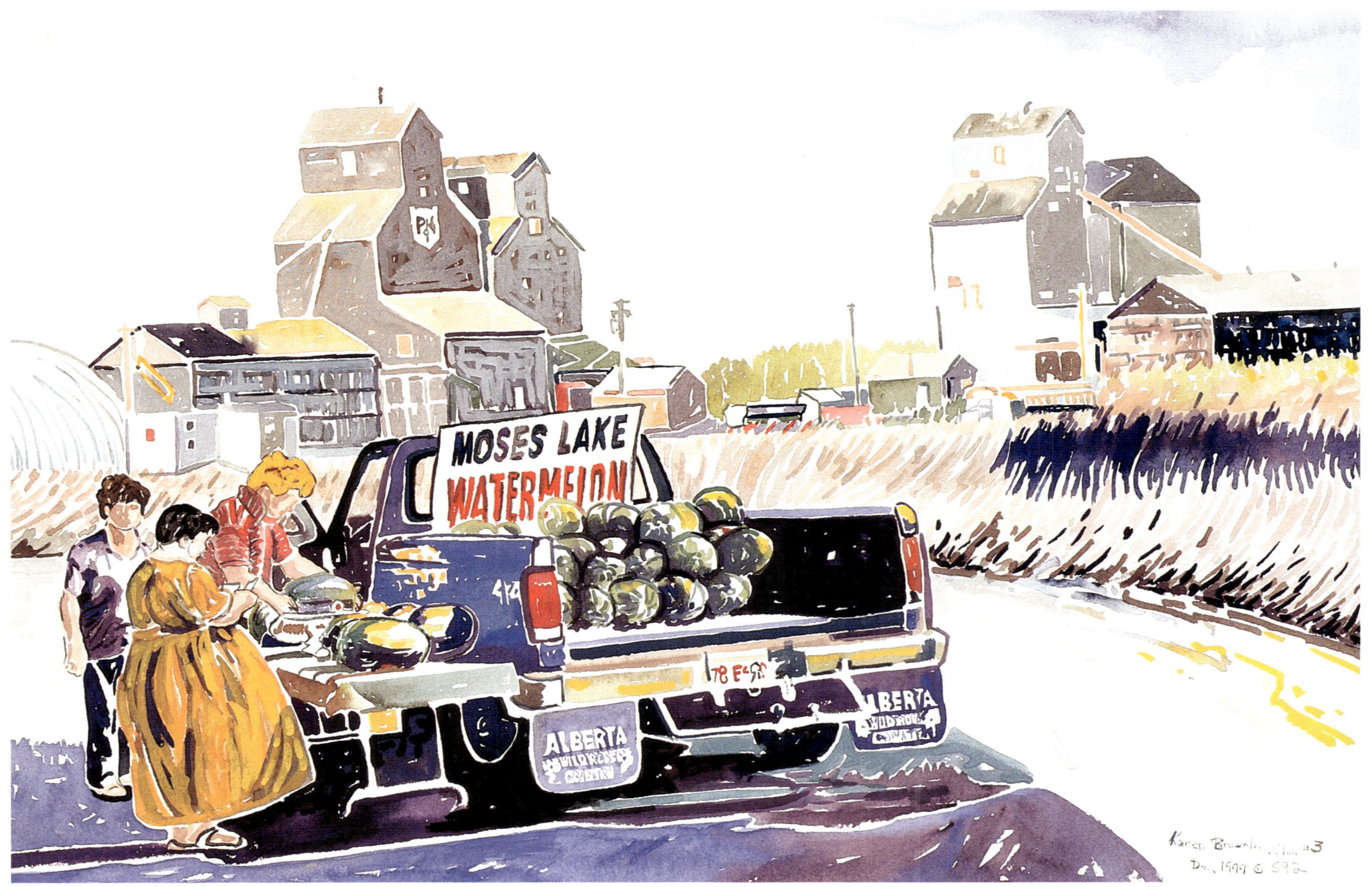

The artist's family often shipped grain at Chin. She recalls there being a watermelon truck parked in the general store parking lot by the highway. "They were Moses Lake, Washington, watermelons. My mother, my sister and I would wait in the car while my father would buy one for us, knocking on them with his large hands."

CHIN #3, 1999, 18" X 12", CIRCA JUNE 1996.

In 1920 the Alberta Railway and Irrigation Company canal from Chin Coulee to Taber was completed at a cost of $272,000. With irrigation, grain farming became a more certain enterprise. Elevators were erected in Chin earlier than other towns. Tempest, for example, did not have its first elevator raised until 1928. As a result, Chin did much of the district's early grain business.

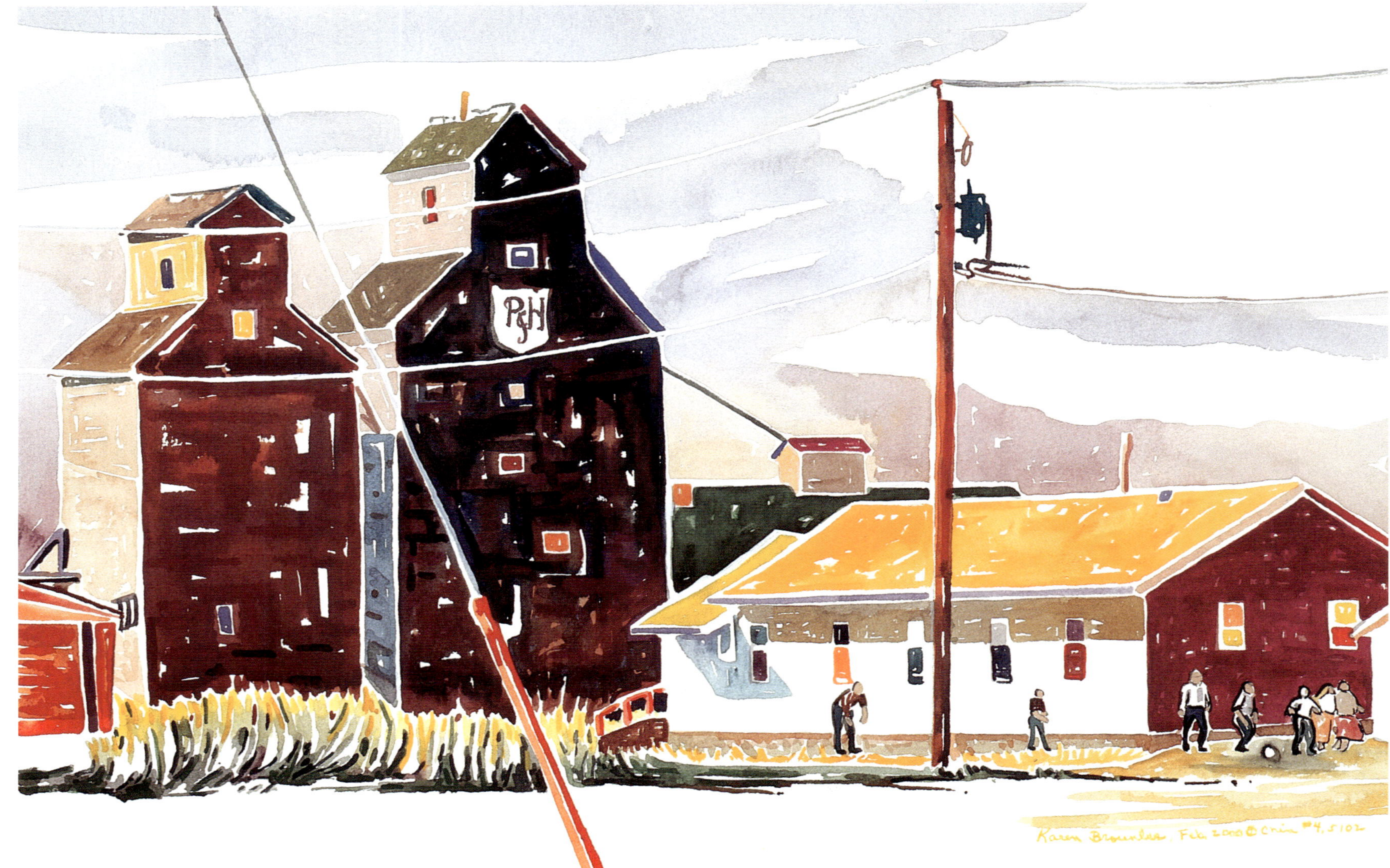

Chin #4, 2000, 18" x 12", circa Oct. 1999.

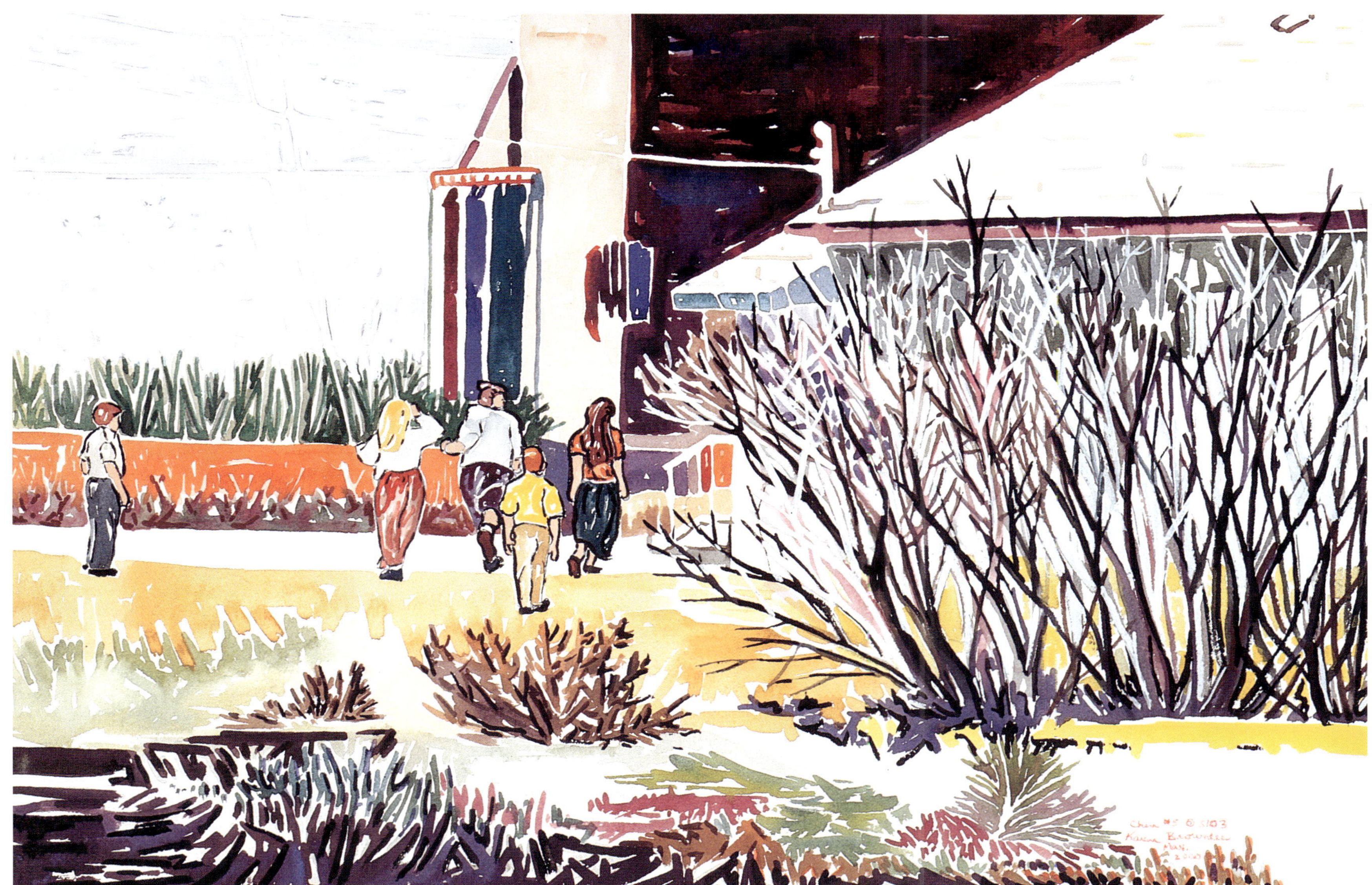

Chin has a diverse history, shaped by efforts to build a community, present and future. In 1930 N.F. Priestly wrote: "Elevators loom large in the life of the Canadian prairies. Their great bulk silhouetted against the prairie skies have not dominated the view more than the struggle to make them serve the interests of the farming community has affected the thought and action of its people."

CHIN #5, 2000, 18" X 12", CIRCA OCTOBER 1999.

Taber was initially known for the coal seams in the area. Settlement was not far behind. James Hull's 1903 house was the first, built in the year that the Canadian Pacific Railway spur line arrived in town. Grain elevators were among the selling points for places intent on attracting commerce and were featured prominently as illustrations in Taber's advertising.

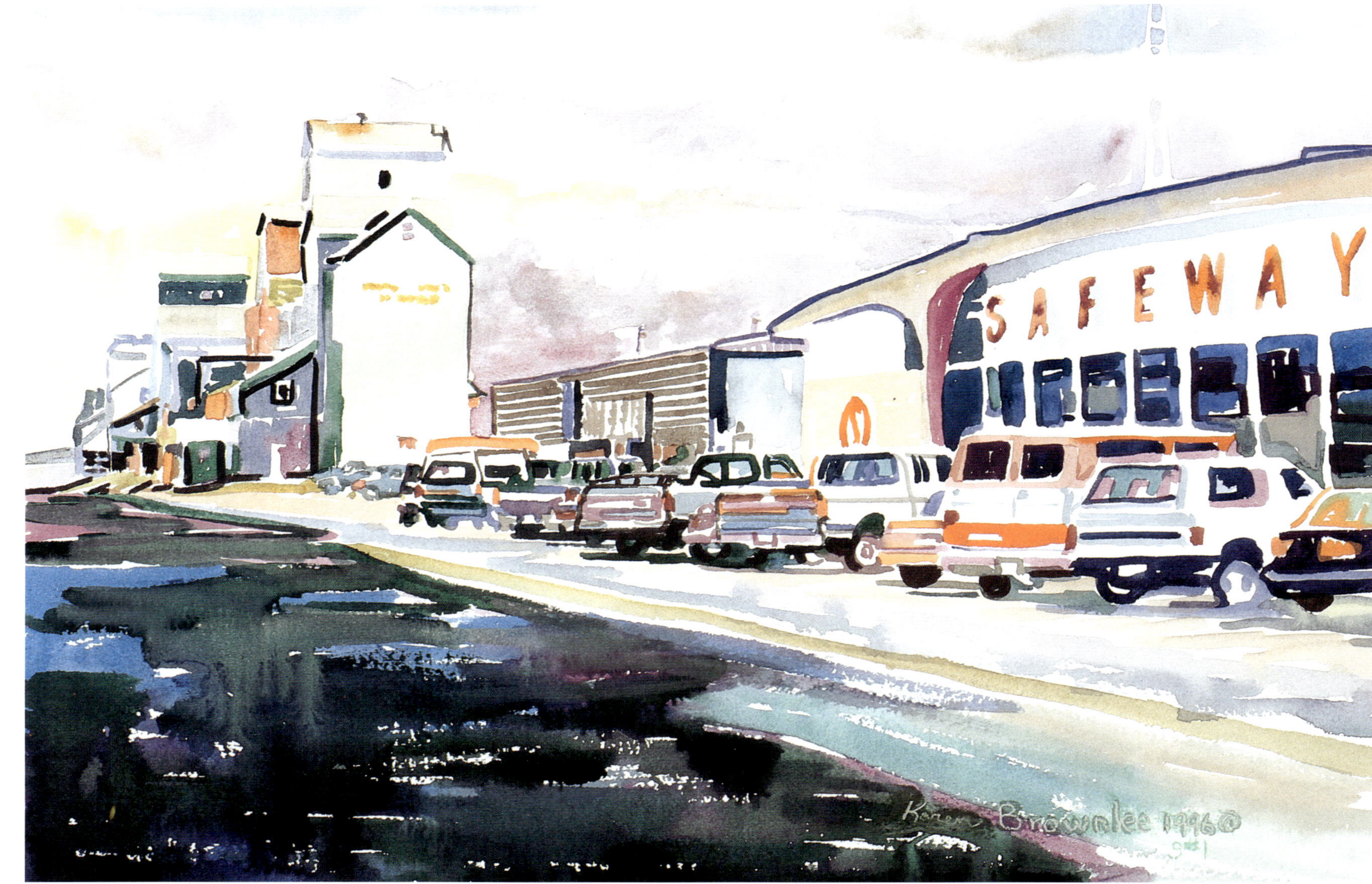

 TABER #1, 1996, 18" x 12", CIRCA JUNE 1996.

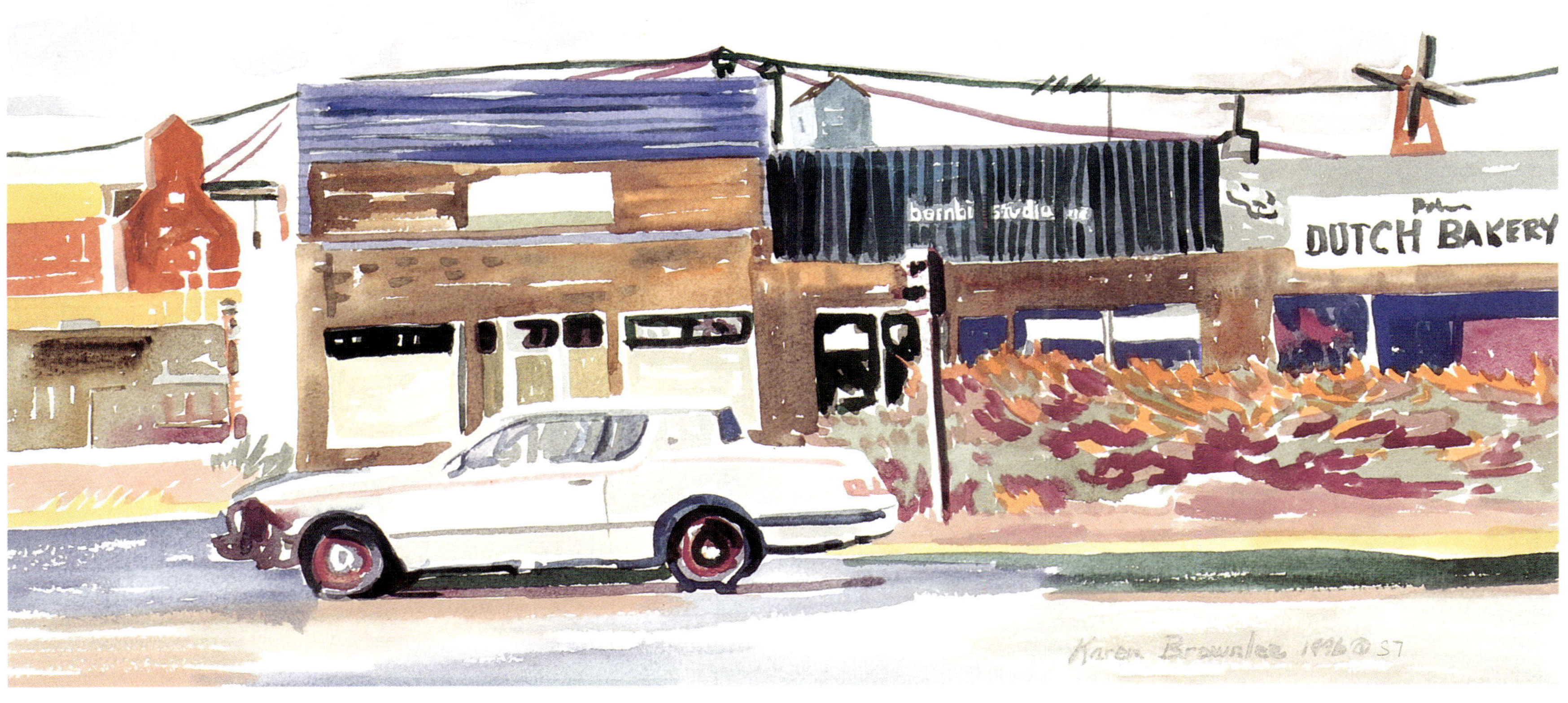

Before irrigation arrived in Taber in 1920, crops suffered periodic drought. In 1911, a year of plenty, two million bushels were shipped, but other years in this decade saw a generally low yield.

TABER #2, 1996, 18" x 12", CIRCA JUNE 1996.

Although substantial irrigated acreage was converted to vegetables, root crops and cattle feed by 1925, grain was still important. One freighter had 12 teams of mules, and residents would gather to watch the parade of grain wagons as it pulled into the elevators. Company elevators shared the market with farmer-owned facilities, built to ensure that fair profits went to the producers.

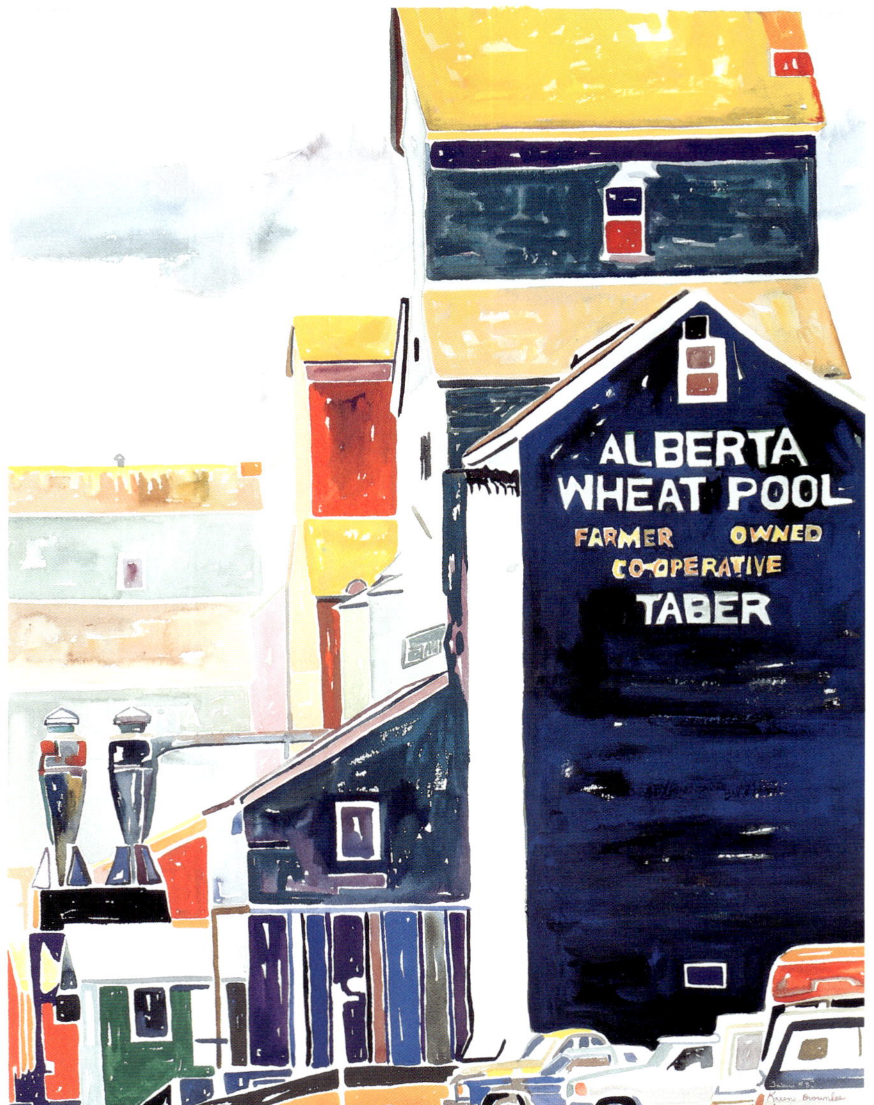

 TABER #3, 1998, 21" x 28", CIRCA JUNE 1996.

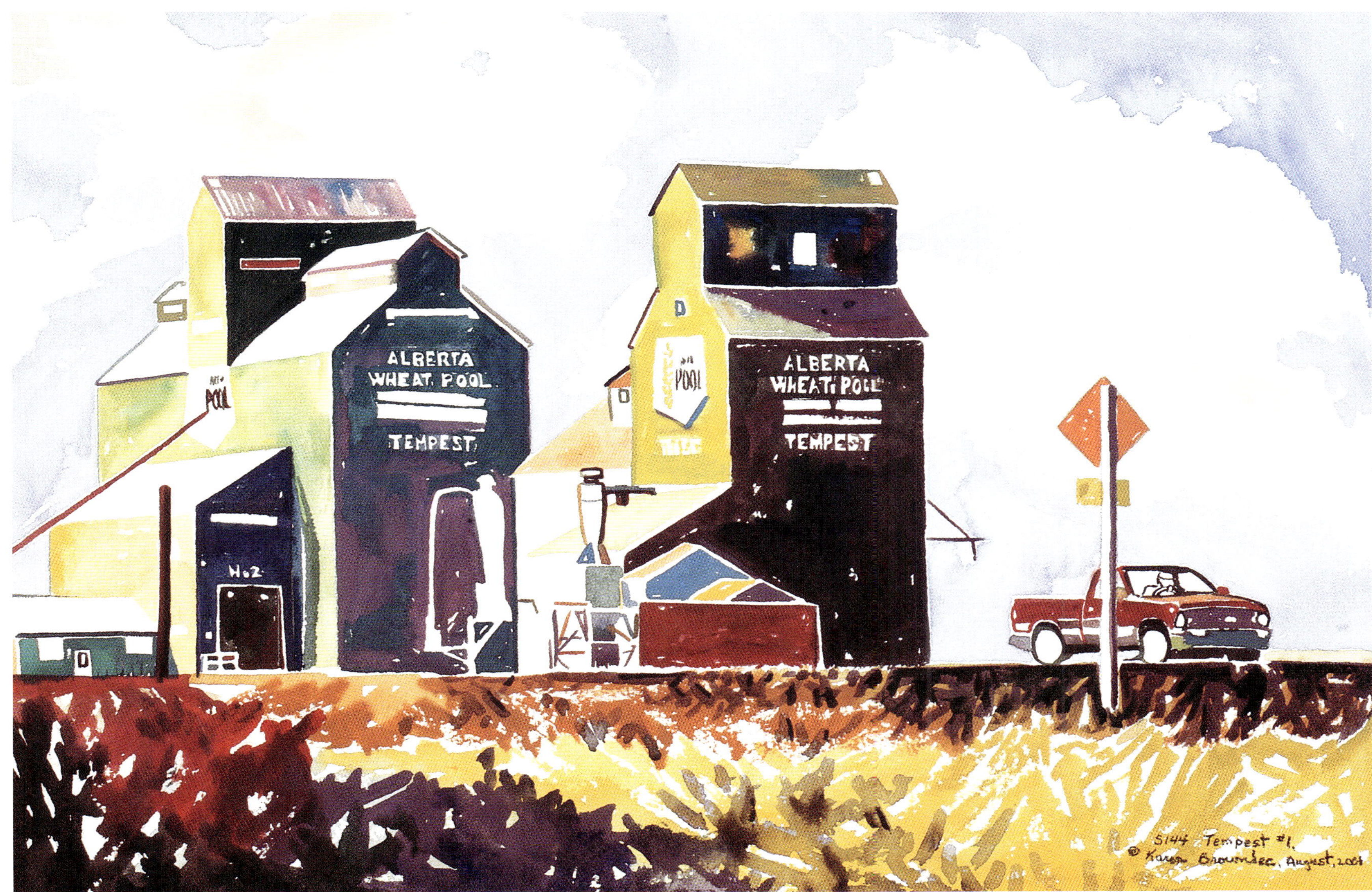

Tempest, a post office named for English opera singer Marie Tempest, opened in 1913 and closed in 1916, but Alberta Wheat Pool and Alberta Pacific Grain Company elevators revived the settlement. In 1928 nearby farmers, who had previously shipped grain through Chin or Coaldale, came to Tempest. The Federated Grain Company bought the Alberta Pacific elevator in 1972, later selling it to the Wheat Pool.

TEMPEST #1, 2001, 18" x 12", CIRCA NOVEMBER 1995.

Fort Macleod, founded in 1874, was Alberta's first North-West Mounted Police post. Oats were planted to supplement the natural grass that fed the police horses. Francis Willock grew the first wheat in 1882 near Pincher Creek. Shortly after, Fort Macleod's Dave Grier planted five bushels of seed acquired from Brandon, becoming credited with growing Alberta's first commercial wheat crop.

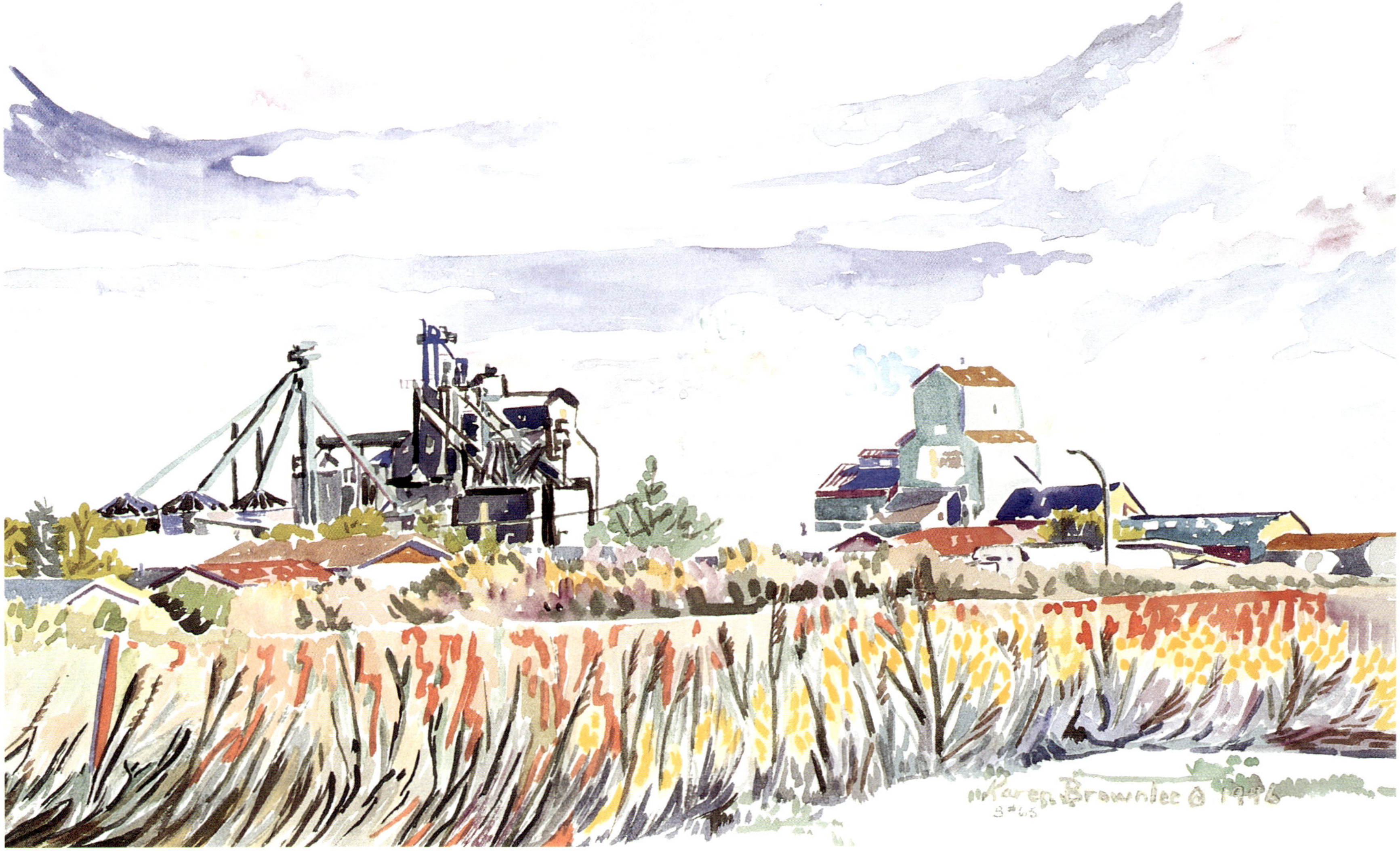

Fort Macleod #1, 1996, 18" x 12", circa August 1996.

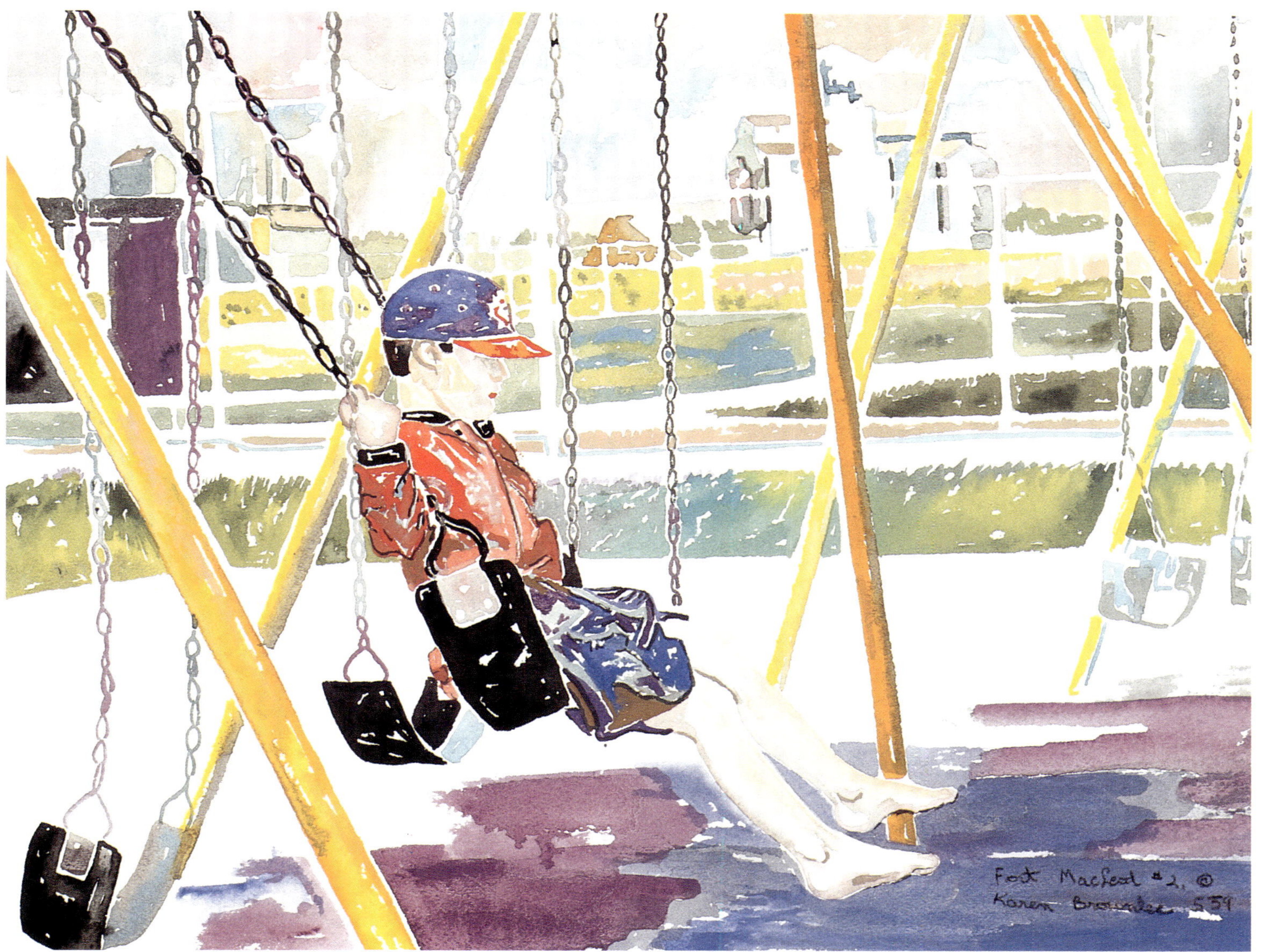

George Duce delivered 14,000 bushels of wheat to Fort Macleod in 1899, reportedly southern Alberta's first carload shipment. In 1913 local farmers created the Alberta Farmers' Co-operative Elevator Company to safeguard collective profits. This community cooperative spirit lives on, as evidenced by the town playground, where the artist's son, Logan, waits in July 1998 for the second ballgame of a double header.

Fort Macleod #2, 1998, 12" x 9", circa July 1998.

The name Coaldale, reflecting the resource that first attracted interest to the area, is mentioned as early as 1886. Eliot T. Galt—of coal, railway and irrigation fame—built railways to move locally mined coal to market, receiving land grants in exchange for constructing the railways. These land grants included the land around Coaldale, which would become as important for agriculture as for coal in future years.

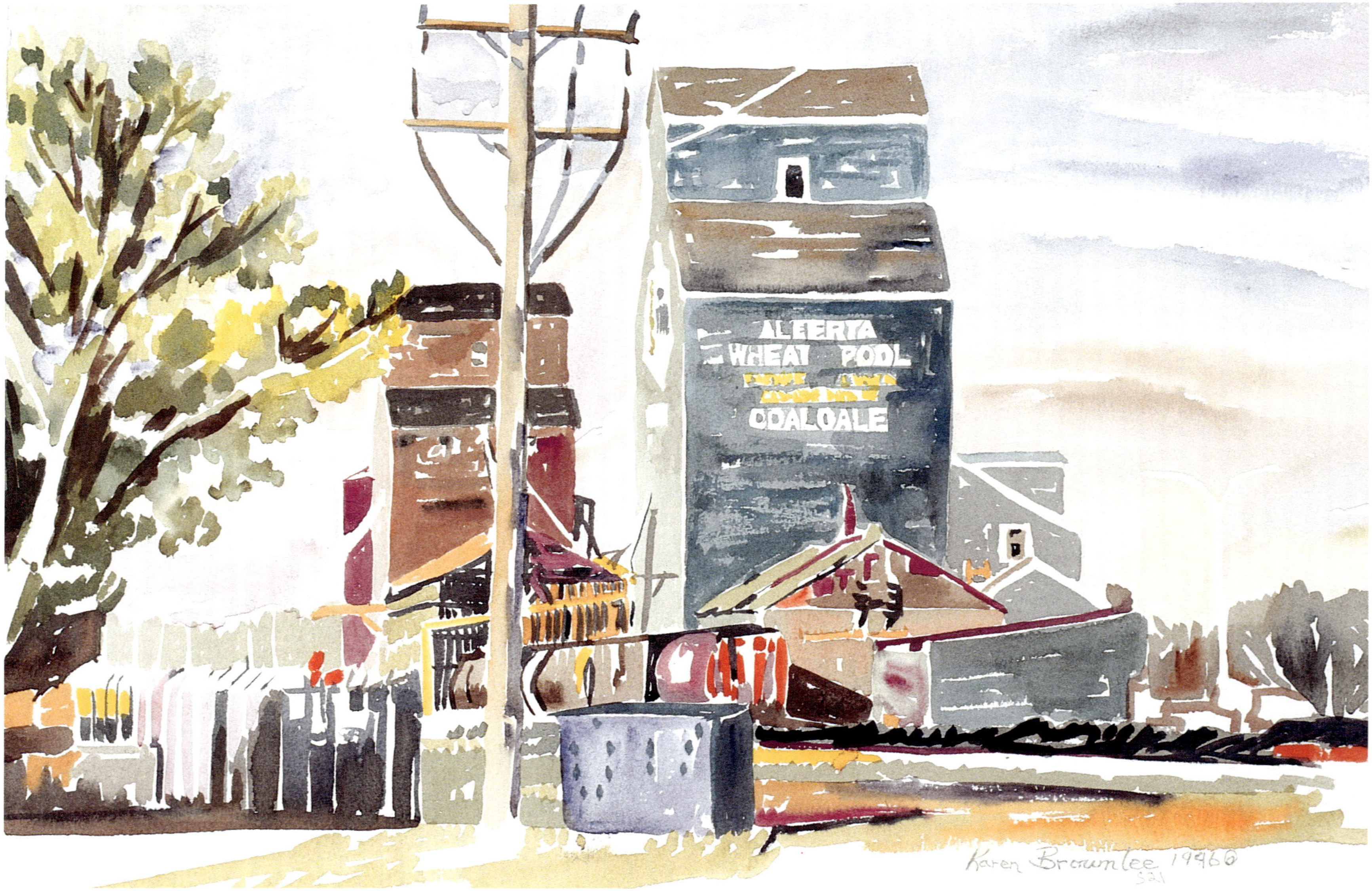

 Coaldale #1, 1996, 18" x 12", circa June 1995.

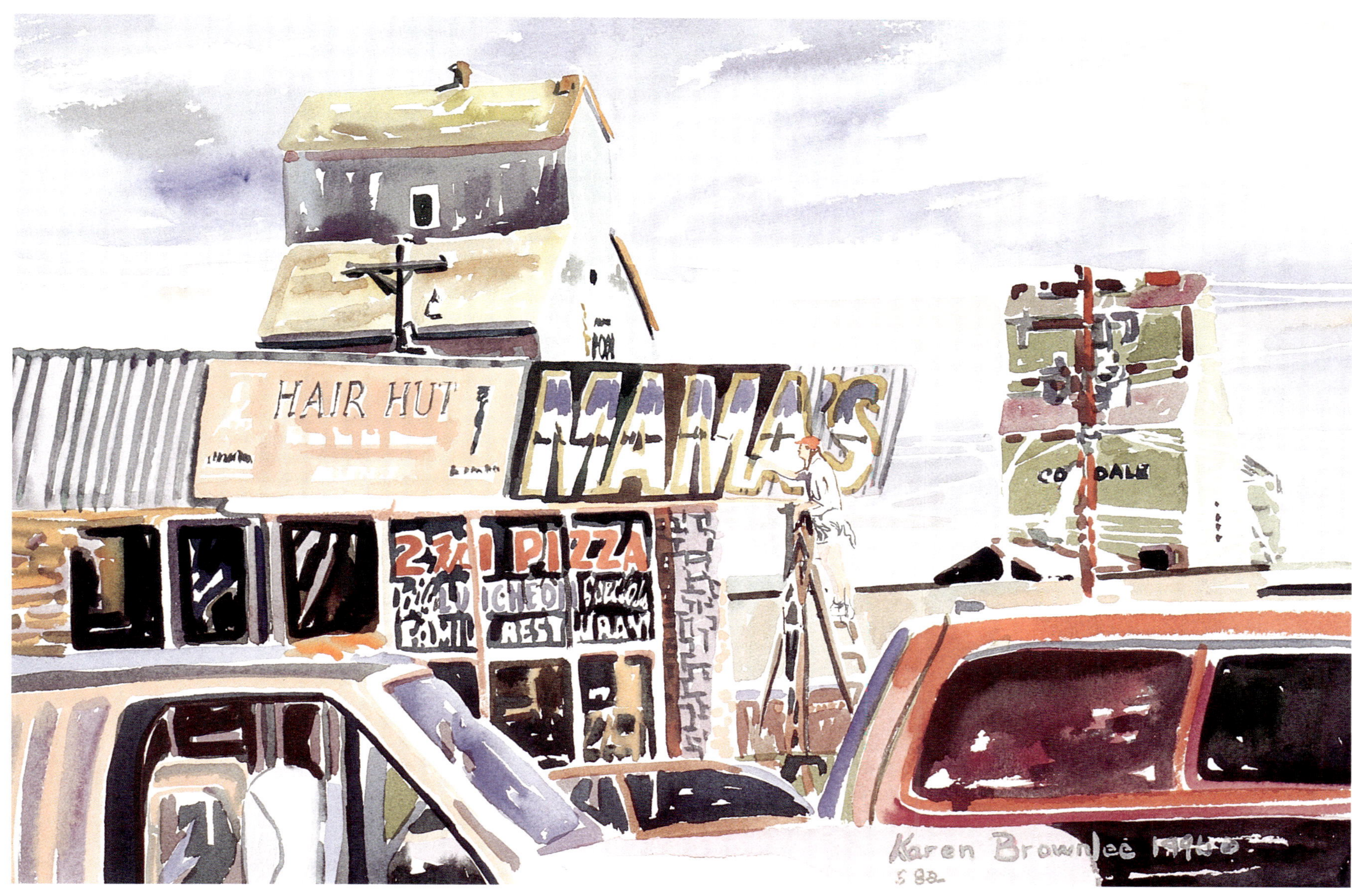

Captain John Palliser surveyed this semi-arid region in 1857–60 during a period of drought. He reported that the area was unsuitable for agriculture. Wetter years and the introduction of irrigation proved this opinion wrong. In 1915–16 elevators were crucial as the area produced a world record wheat crop, raising 54,389 bushels on a thousand acre block within 30 miles of Coaldale.

Coaldale #2, 1996, 18" x 12", circa August 1996.

In 1905 large company farms were prevalent around Coaldale, including the Southern Alberta Irrigated Farms Company, headed by J.A. Suggitt with farmers from Nebraska and Illinois. The size of these holdings made management of the irrigated crops less efficient, and yields were less than expected. Larger farms were subsequently broken up into 80-acre parcels. These smaller farms handled irrigation more successfully, increasing the area's prosperity.

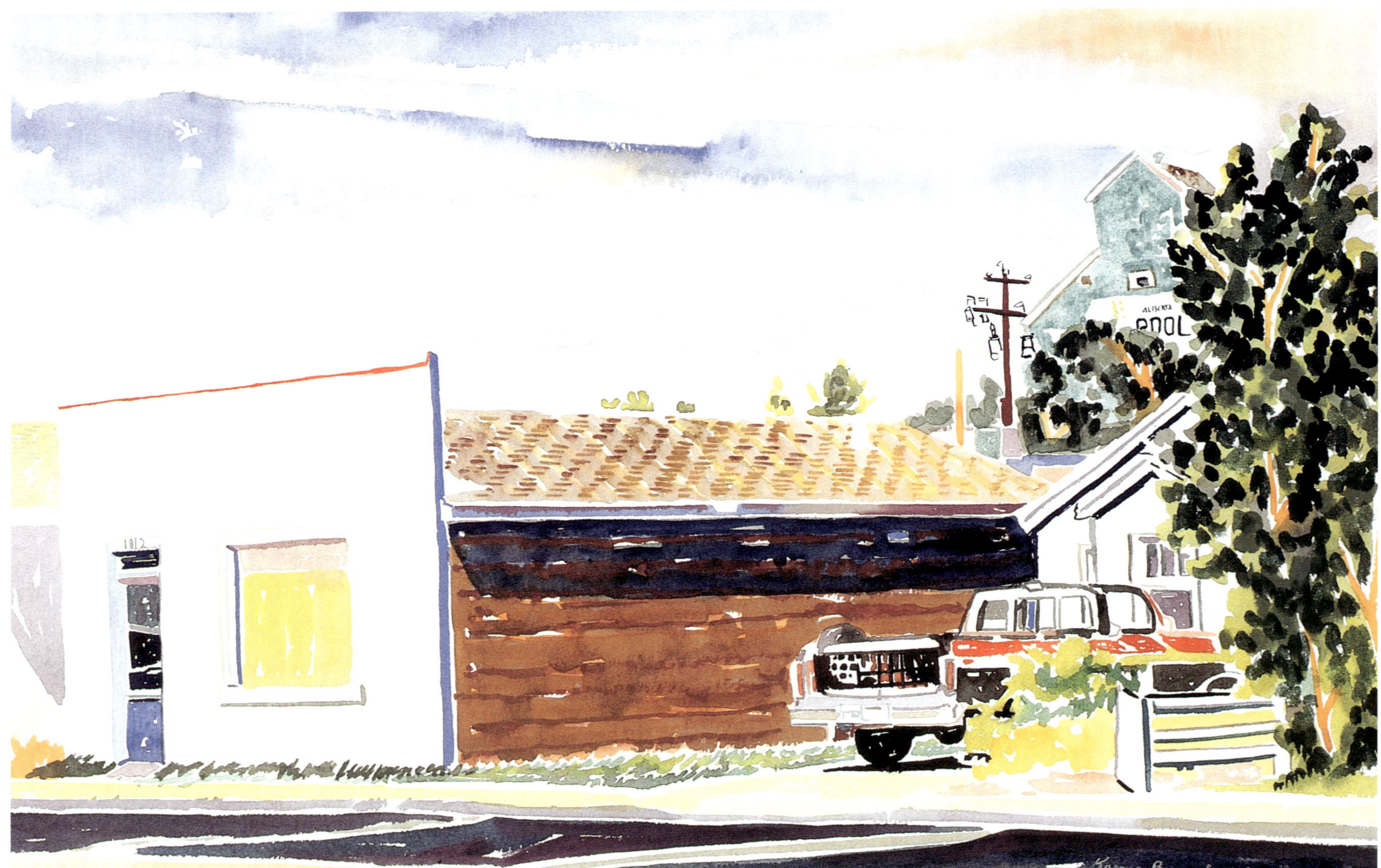

Coaldale #3, 1998, 18" x 12", circa August 1996.

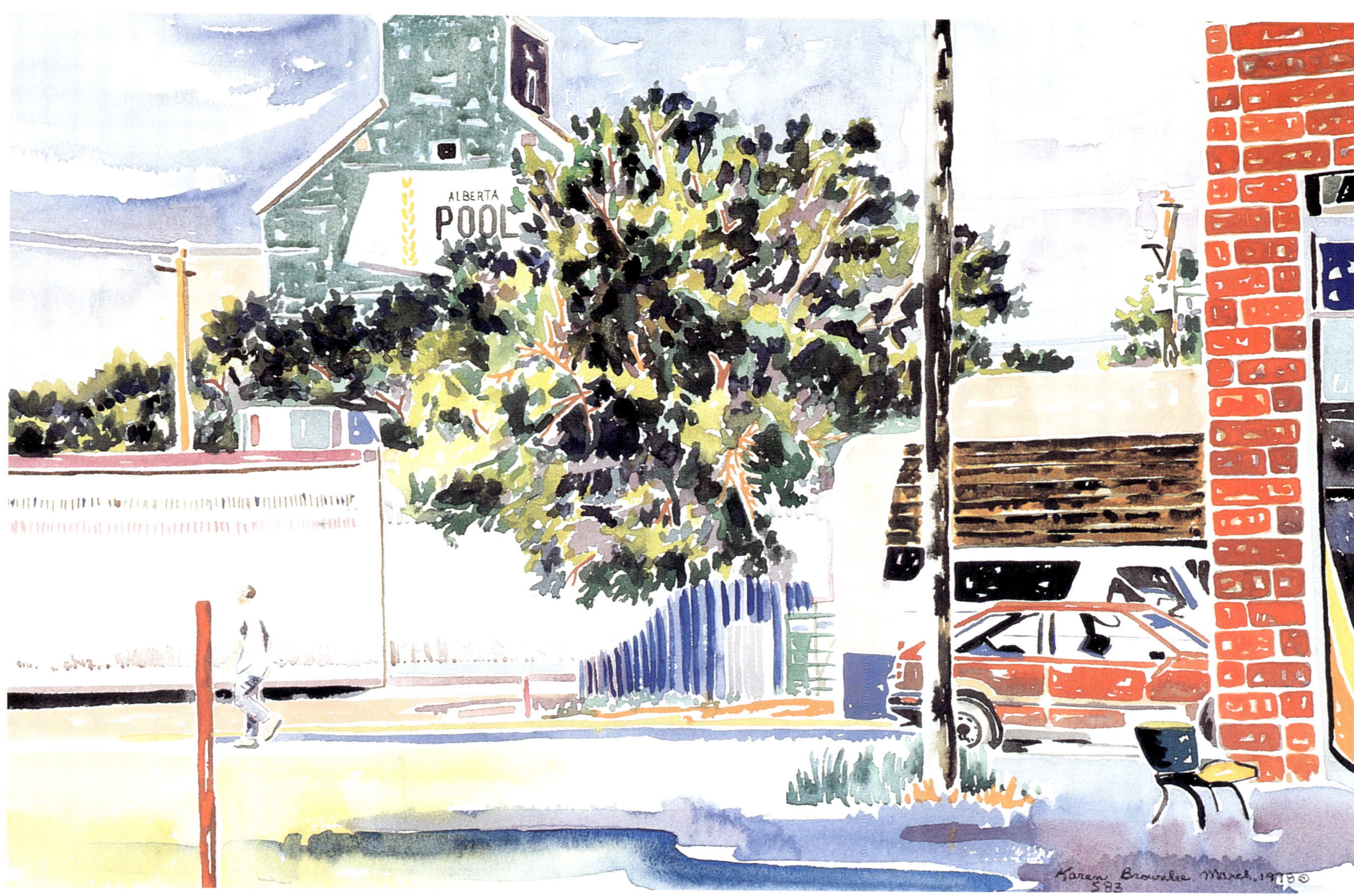

Coaldale's West Coast Grain Company elevator rose in 1908. Purchased by Ellison Milling and Elevator in 1911, it was for years the only elevator between Lethbridge and Taber. Grain was hauled up to 30 miles from the Iron Springs–Turin area. In 1920 the Coaldale Co-Operative Elevator (bought by the Alberta Wheat Pool in 1926) was constructed, followed by the Alberta Pacific elevator in 1925.

COALDALE #4, 1998, 18" x 12", CIRCA AUGUST 1996.

Coaldale's first building boom began in 1917. A general store opened, followed by a harness shop, hardware store, hay market sheds, a butcher shop, a Chinese laundry, two restaurants, and a billiard hall and barbershop. The first Fair and Exhibition was held in 1919, attracting townspeople, farmers and workers from larger farms, such the Canadian Pacific's Central Farm.

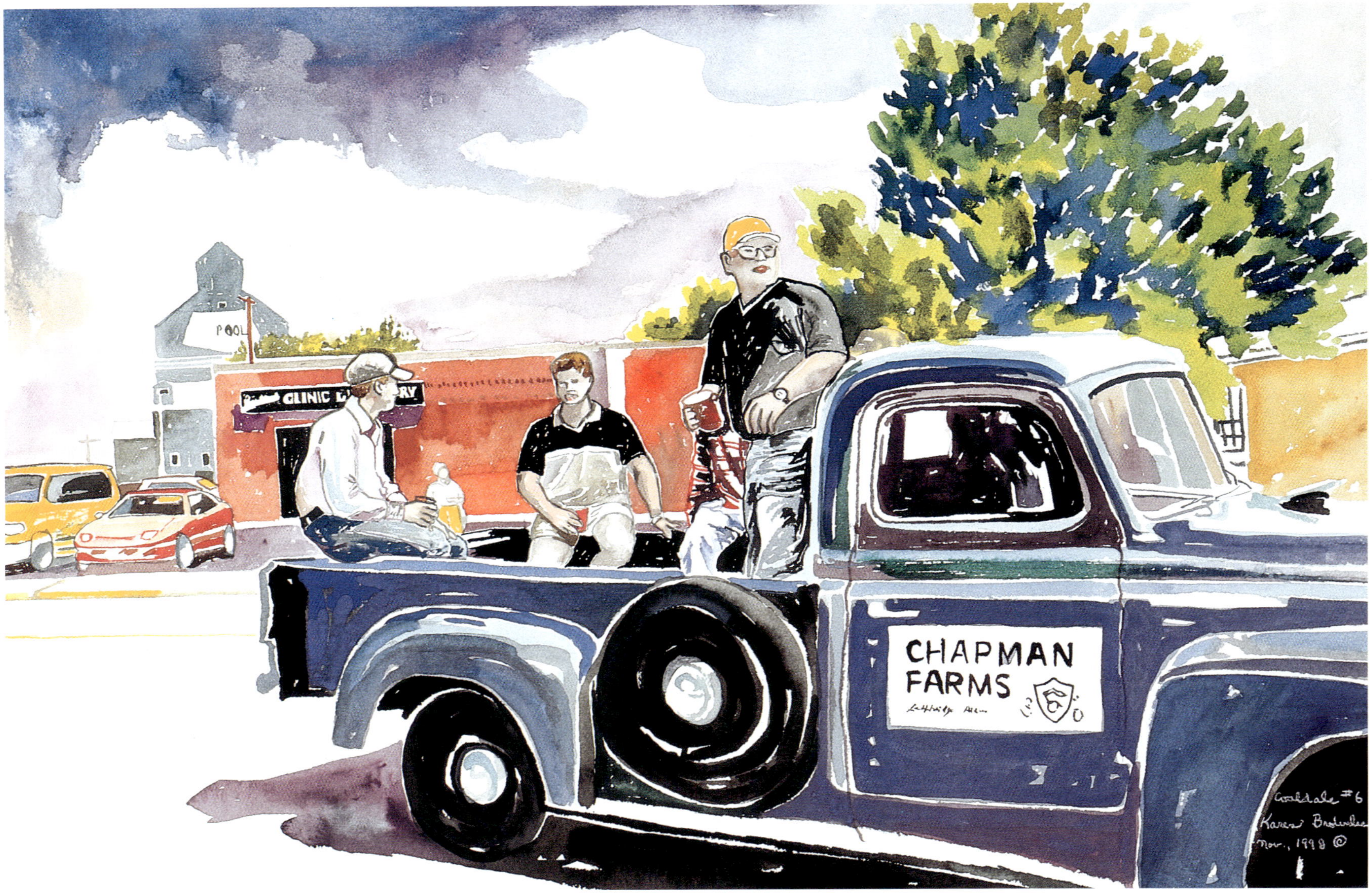

 COALDALE #6, 1998, 18" x 12", CIRCA JULY 1998.

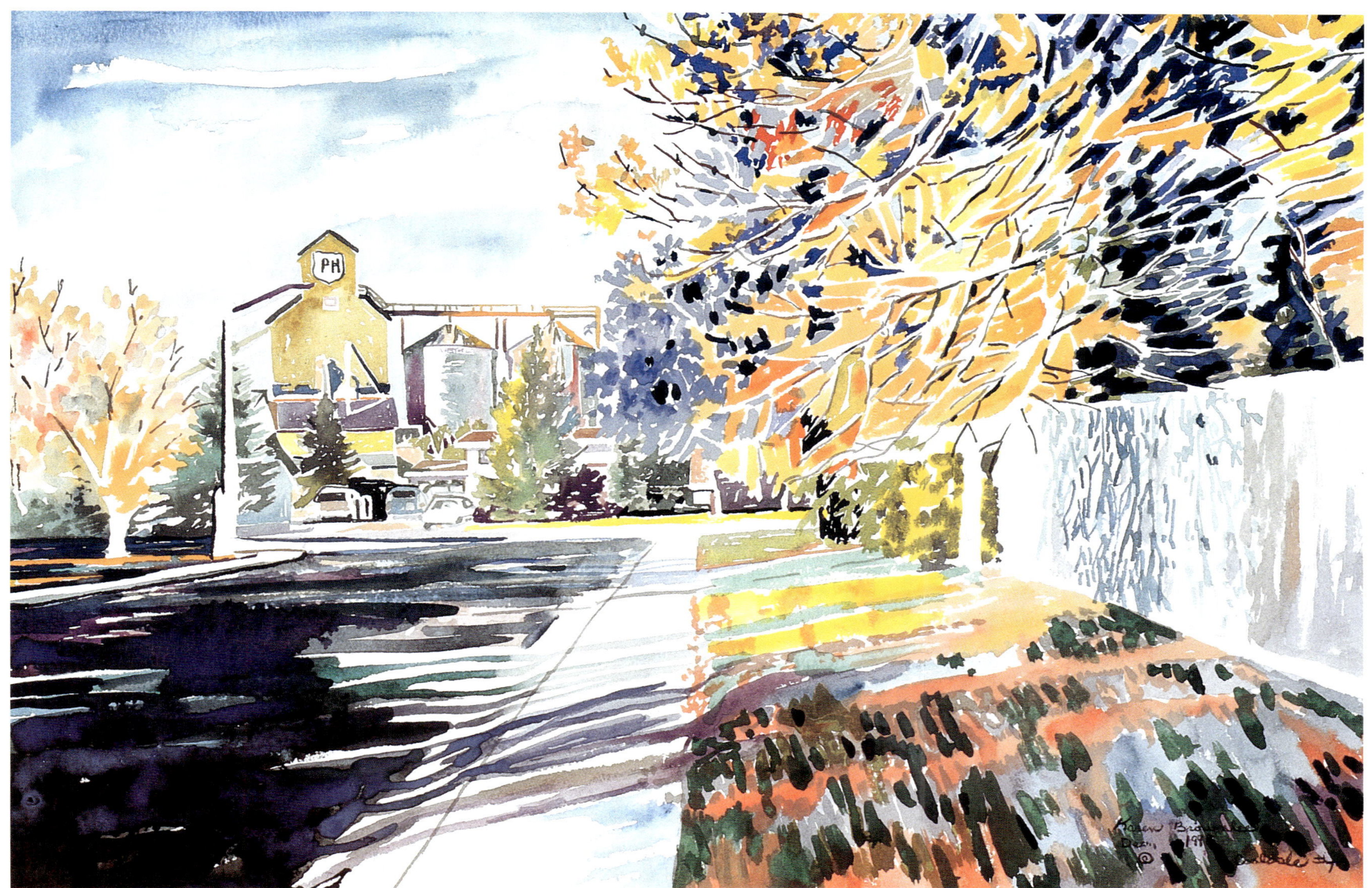

Coaldale's early tradition of agricultural innovation continues, evident in this modern elevator. The Canadian Pacific's Central Farm experimented with irrigation and crop diversification from 1916 to 1945, growing sugar beets for the Raymond factory in 1926. Ellison Milling and Elevator introduced soft white Idaho wheat for pastry flour in 1925. Ellison also built an early electric-powered elevator here after a 1937 fire destroyed one of their facilities.

Coaldale #7, 1998, 18" x 12", circa October 1998.

Coaldale has been community oriented since its beginnings. The town, benefiting from irrigation, held its first fair in 1919, despite the drought that cancelled events in neighbouring communities. Large buildings, constructed from alfalfa bails, housed exhibits and a dance hall. Baseball games, a team pulling contest and a parade were highlights. Parades remain popular, with this contemporary family cycling to one such event.

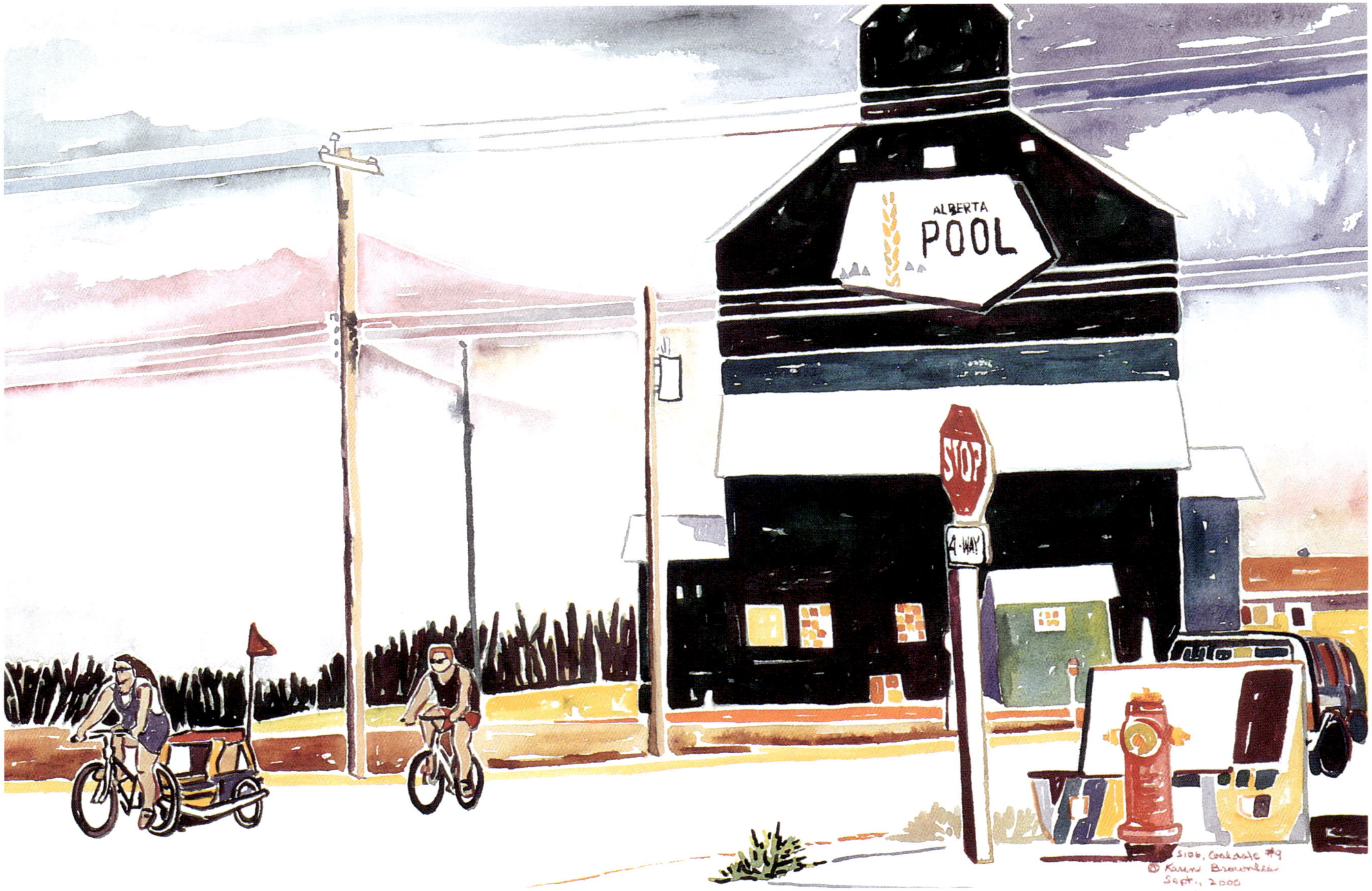

 Coaldale #9, 2000, 18" x 12", circa July 1998.

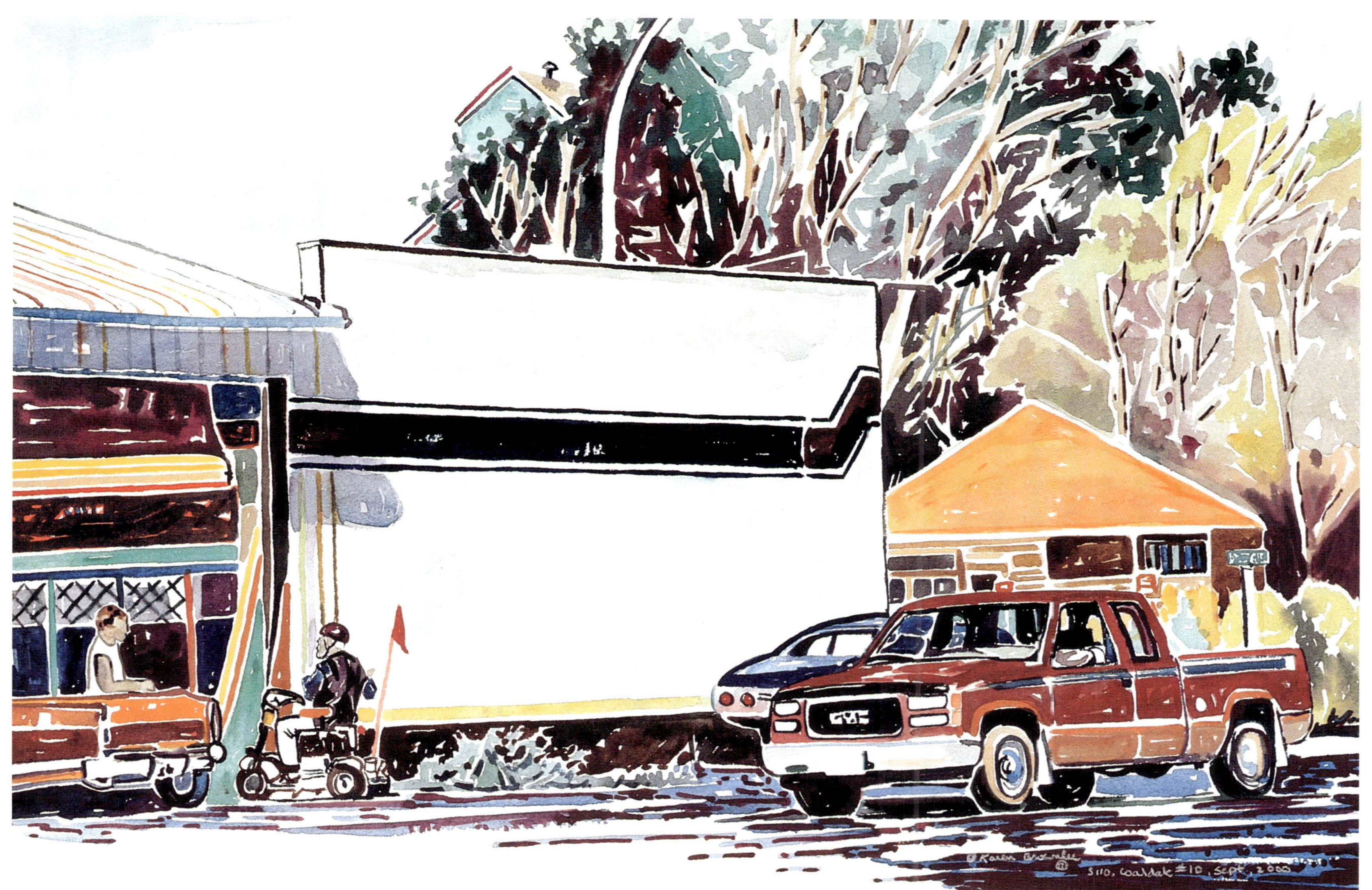

Coaldale's long and varied settlement history includes early settlers from the United States, Europe and eastern Canada, as well as Japanese families forcibly resettled here during the Second World War. The varied experiences and backgrounds of Coaldale's citizens contributed to their enthusiastic support of Sunrise Ranch, built near Coaldale, which provided employment and community integration for mentally challenged individuals from 1969 to 1981.

Coaldale #10, 2000, 18" x 12", circa August 1996.

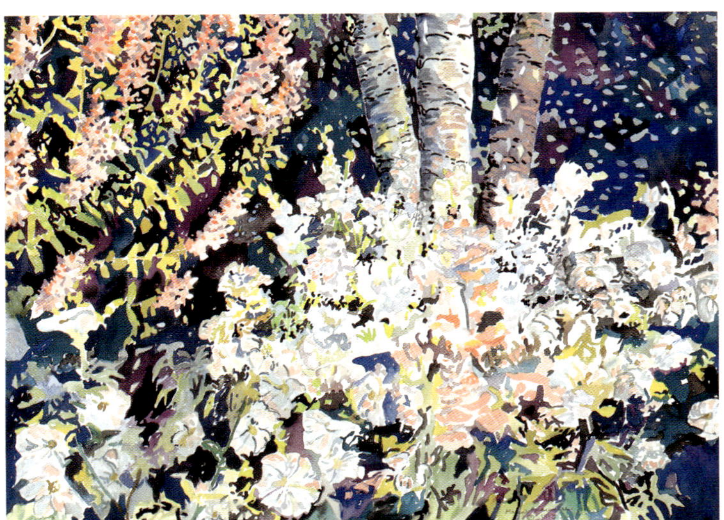

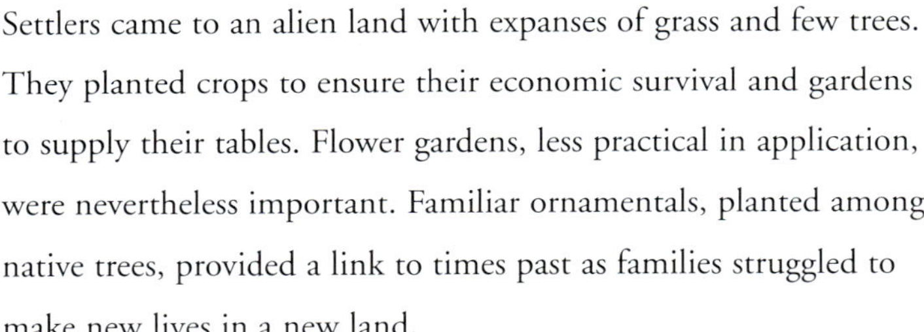

Settlers came to an alien land with expanses of grass and few trees. They planted crops to ensure their economic survival and gardens to supply their tables. Flower gardens, less practical in application, were nevertheless important. Familiar ornamentals, planted among native trees, provided a link to times past as families struggled to make new lives in a new land.

INTIMATE GARDENS, 1993, 24" x 18".

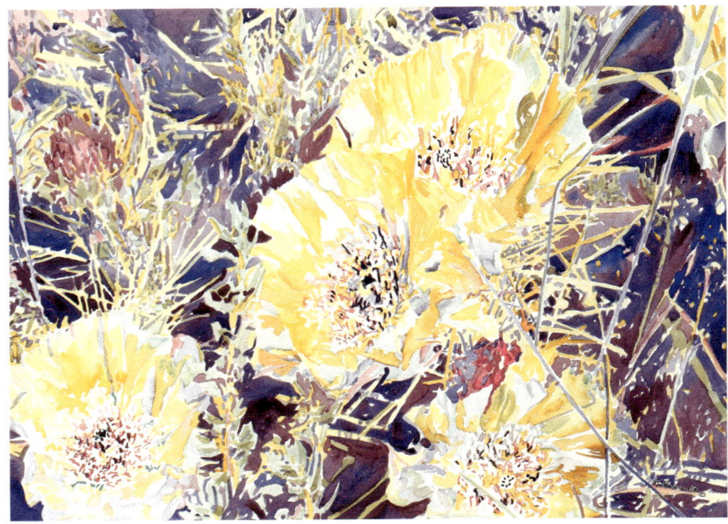

Palliser's expedition (1857–60) travelled through what is now southern Alberta during a drought. Palliser referred to the region as part of the Great American Desert. Prickly pear cactus, blooming in profusion, supported his opinion. The flat, fleshy stems function in water conservation, photosynthesis and flower production.

PRICKLY PEAR CACTUS #1, 1992, 28" x 21".

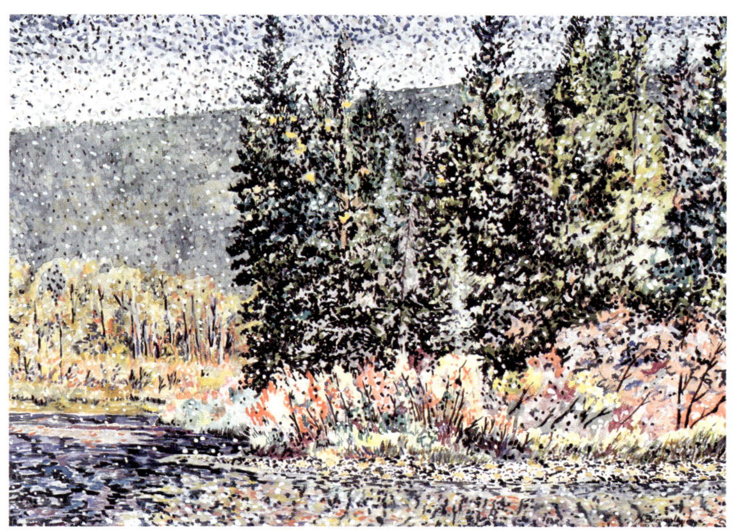

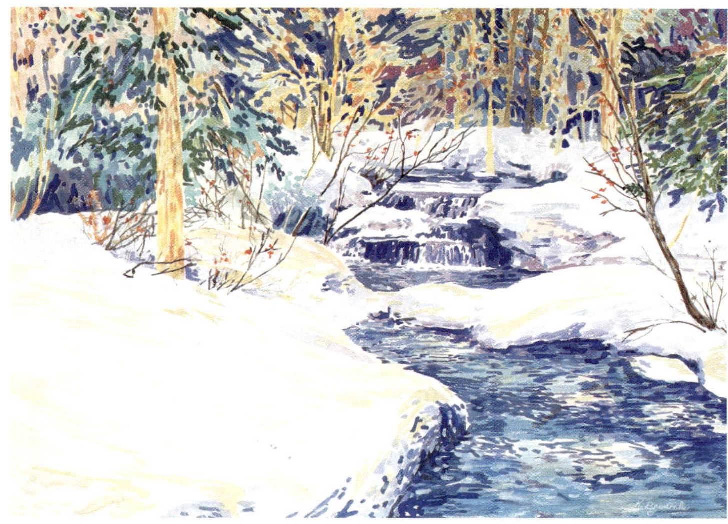

The name Cameron, associated with this marvellous lake, a creek and a spectacular falls in Waterton Lakes National Park, honours Captain Donald Roderick Cameron, the British Commissioner on the International Boundary Commission of 1872–76. In establishing the Canadian–American border, the Commission was essential to Canadian sovereignty. It also supported the work of the North-West Mounted Police and the development of railways, both central to orderly settlement.

William Aldridge sold axel grease made from oil collected from seeps near Oil Creek, later renamed Cameron Creek. In 1902 Patrick, Leeson and Lineham imported a rig from Canada's first oil well in Petrolia, Ontario. They struck oil. Alberta's first producing well, 311 meters deep, yielded 300 barrels a day. Although short-lived, this first signalled the oil derrick's challenge to the elevator for Alberta's skyline.

Cameron Lake in Fall, 1992, 28" x 21".

Cameron Creek, 1992, 28" x 21".

The Ellison Milling and Elevator Company began milling, storage and elevator operations at Lethbridge in 1907. Ellison, originally the 1902 Raymond Milling and Elevator Company, grew rapidly, employing 140 people by 1955. Lethbridge's distinctive Canadian Grain Commission inland terminal was finished in 1931 with a handling capacity of 1,125,000 bushels. A precursor of modern concrete elevators, it was privatized in 1979 as Alberta Terminals Ltd., then sold in 1992 to Cargill.

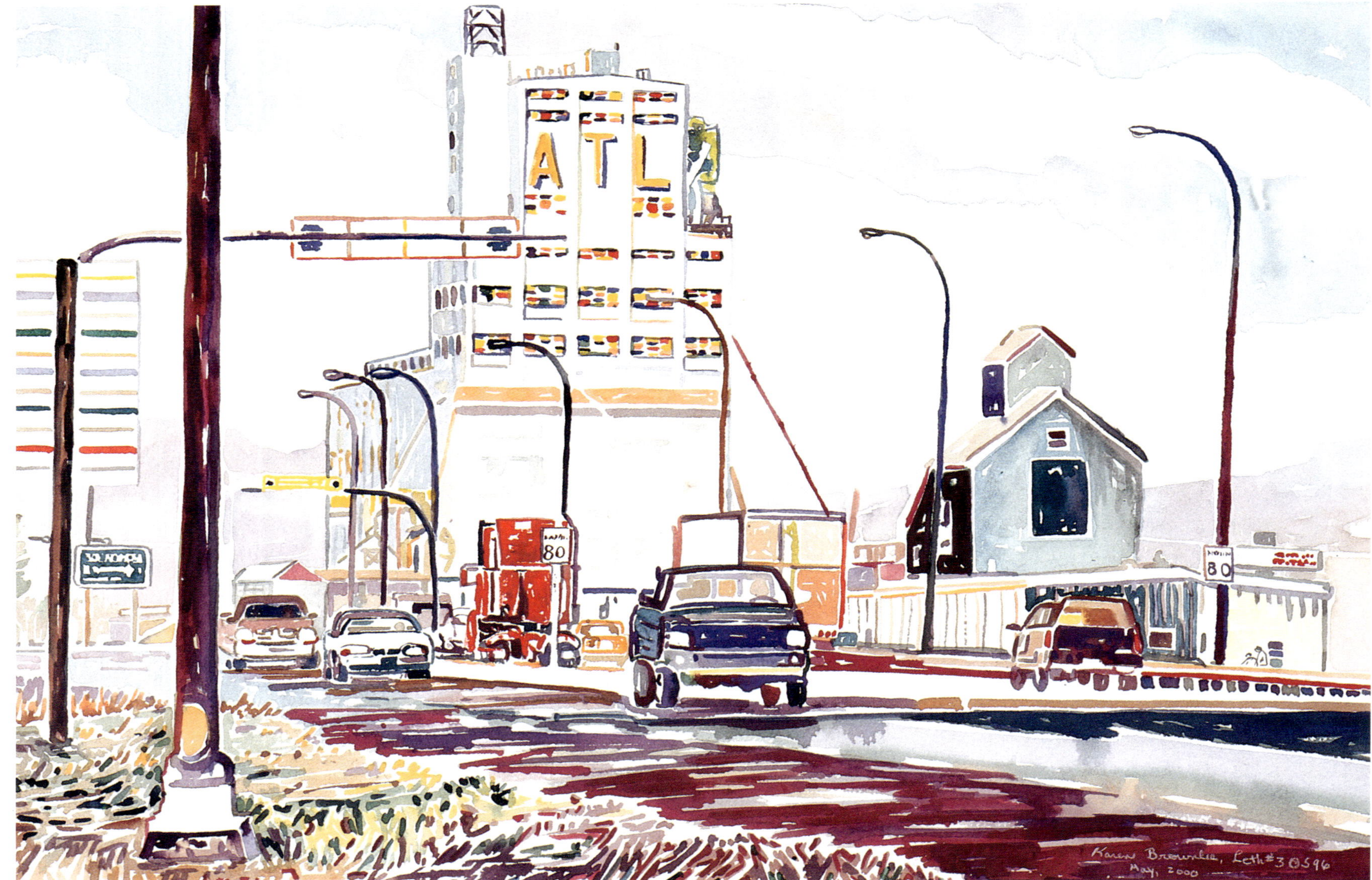

LETHBRIDGE #3, 2000, 18" X 12", CIRCA OCTOBER 1999.

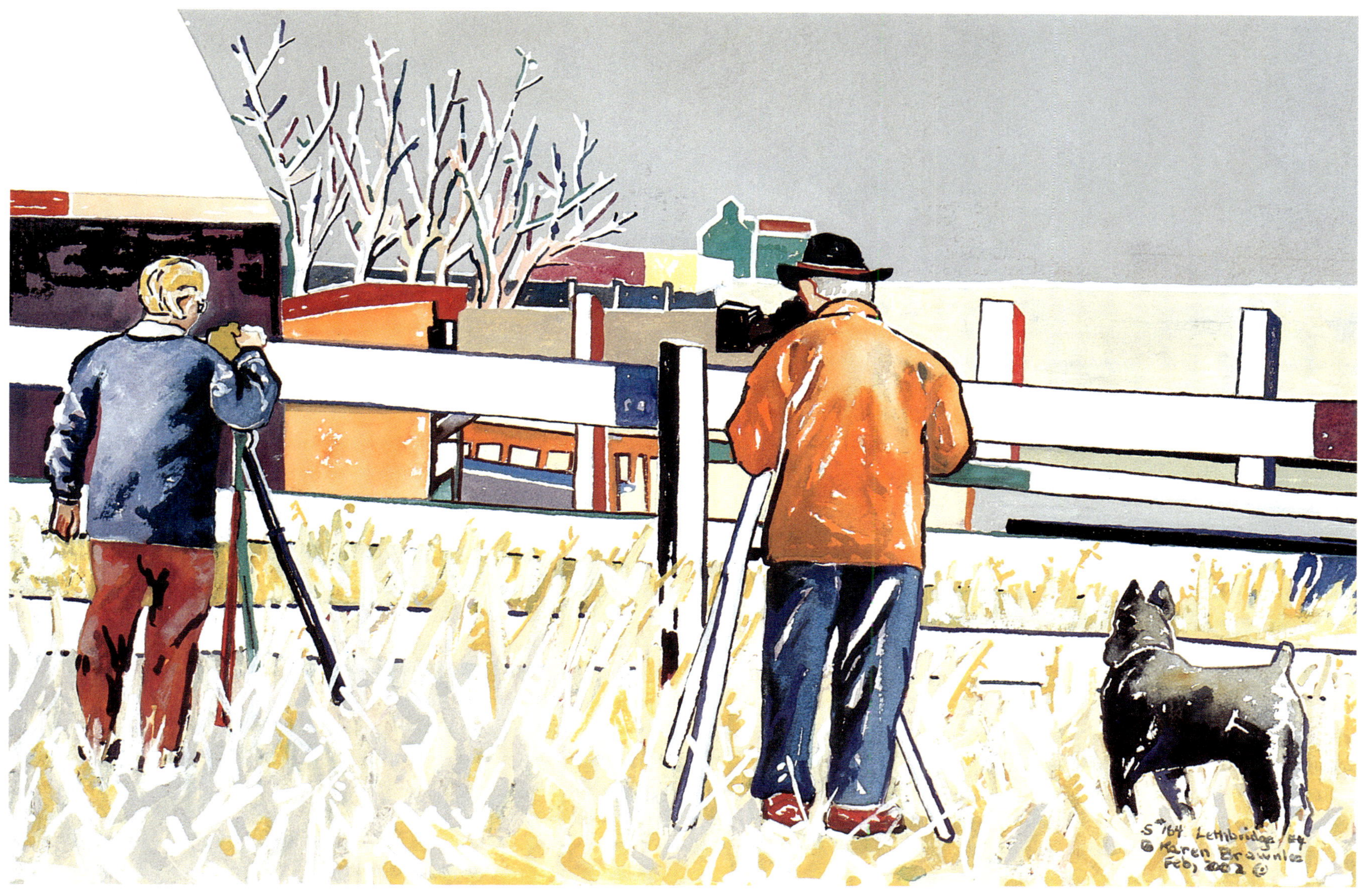

Lethbridge elevators can be seen in the distance from the artist's family farm. The artist's father, Mike Hazuda, and her husband, Ray Brownlee, built the corrals. Professional fine art photographers Rhonda Kupsch and Morry Katz, friends of Karen, are in the foreground with Morry's dog, Jammer.

Lethbridge #4, 2002, 13" x 12", circa September 2000.

Wilson Siding, named for Ernest Henry Wilson, a pioneer and comptroller of the Alberta Railway and Irrigation Company, was built 11 miles, or one day's journey, from the next elevator on the line. The Cardston Milling Company and the Nicholas Bawlf Grain Company constructed the first two elevators here. In 1914 Ogilvie Flour Mills also built at Wilson Siding.

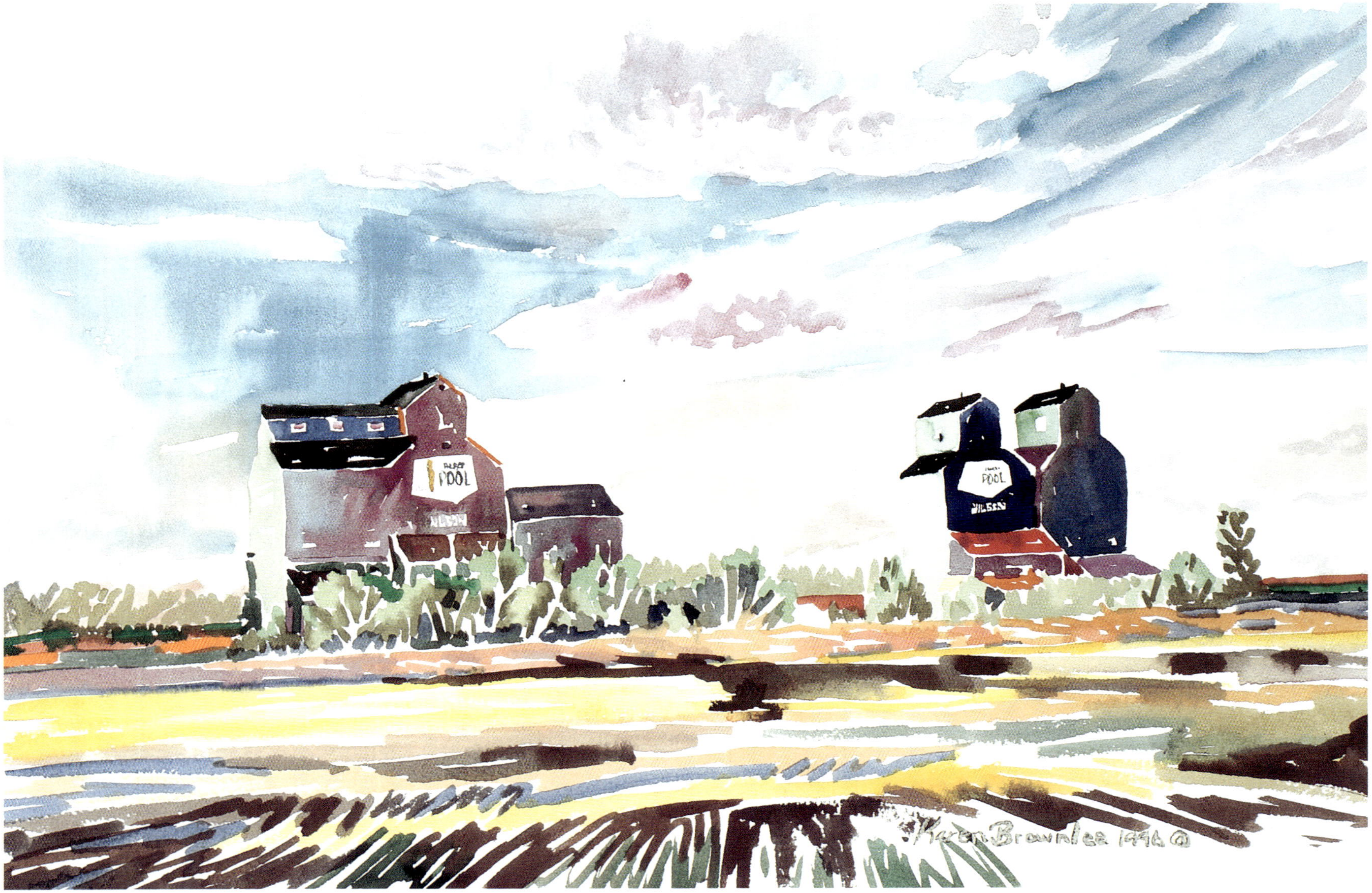

 WILSON SIDING #1, 1996, 18" x 12", CIRCA JUNE 1995.

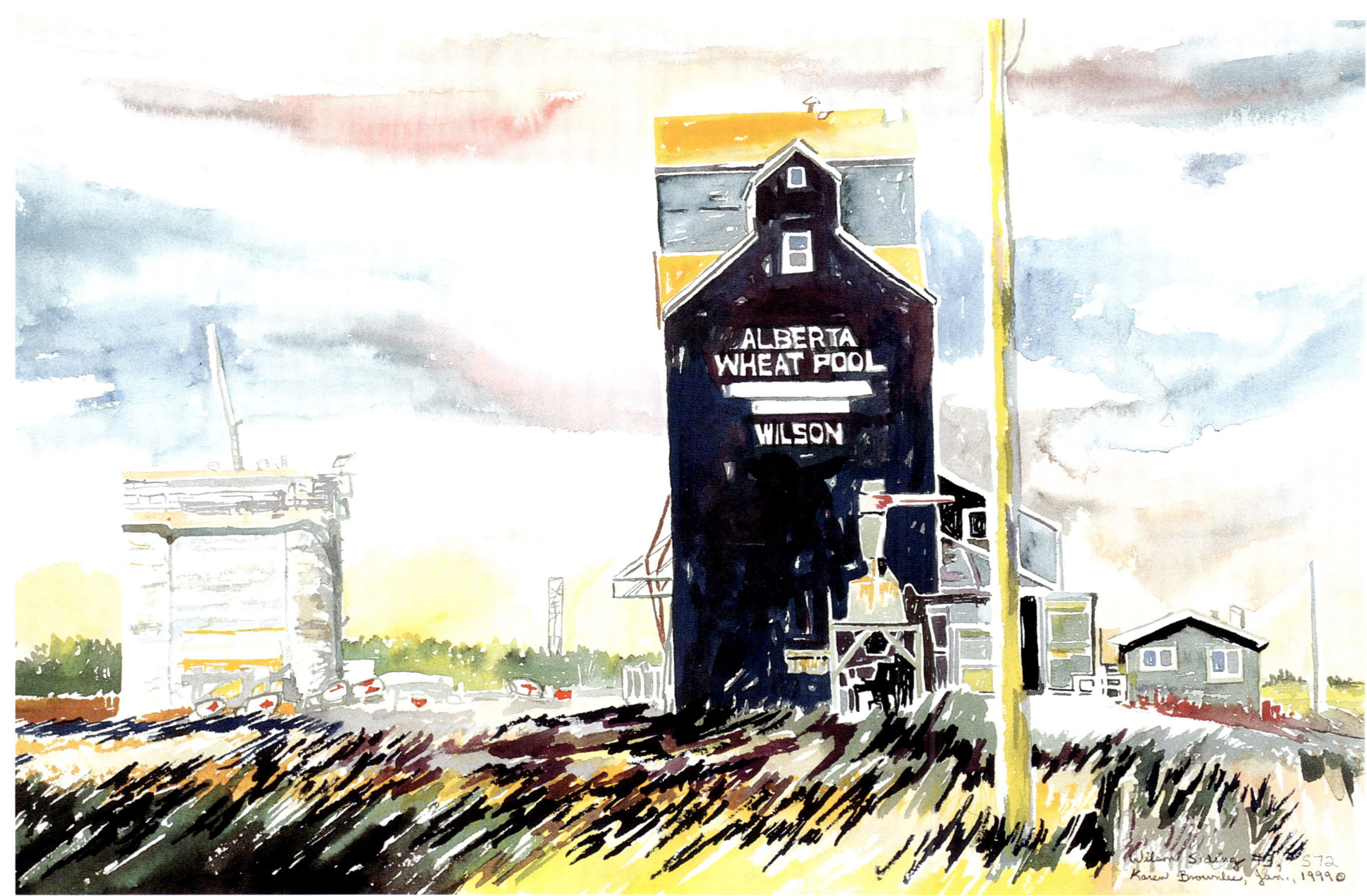

By 1994 the only elevator company operating at Wilson Siding was the Alberta Wheat Pool. With the CPR shutting down branch lines, elevators too disappeared. Small communities such as this, bustling centres of activity in their day with elevator operators, railway section men and express and telegraph offices, slowly return to the obscurity implied by the word *siding* in the name.

Wilson Siding #3, 1999, 18" x 12", circa July 1998.

The CPR established a siding at Brocket in 1897–1898, along the new Crowsnest Pass route to the Pacific. Two elevators were built here in 1907. The Alberta Pacific Grain Elevator Company and Pincher Creek merchant Timothé Lebel erected grain warehouses and loading docks. For nearly a century, elevators stood at Brocket, sentinels overlooking the Oldman River winding through the deep valley below.

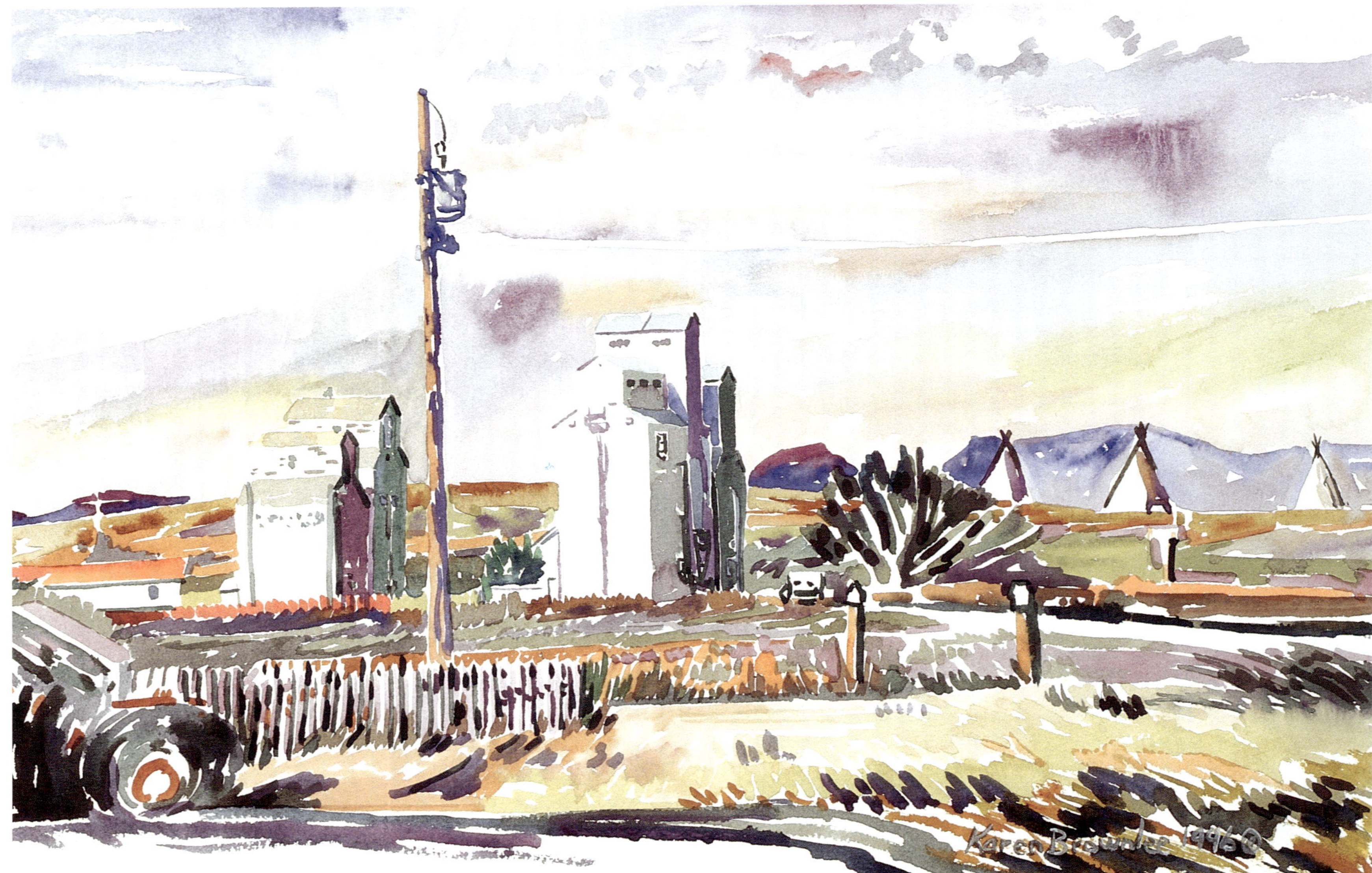

Brocket #1, 1996, 18" x 12", circa July 1996.

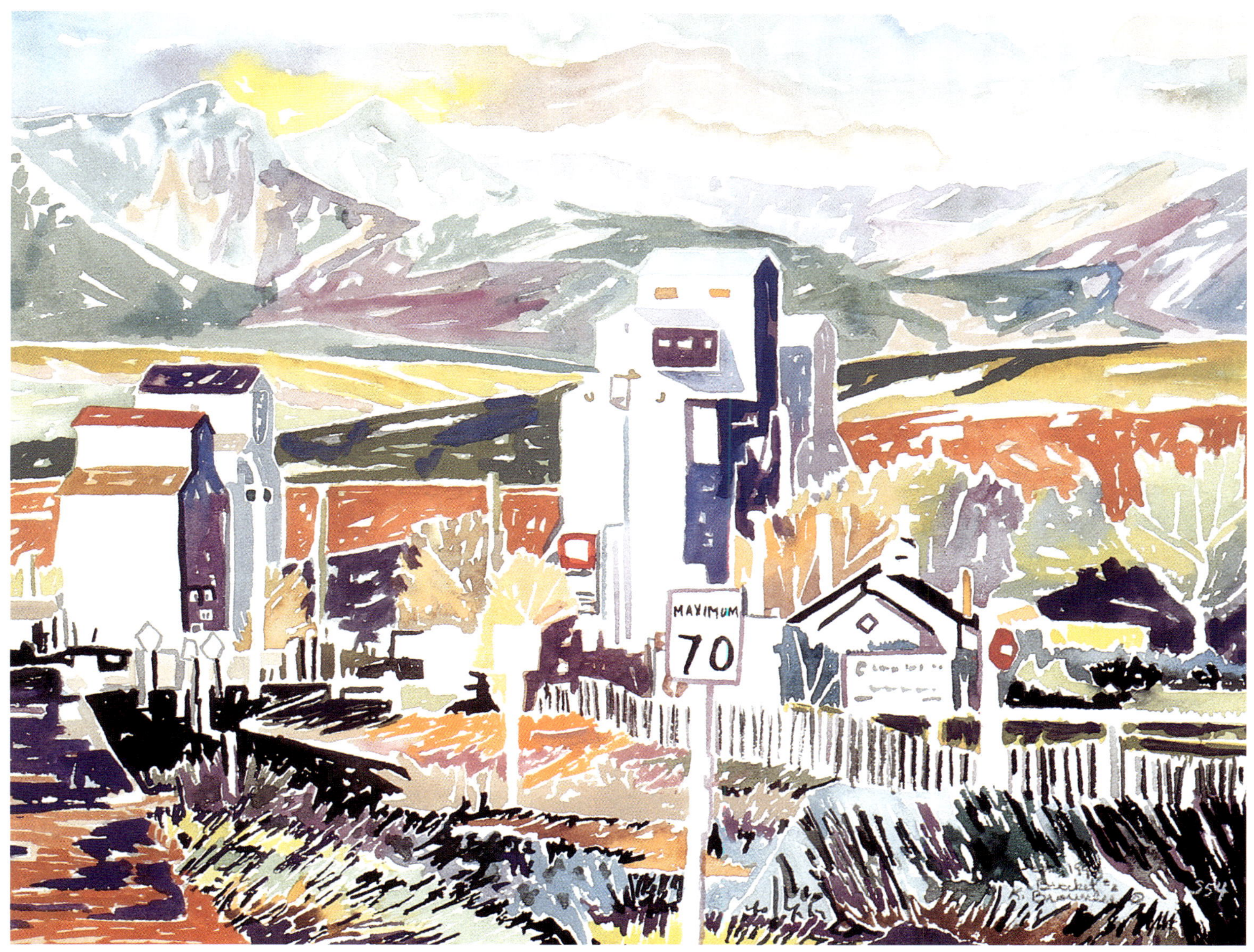

By 2001 the larger United Grain Growers metal-clad structure had been moved to Heritage Acres Museum and the smaller, older Alberta Pacific Elevator had been torn down.

Brocket #2, 1998, 12" x 9", circa September 1998.

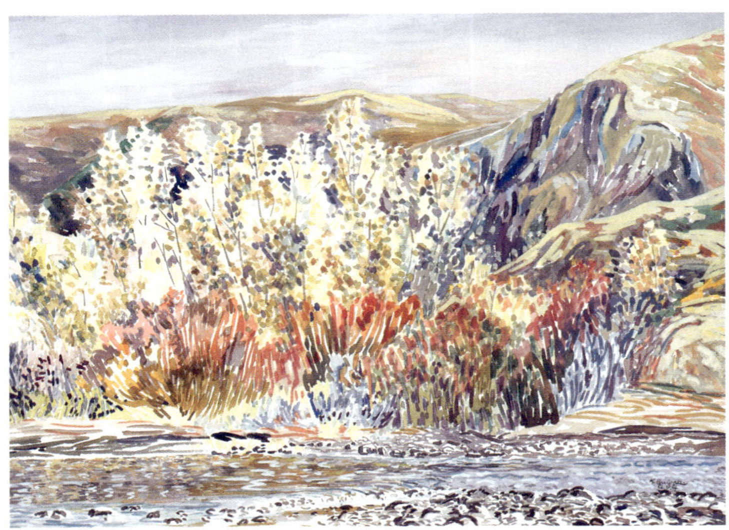

Glaciers shaped Canada's plains. The eastern portion is the flat bottom of glacial Lake Agassiz, with an escarpment along the Manitoba border signalling the rolling land to the west. Central Saskatchewan's Missouri Coteau defines the westernmost area. Valleys are deep here, with the 15 to 60 metre-high banks of the Oldman River being typical. The profile of the land challenged railway and road builders.

OLDMAN RIVER TOPOGRAPHY, 1994, 28" x 21".

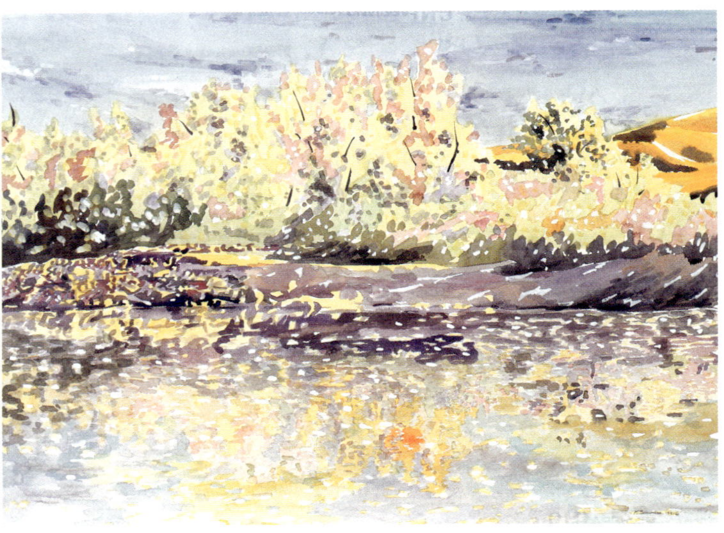

These huge cottonwood trees in their autumn glory depend on spring floods for germination. Cottonwoods, living an average of 30 years, are an important native tree of arid regions. In 1981, two decades after damming on the St. Mary and Waterton rivers, a survey showed that cottonwood groves had been reduced by 48 and 23 percent respectively. Concern for the loss of cottonwoods escalates as rivers are increasingly managed for human use.

OLDMAN RIVER COLOURS, 1991, 28" x 21".

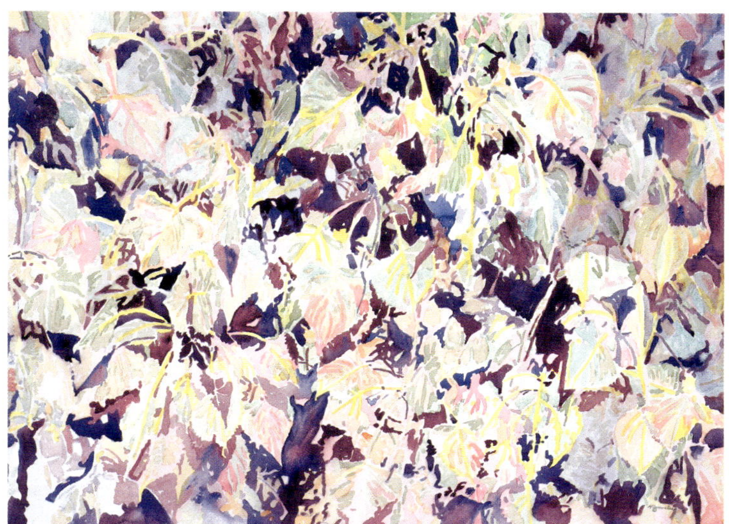

Trembling aspen roots are suited to arid southern Alberta. Most saplings are clones, emerging from root systems that survive floods and fires, allowing the fast-growing trees to re-populate areas. A Wasatch Mountains, Utah, grove, with 47,000 stems from one root system, is currently cited as the world's largest living organism. Poplars, prone to heart rot, are ideal nesting habitat for birds, and create splashes of fall colour on the prairie.

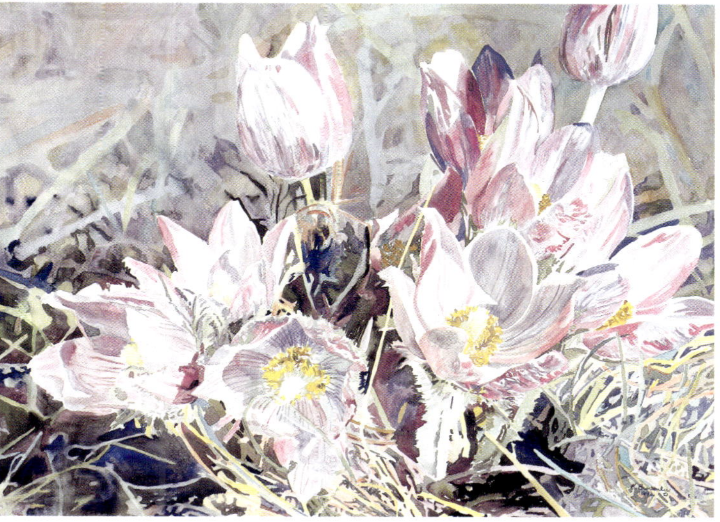

Crocuses, or pasque flowers, signalled the coming of spring to settlers. Using melting snow for moisture, they adapt to the elements by growing at ground level with a jacket of fine hairs that traps heat and moisture. The petals create a parabolic disk, allowing solar heat to warm the flower's interior by as much as 10°C and encouraging the emergence of the fluffy seed head before other flowers even bloom.

Poplar Leaves #1, 1992, 28" x 21".

Prairie Crocus #1, 1992, 28" x 21".

Craddock, located between Stirling and New Dayton, originally had Alberta Pacific and Alberta Wheat Pool elevators, which were moved to a feed facility between the CPR tracks and the junction of Highways 52 and 4. In 1982 Agricore built a new barley elevator, using 562,951 board feet of spruce lumber. In 1984 the company purchased a smaller depression-era elevator for fertilizer storage, saving it from destruction.

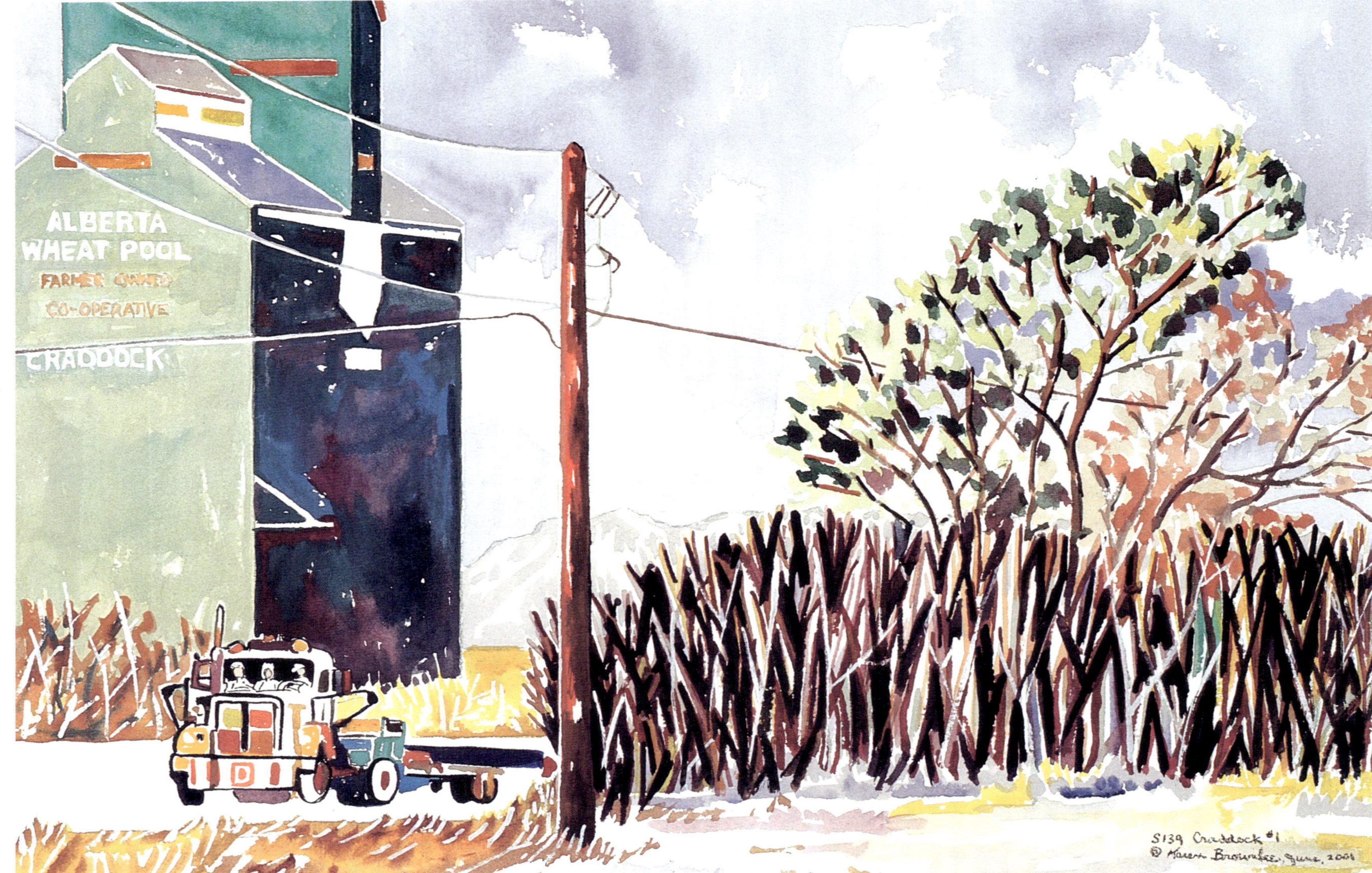

 CRADDOCK #1, 2001, 18" x 12", CIRCA MAY 1998.

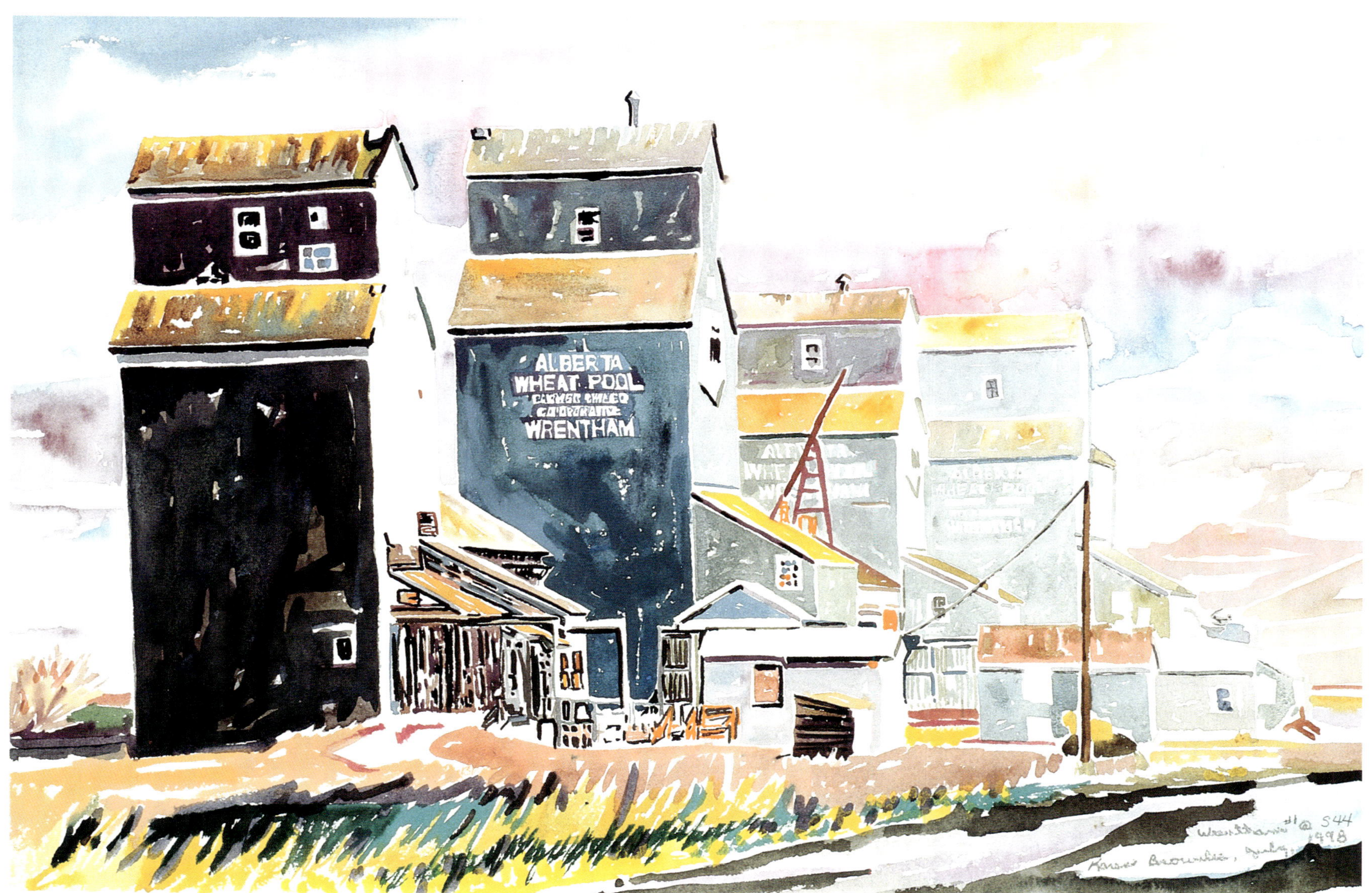

Wrentham's first elevator, built in 1915 by Randle Gee and Mitchell, made loading boxcars much easier. Unfortunately the first grain, delivered by Lief Erickson, came before construction was finished and had to be hand-loaded in any case. By 1930 this first facility had been joined by Midland Grain Company, N. Bawlf Grain Company and the Alberta Wheat Pool.

WRENTHAM #1, 1998, 18" x 12", CIRCA MAY 1998.

Wrentham was home to Alberta Pacific, Ogilvie and Federal grain elevators. The construction of the 113,000-bushel No. 2 Alberta Wheat Pool elevator in 1968 was an event cited in local history. The "Pool green" paint was applied to the west side even before construction was completed.

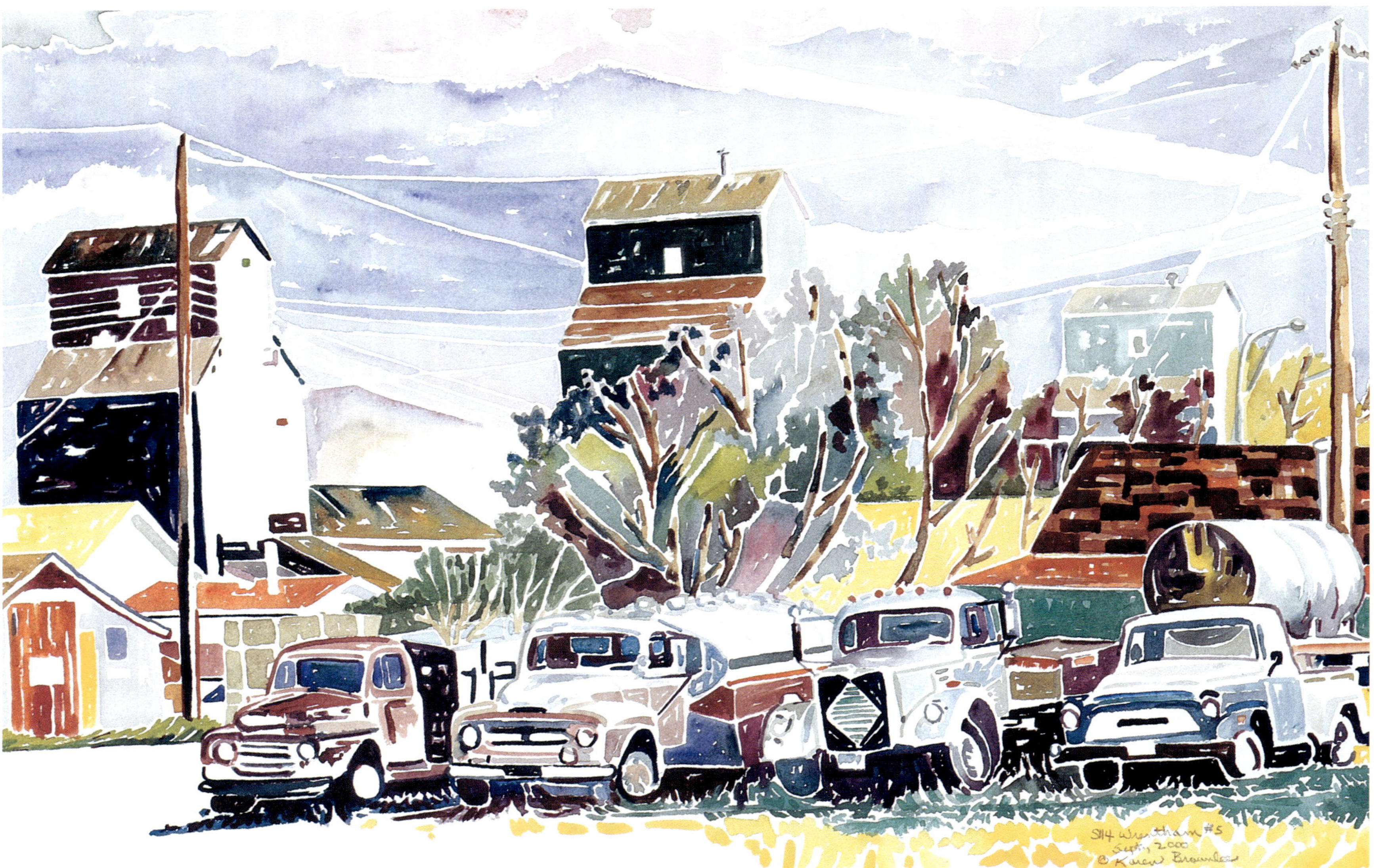

 WRENTHAM #5, 2000, 18" x 12", CIRCA MAY 1998.

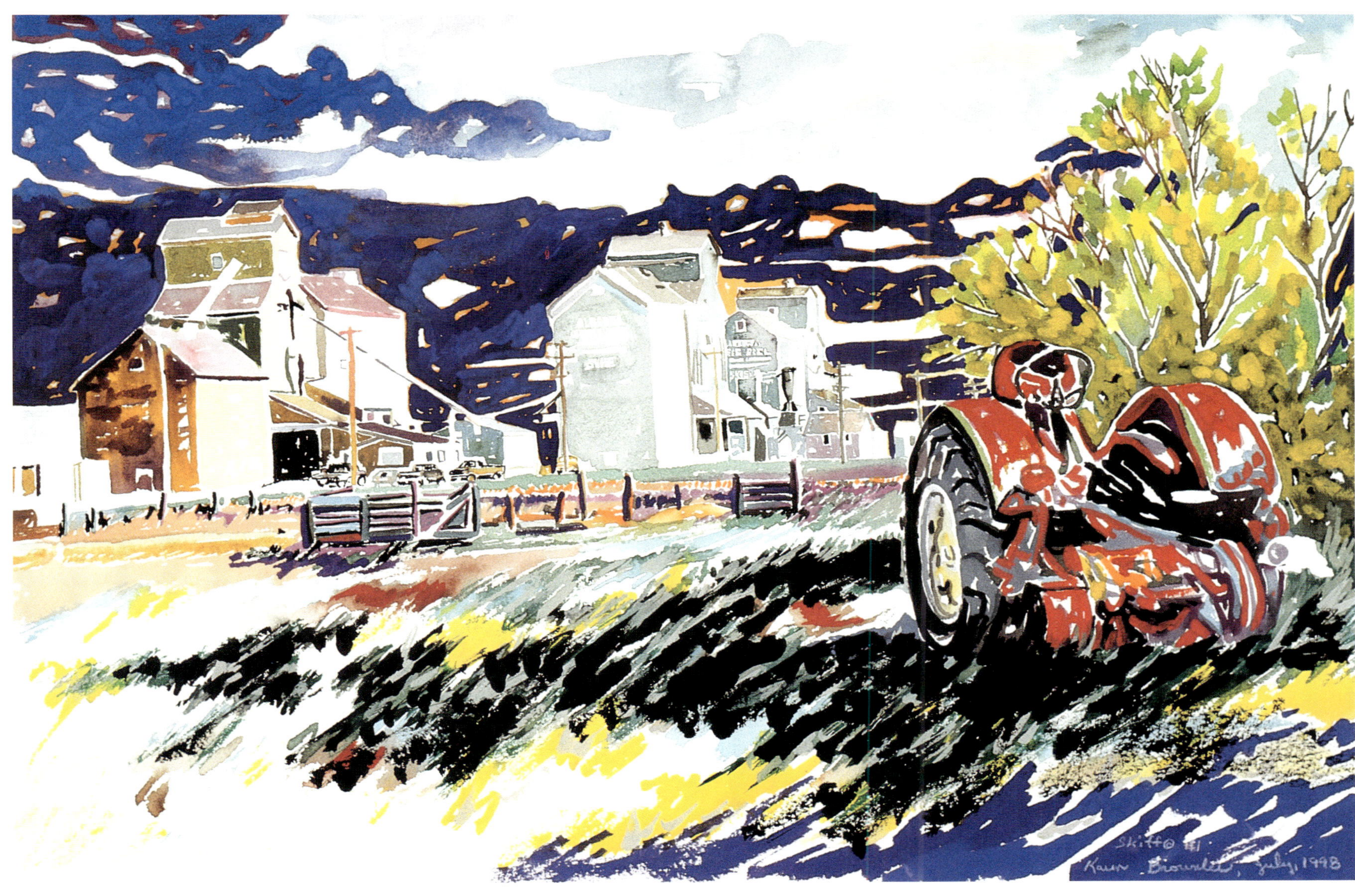

The Alberta Wheat Pool built elevators in Skiff in 1929 and 1954. Ellison Milling and Elevator also constructed an elevator in the town in 1929. Parrish & Heimbecker purchased the Ellison facility in 1975. The Albert Wheat Pool reported its highest handling of grain at Skiff—1,014,232 bushels—in 1975–76.

Skiff #1, 1998, 18" x 12", circa May 1998.

Gail Holland, a friend of the artist, is from the Skiff area. Her father was the elevator agent for the Ellison elevator, which later was purchased by Parrish & Heimbecker. Parrish & Heimbecker, formed in 1909, still has operations in Canada, employing more than 1,000 people.

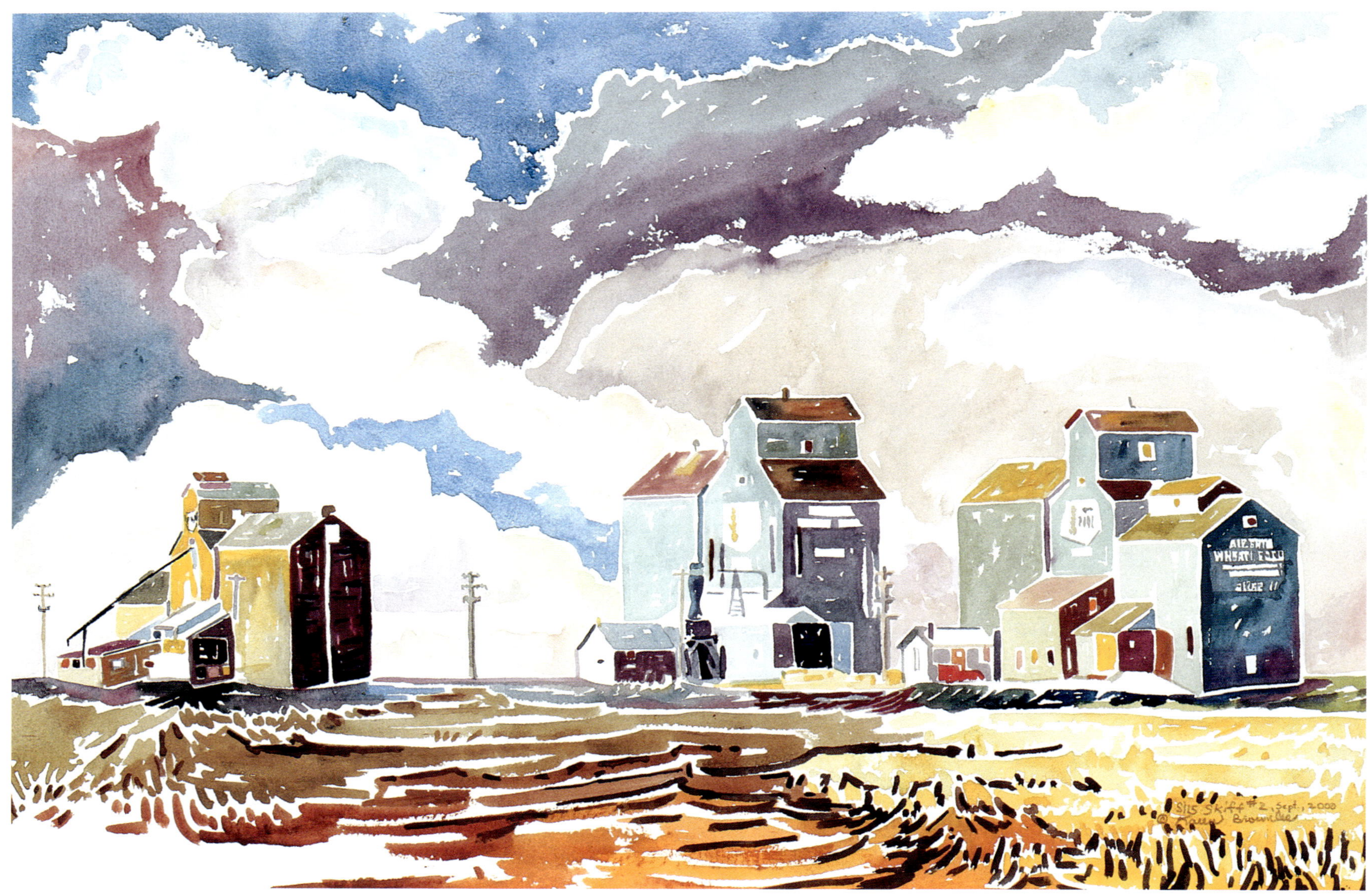

 Skiff #2, 2000, 18" x 12", circa May 1998.

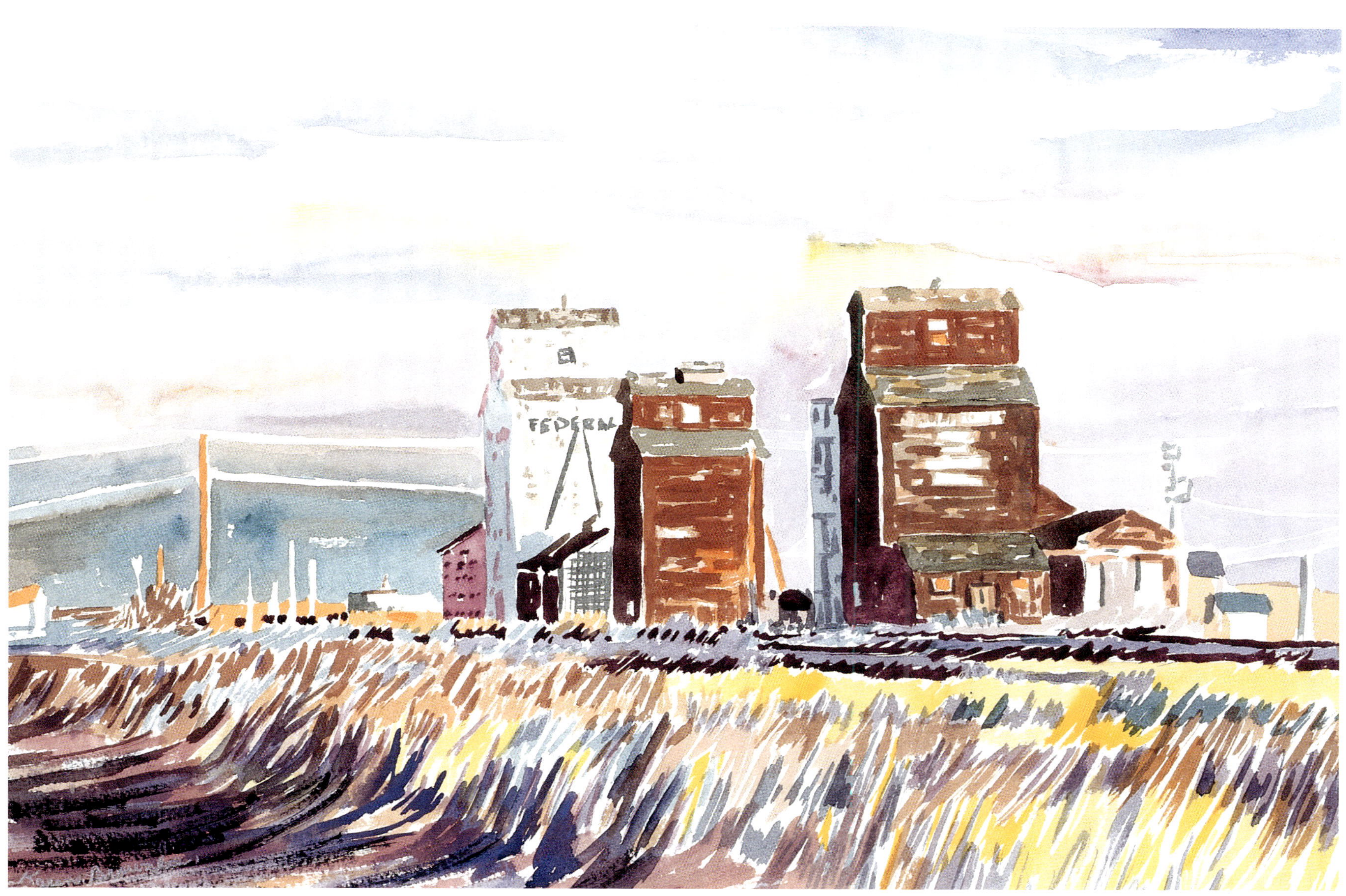

Taylor Milling and Elevator built Stirling's 40,000 bushel elevator in 1911. Stirling responded. The following year, the *Lethbridge Herald* reported that 40,000 acres of wheat had been planted in the area. The locality is still a major producer. Agricore United's cutting-edge concrete silo, constructed in 1999 at a cost of $11,000,000, is about a kilometre away from the existing village, a decision reminiscent of early railway choices to bypass settlements and create company locations.

STIRLING #1, 1997, 18" X 12", CIRCA NOVEMBER 1995.

In 1898 the CPR's Crowsnest line followed the high ground north of Pincher Creek. The company constructed a station to accommodate passengers, and Pincher Station, which first called itself Pincher City, was born. By 1904 Pincher City had an elevator, a flat warehouse for storing grain and some dwellings. After struggles with debt, Pincher City reverted to the name Pincher Station in 1932.

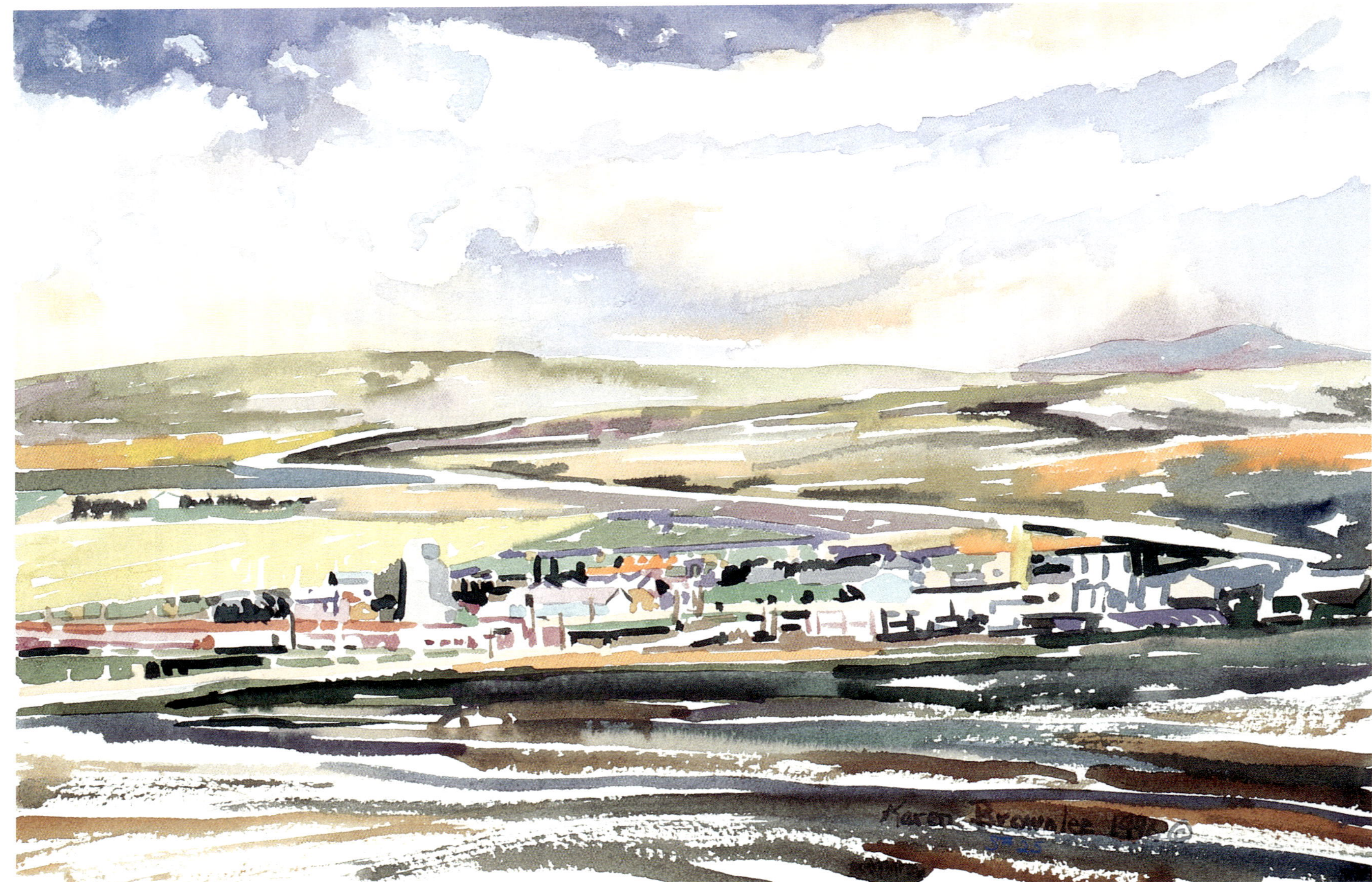

PINCHER STATION #1, 1996, 18" x 12", CIRCA AUGUST 1996.

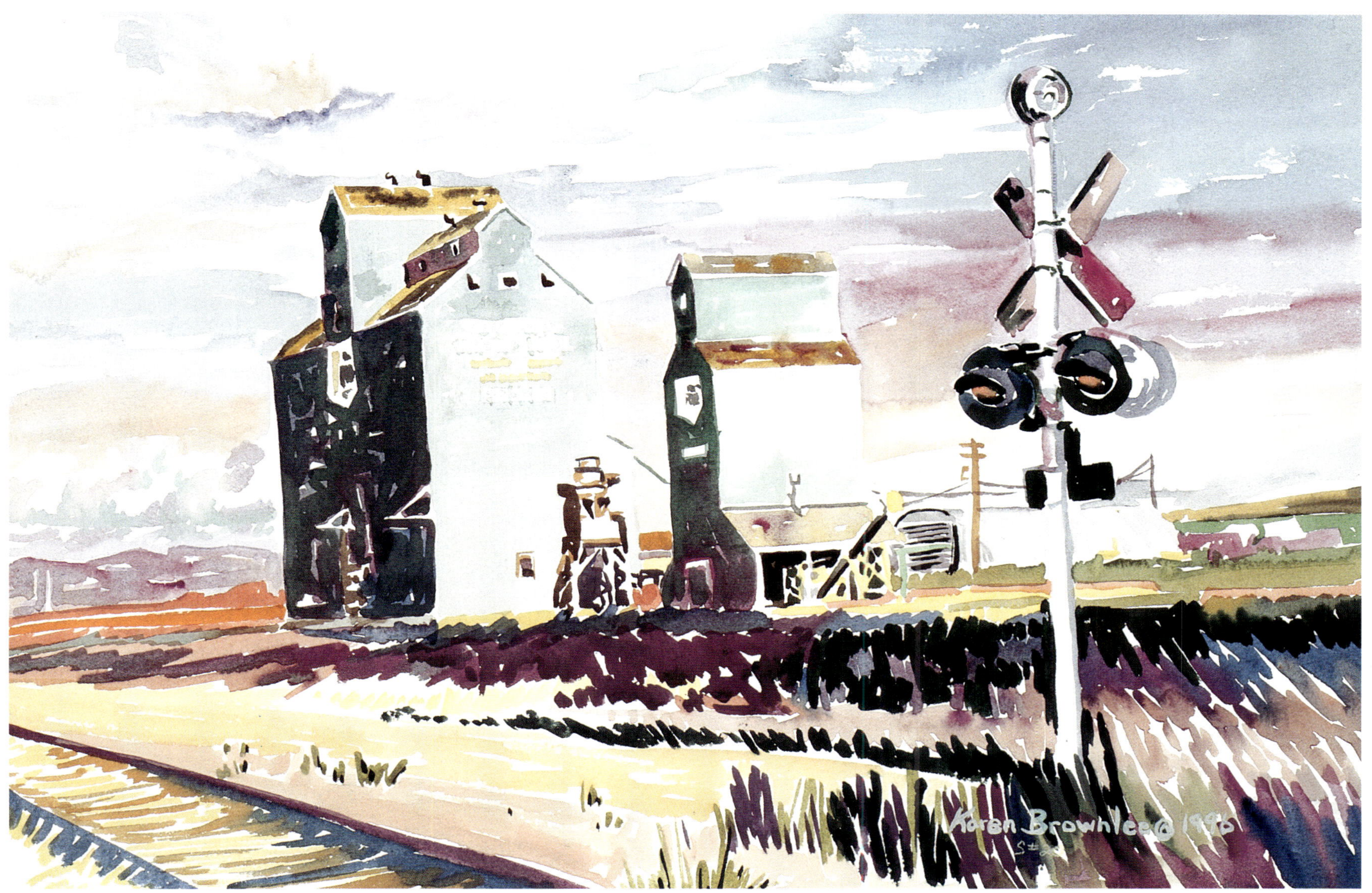

Former Mountie Charles Kettles laid out the Pincher Creek town site in 1882. Kettles contracted the building of an elevator and flour mill in 1907 that produced Pride of the West, Standard Bakers and Choice Graham flours. White Clawson wheat, planted by Frank Willock in the early 1880s, was shared as seed with neighbours. A sample grown by A.M. Morden won a prize at Chicago's 1893 World Fair.

PINCHER CREEK #1, 1996, 18" X 12", CIRCA JULY 1995.

In this locality, homesteaders were allowed to "preempt," or buy at low cost, an additional 160 acres because the land was not as productive as other regions. On the railway between Foremost and Skiff, Legend has rich brown soil that produces good yields when moisture is right. Too often, however, drought is the norm, and the population has dwindled over the years.

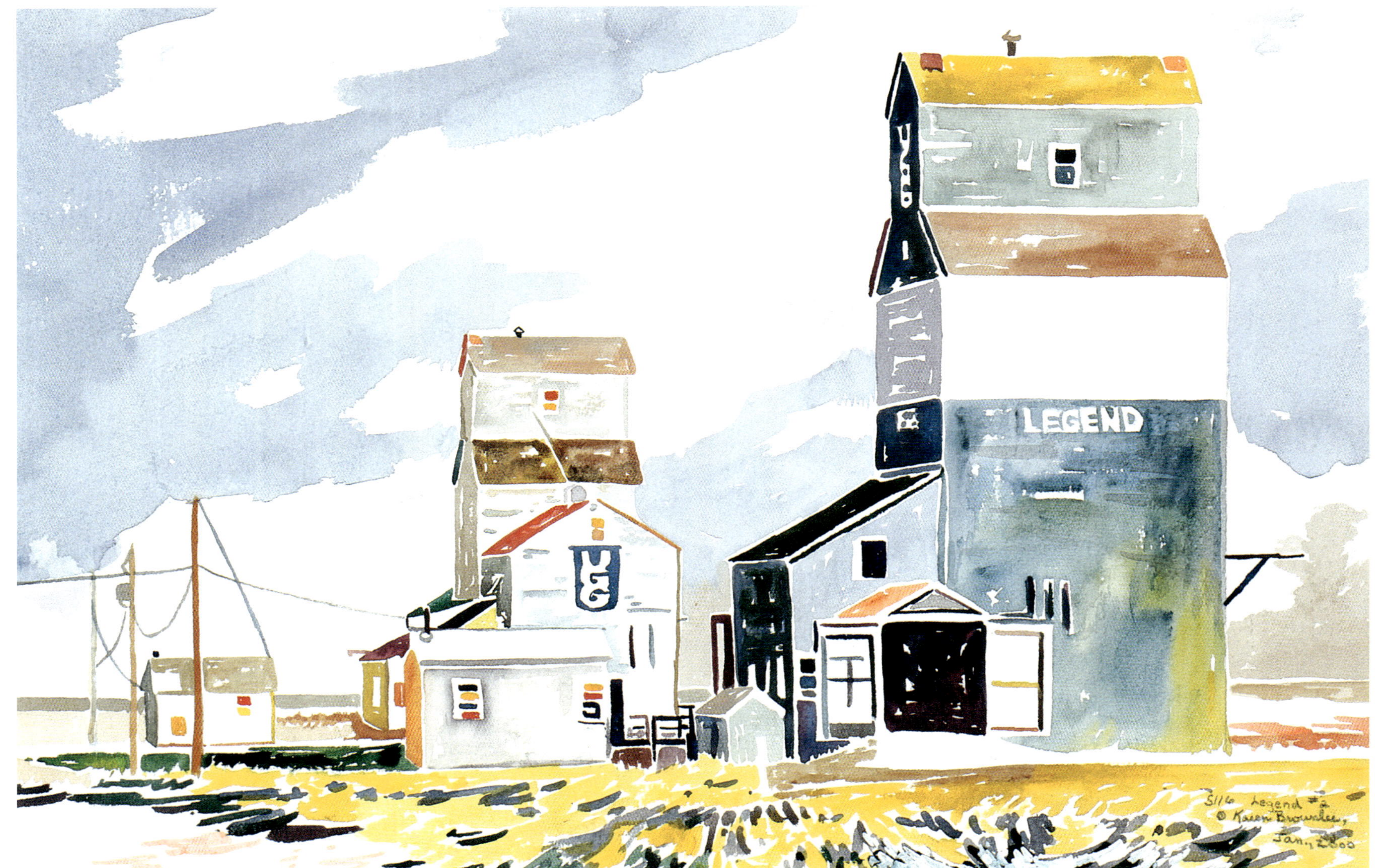

Legend #2, 2000, 18" x 12", circa June 1996.

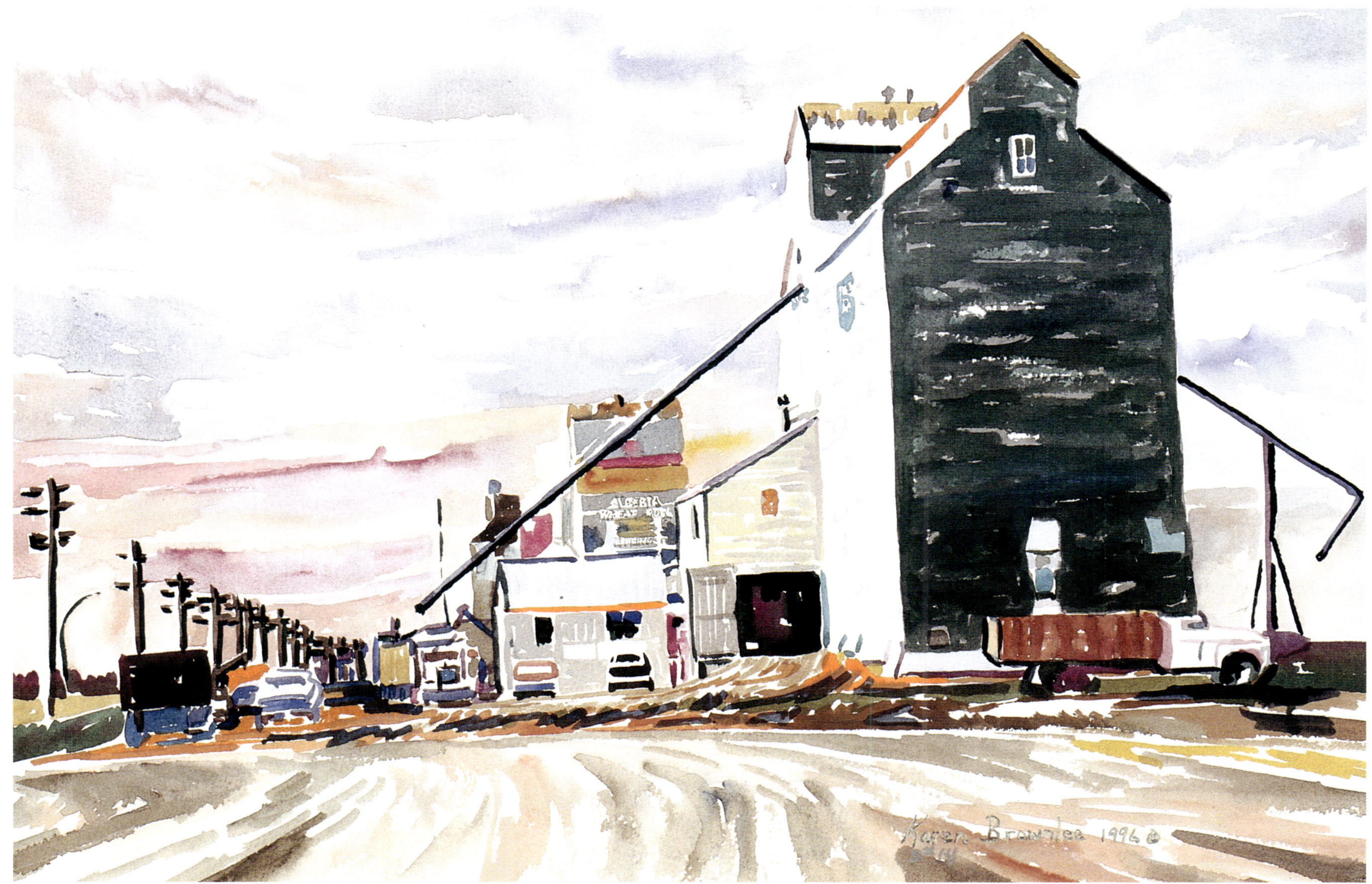

The CPR line from Lethbridge to Weyburn, Saskatchewan, arrived in Foremost in 1913, and the town grew overnight. The National and Farmers' Co-operative elevators were constructed immediately. Before the first official date of sale of residential lots, November 9, 1913, two general stores, a pool hall, a restaurant, a carpenter shop, a livery stable, a hardware store, a pharmacy and four residences had been constructed.

Foremost #1, 1996, 18" x 12", circa June 1996.

In 1916 Bingen post office was renamed Nemiskam, from the Blackfoot meaning "the place between two valleys," these being the Chin and Etzicom coulees. Four elevators were built in response to excellent yields: Purity Flour, Alberta Pacific, Victoria and Pioneer. The United Grain Growers built a fifth elevator in 1917. Drought between 1924 and 1927 caused three to be demolished, and over the years the settlement declined.

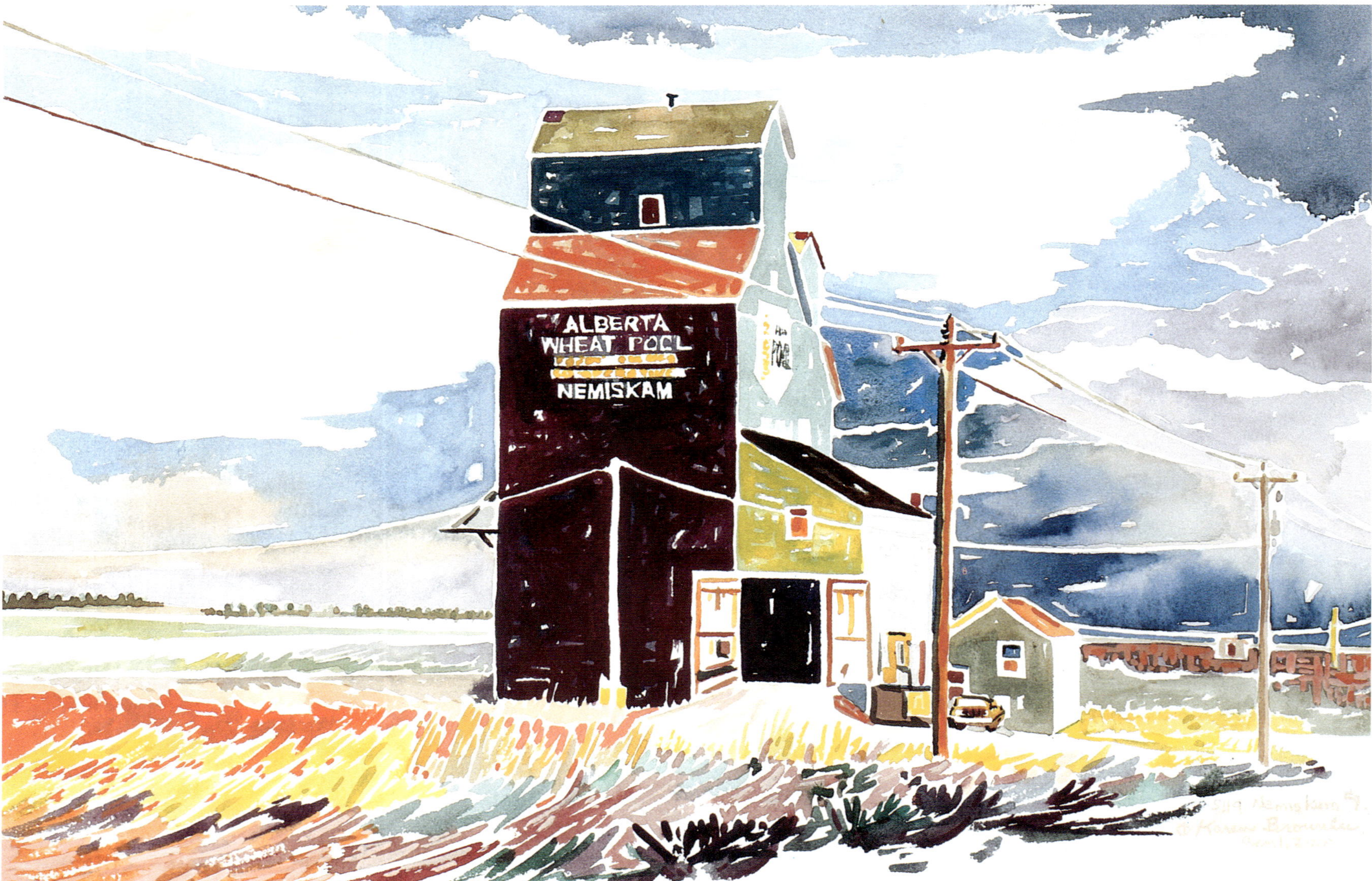

Nemiskam #1, 2000, 18" x 12", circa June 1996.

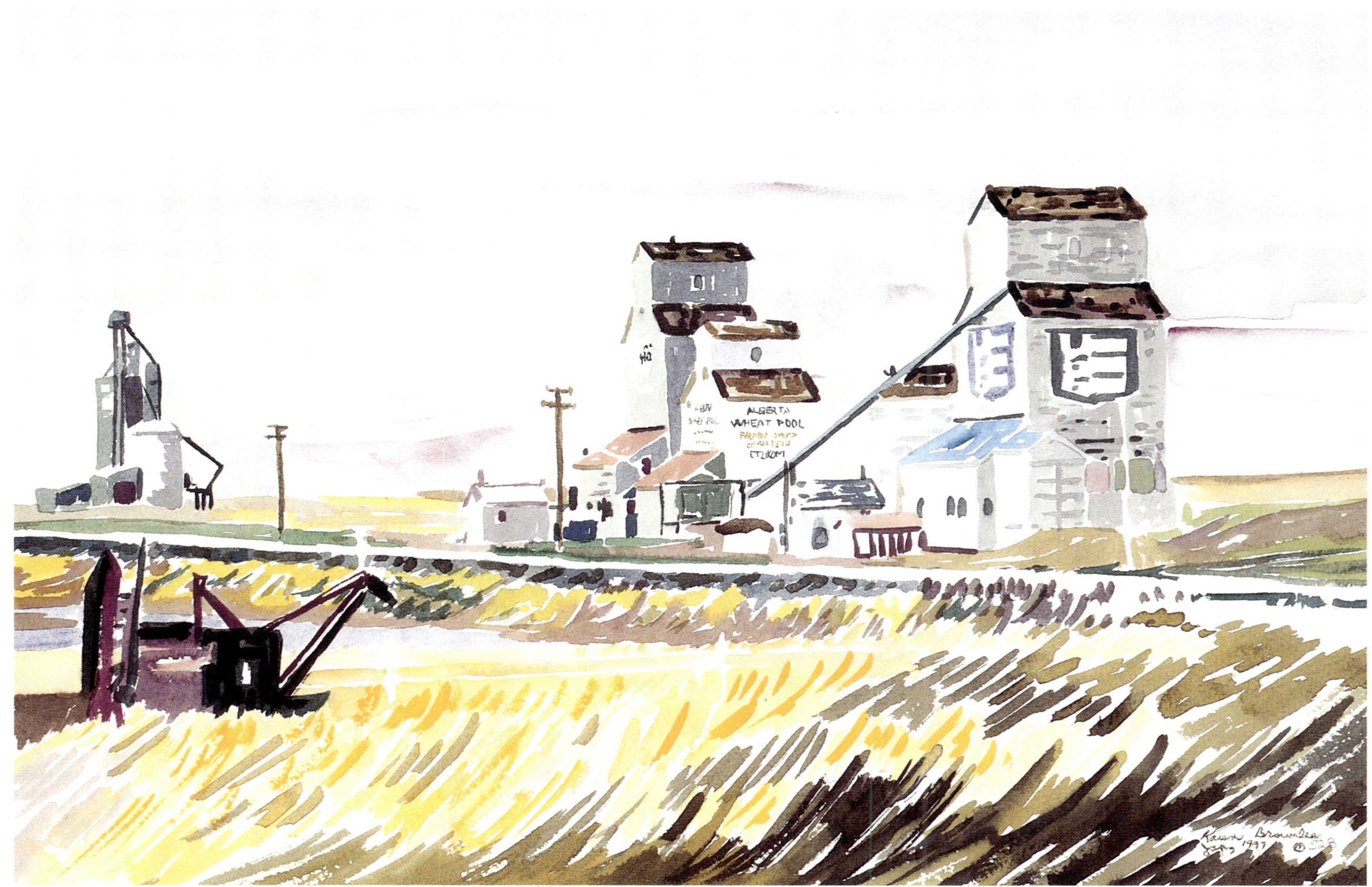

The Alberta Farmers' Co-operative built Etzicom's first elevator upon the arrival of the CPR in 1915. United Grain Growers purchased and replaced this elevator in 1934. Pioneer Grain and Alberta Grain also built in 1916–17. Alberta Pool Elevators Ltd. bought Pioneer's elevator in 1929 and constructed a second in 1933. Elevators changed over time, with the computerized steel Wheat Pool elevator seen here opening in 1988.

Etzikom #1, 1997, 18" x 12", circa May 1998.

The Alberta Pool Elevator company was a major early grain buyer. Organized to give farmers a producer-owned sales option, it often purchased existing elevators and then expanded them. Voss Brothers of Calgary, a contractor frequently employed by the Pool, constructed Etzikom's second Pool elevator in 1933. The Pool had three elevators and a crib annex here before building its steel 150,000 bushel facility in 1988.

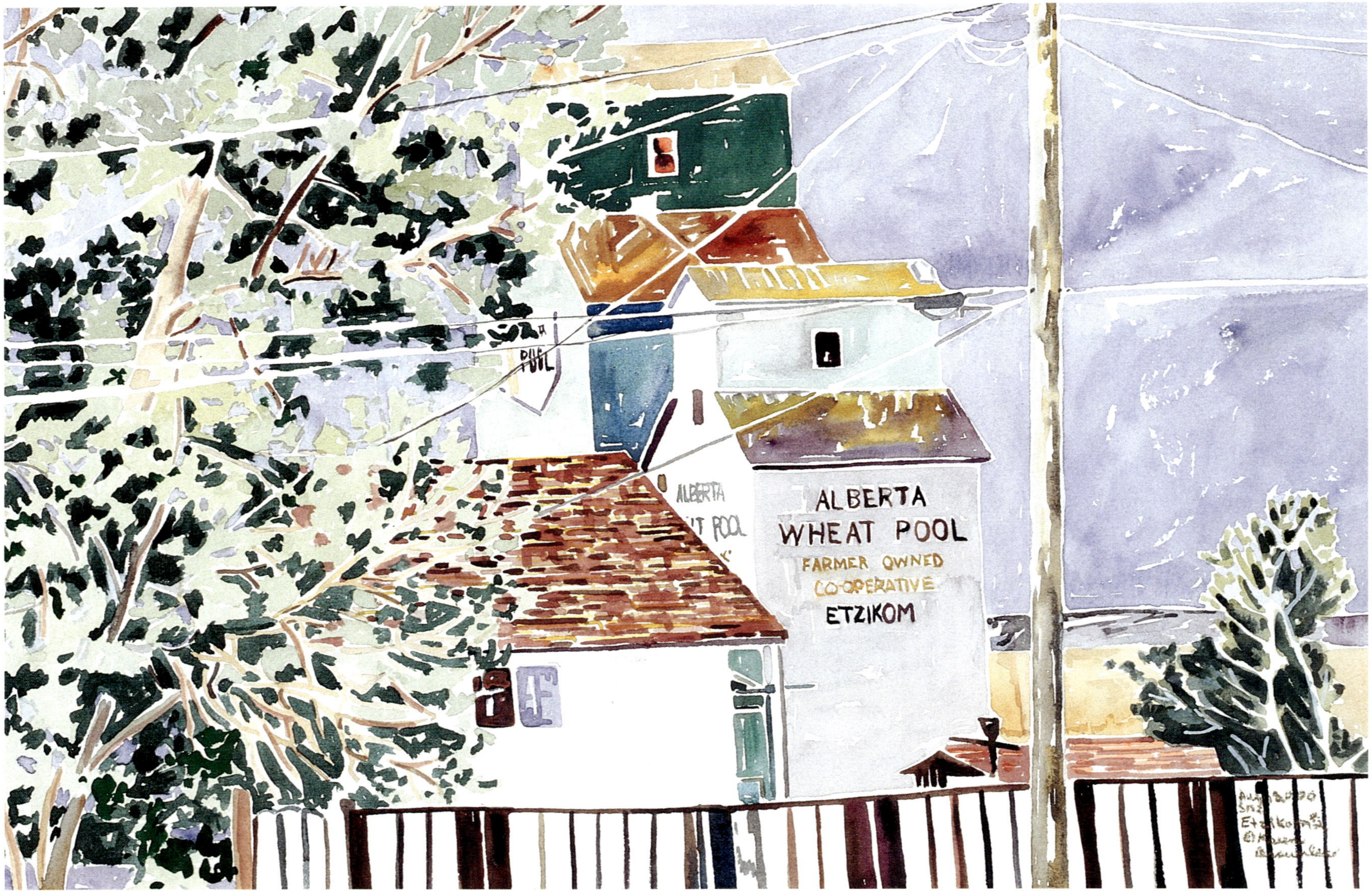

Etzikom #2, 2000, 18" x 12", circa May 1998.

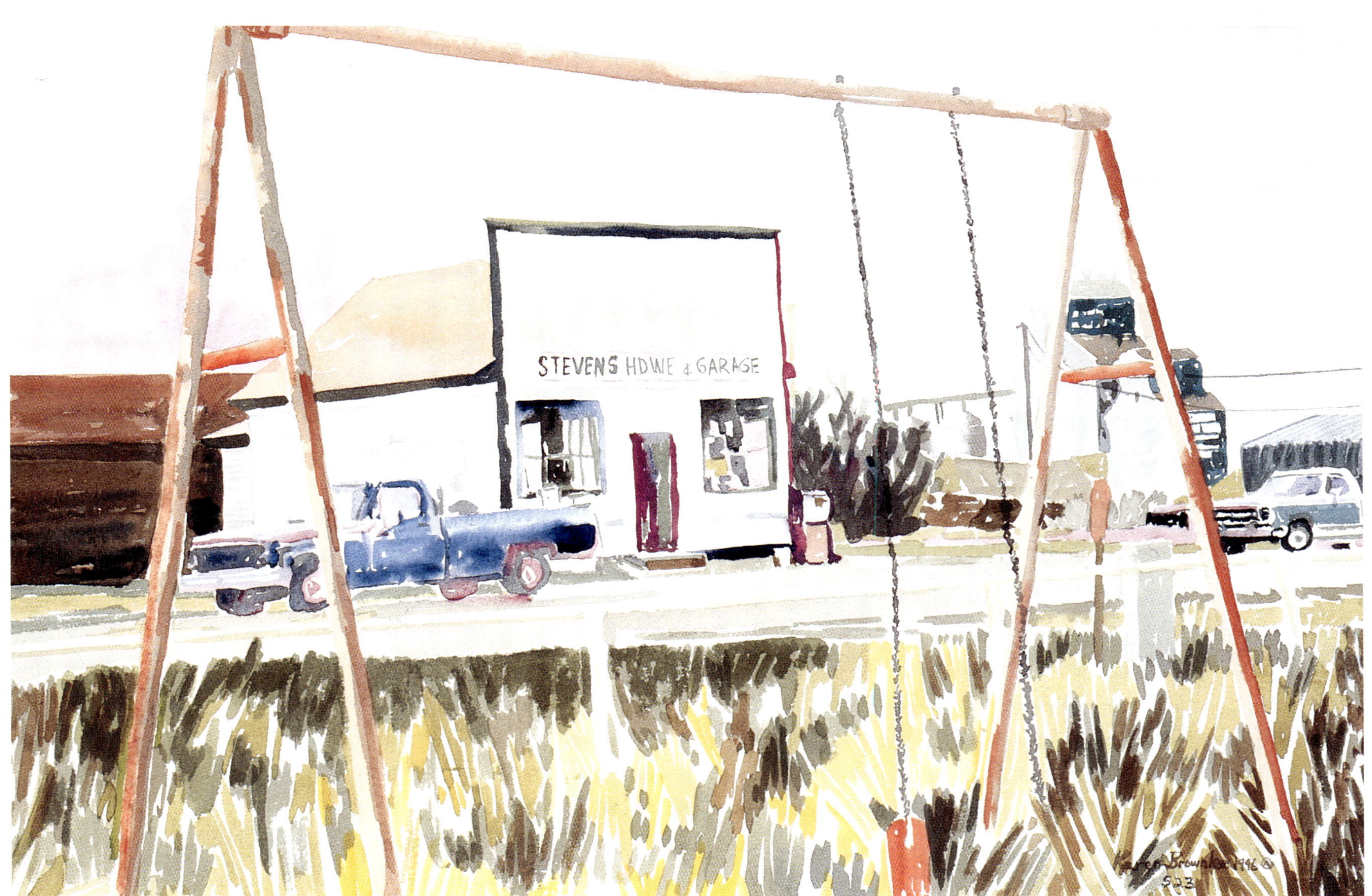

The railway, arriving in 1916, put Orion on the map. Six lots were allocated for elevators. Orion would grow! Drought stretching from 1917 to 1927 dashed these hopes, and the Alberta government provided homesteaders with free transportation to other areas. Then, in 1961, the store burned. Still, the community survived. The Orion Co-op opened, and through families like the Stevens, who own several businesses, the town perseveres.

Orion #1, 1996, 18" x 12", circa June 1996.

Raymond, founded in 1901, was named for Oscar Raymond Knight, one of the earliest settlers, who purchased 30,000 acres from the Canadian Pacific Railway. Sugar beets were as critical to the economy here as grain. A sugar factory soon opened but closed due to depressed prices before the First World War. The town opened another factory in 1925, partly to reduce dependence on grain crops.

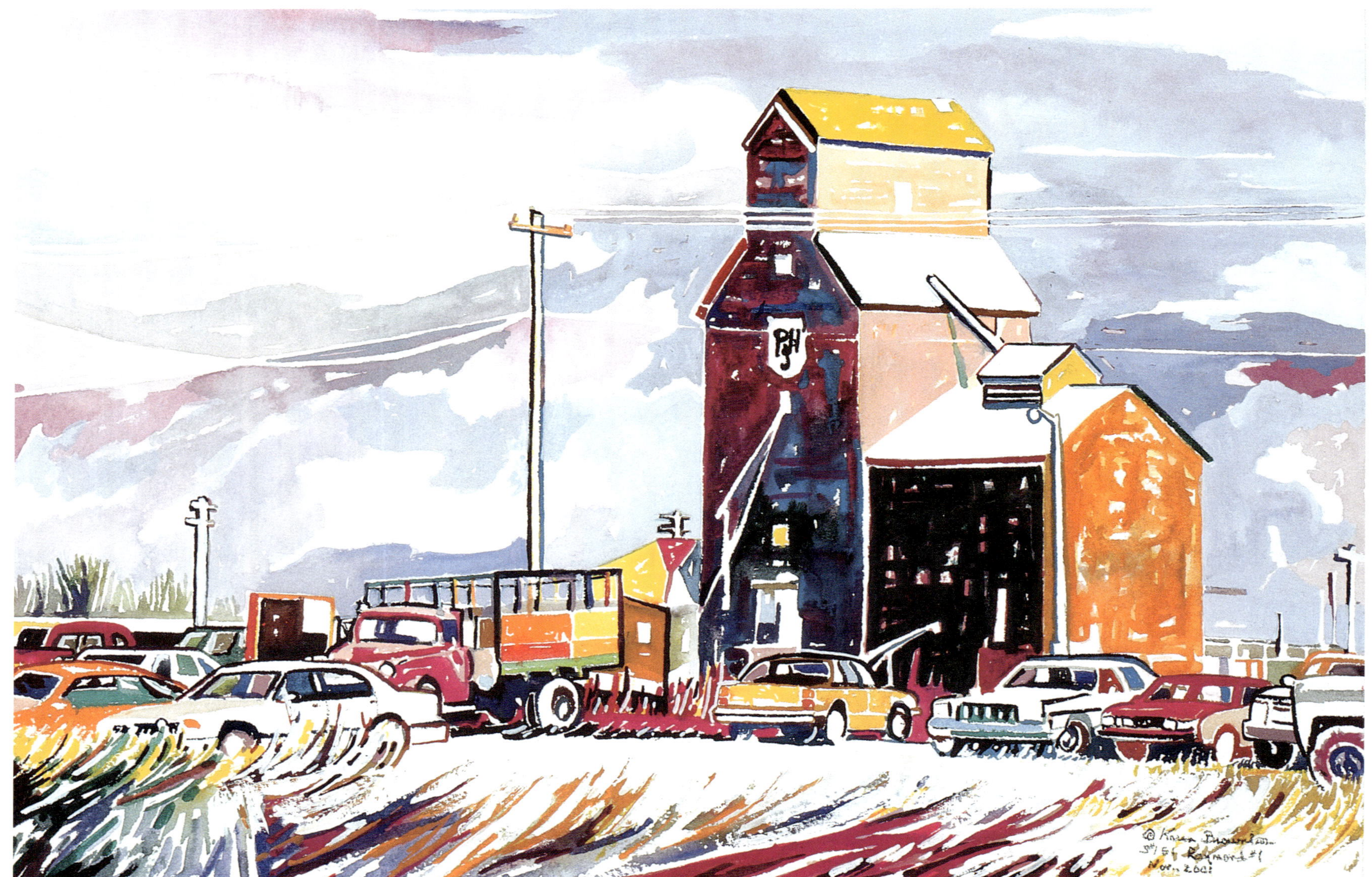

 Raymond #1, 2001, 18" x 12", circa May 2001.

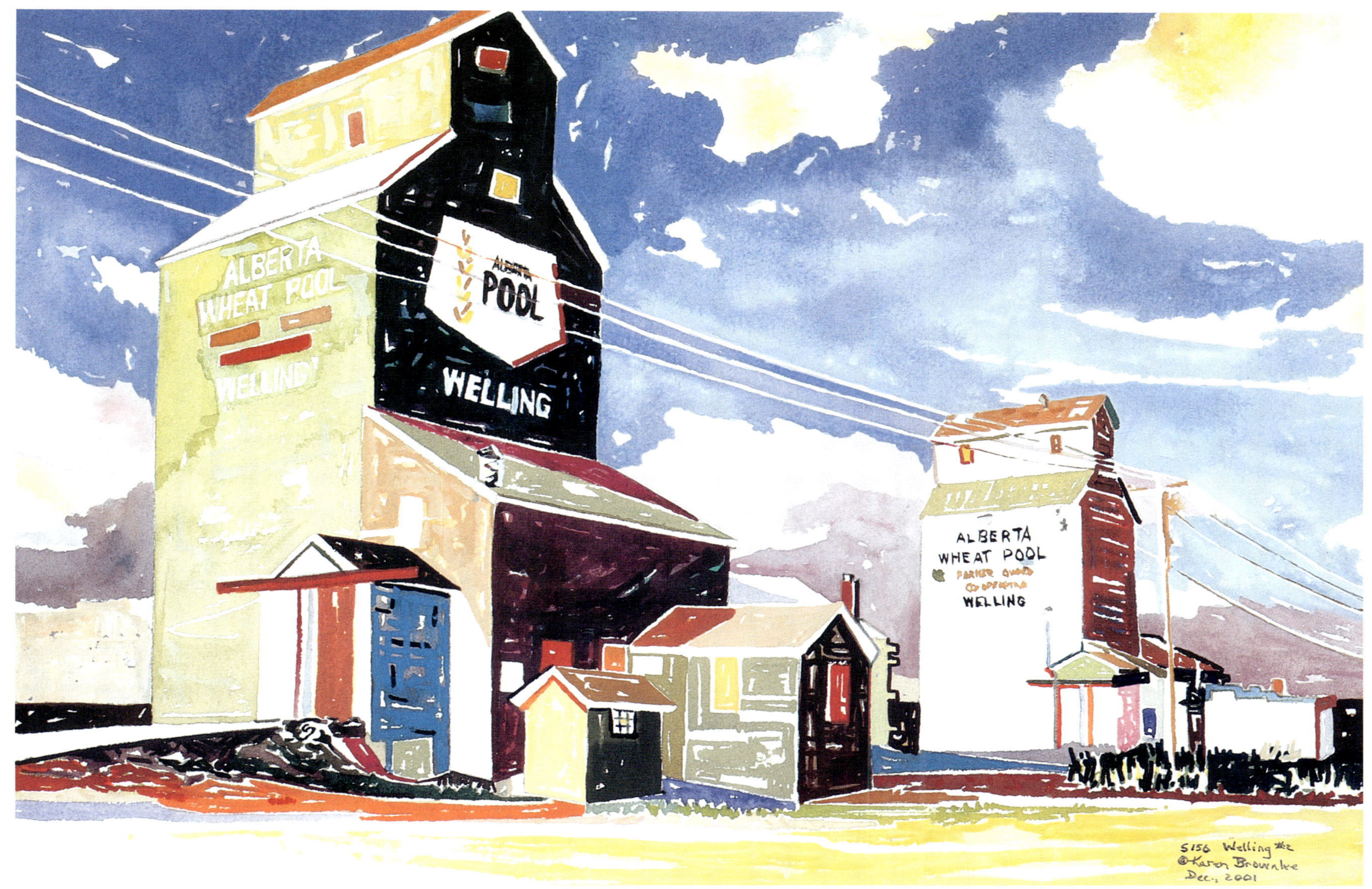

Efficient crop storage and transfer, the impetus for elevator construction, continues to be a concern for farmers. This need led to Gordon Anderson and Barry Beazer's 1963 invention, at Welling, of the Flexa-Hopper. Made of molded plastic, it flexes to fit an auger. Grain is dumped directly into the system, rather than onto the ground, so none is lost.

WELLING #2, 2001, 18" x 12", CIRCA JUNE 1995.

Despite New Dayton's four elevators (Jones and Dill, 1909; Pioneer, 1909; E.P. Page's private elevator, 1913; Alberta Wheat Pool, 1928), farmers, initially suspicious of the elevator companies, loaded boxcars by hand from the platform built for this purpose. Long-serving agents such as New Dayton's Cecil De Pratu built trust as well as business.

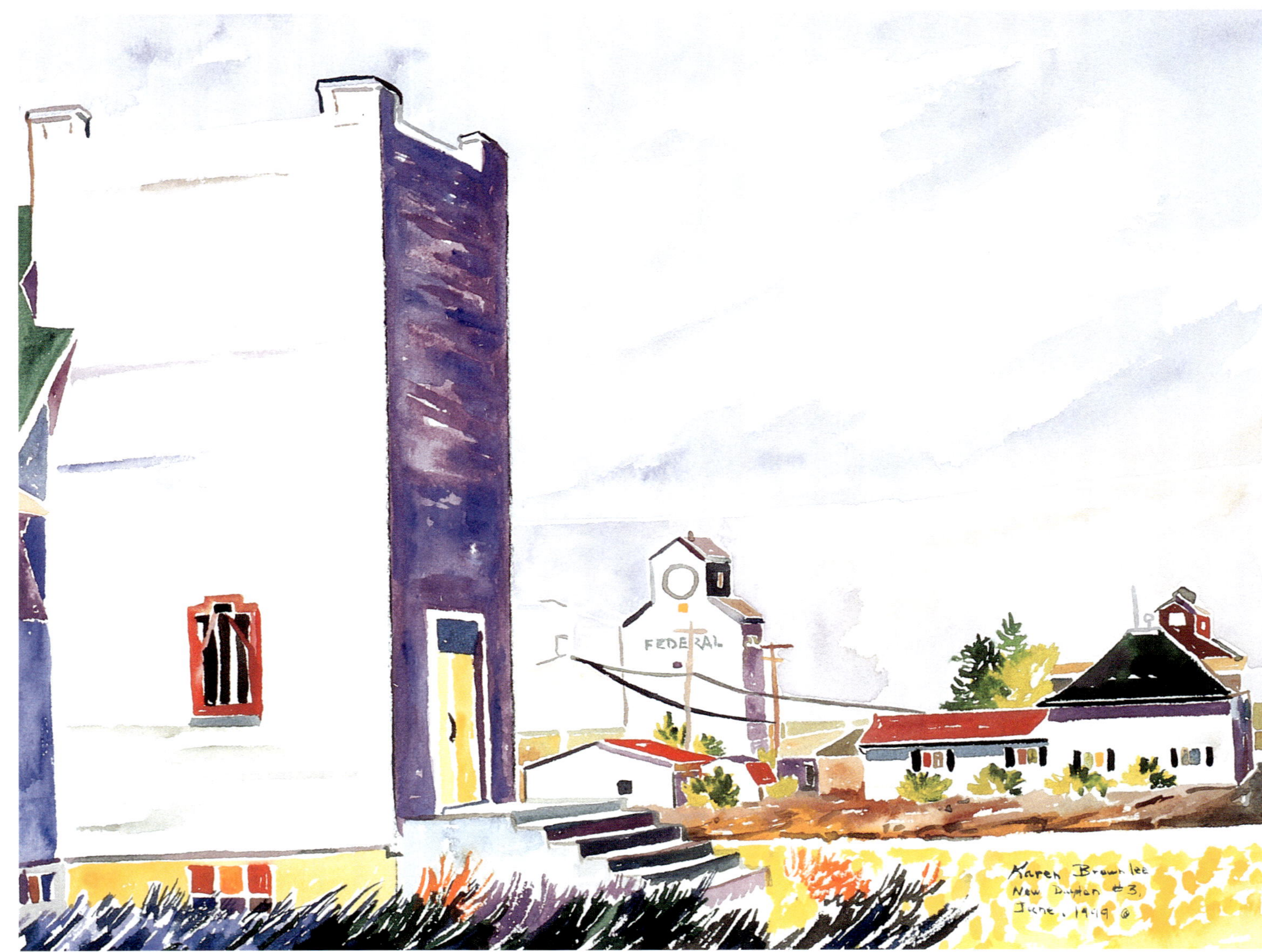

 New Dayton #3, 1999, 14" x 11", circa May 1998.

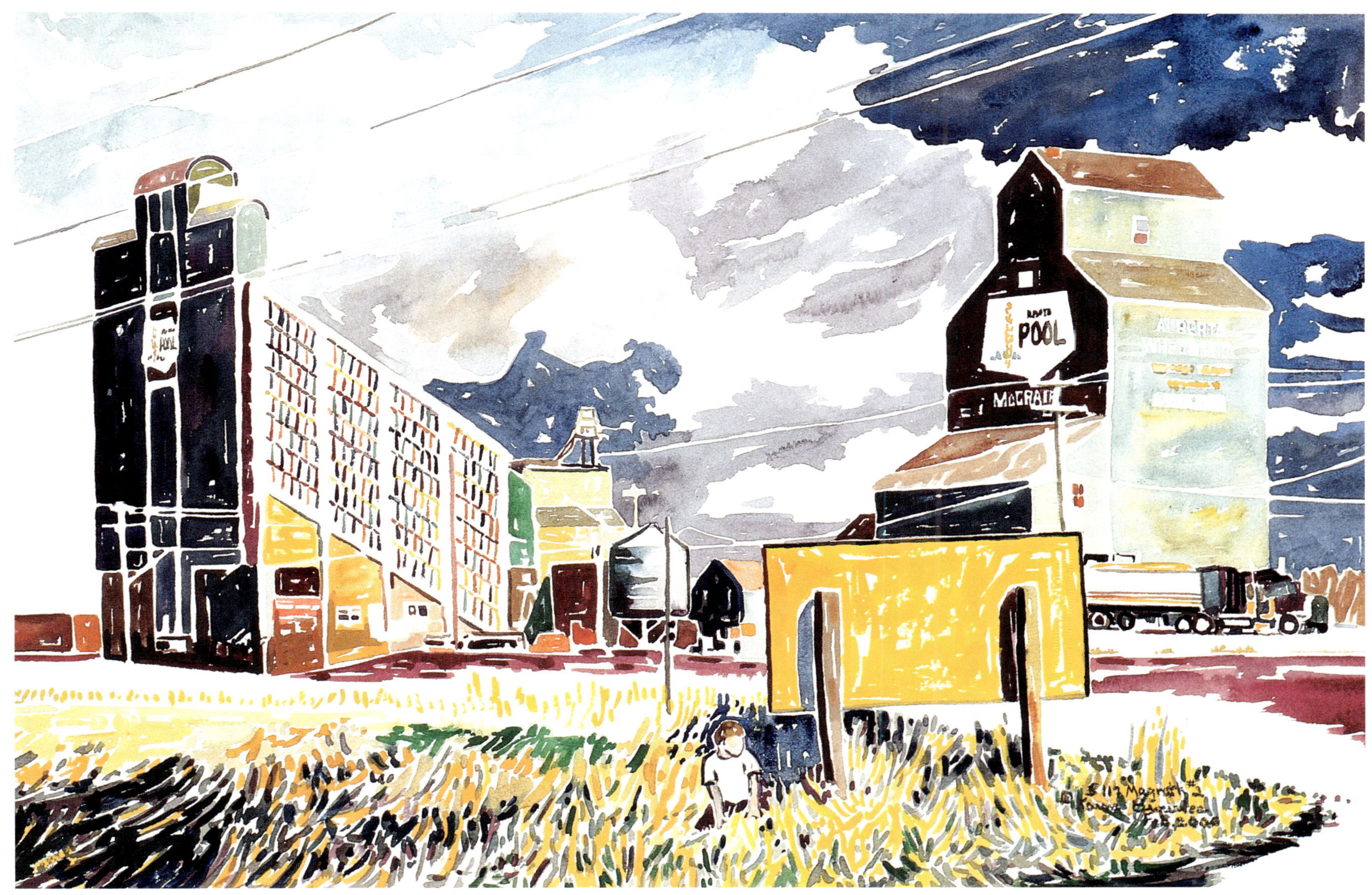

Magrath, settled in 1899, was named for C.A. Magrath, Land Commissioner with the North Western Coal and Navigation Company and a local political leader. Magrath worked with the Latter Day Saints of Utah to settle and irrigate the area for grain production. High yields prompted the Alberta Wheat Pool to build a slope-roof "Buffalo Bin" elevator here in 1980.

Magrath #2, 2000, 18" x 12", circa May 1998.

Magrath's Buffalo Bin was a first in Alberta. These next-generation facilities load grain more rapidly, store it more securely against fire and generally streamline the grain handling business, reducing the need for the older wooden elevators that had served for so many years.

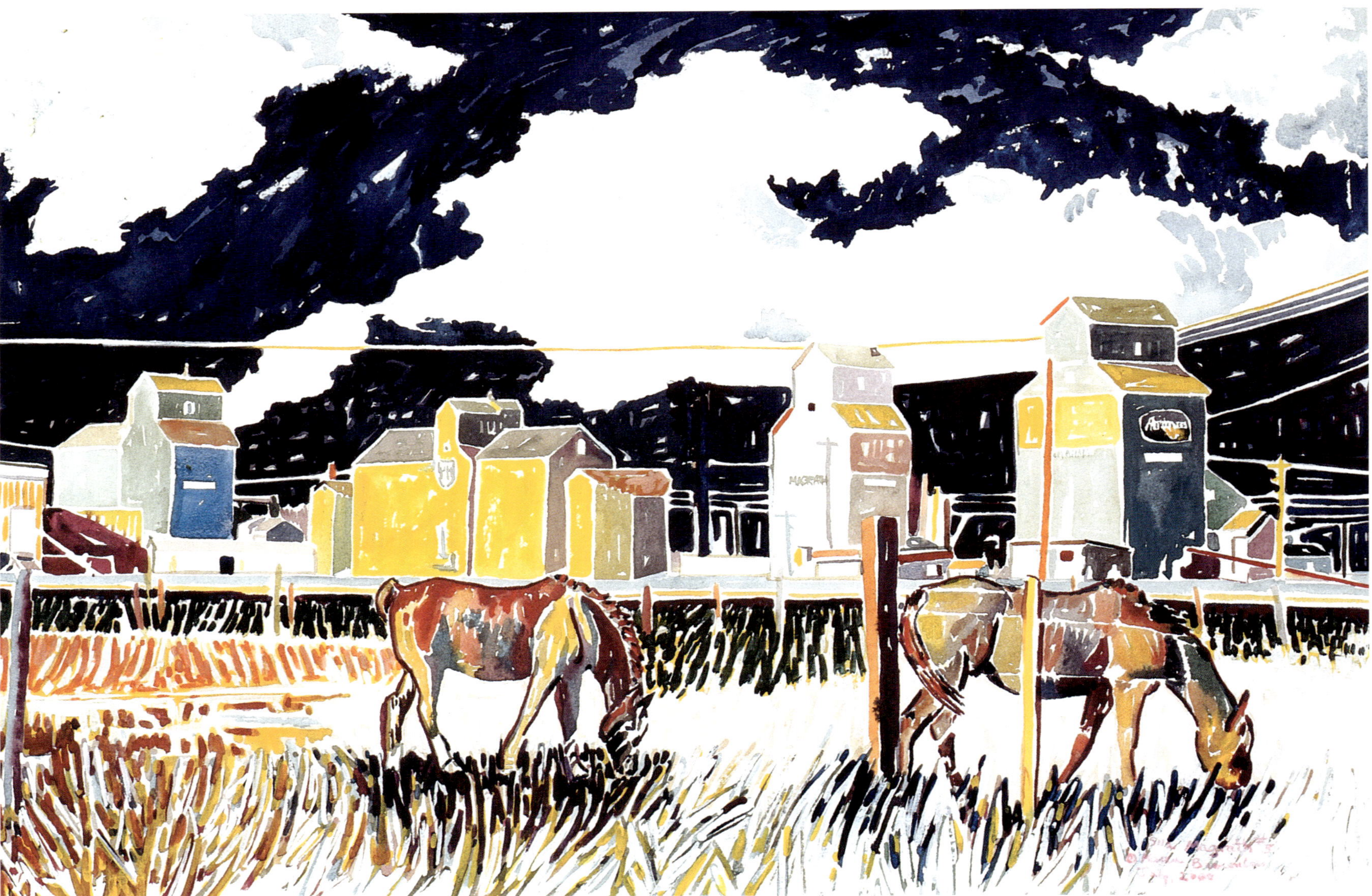

 MAGRATH #3, 2000, 18" x 12", CIRCA NOVEMBER 1999.

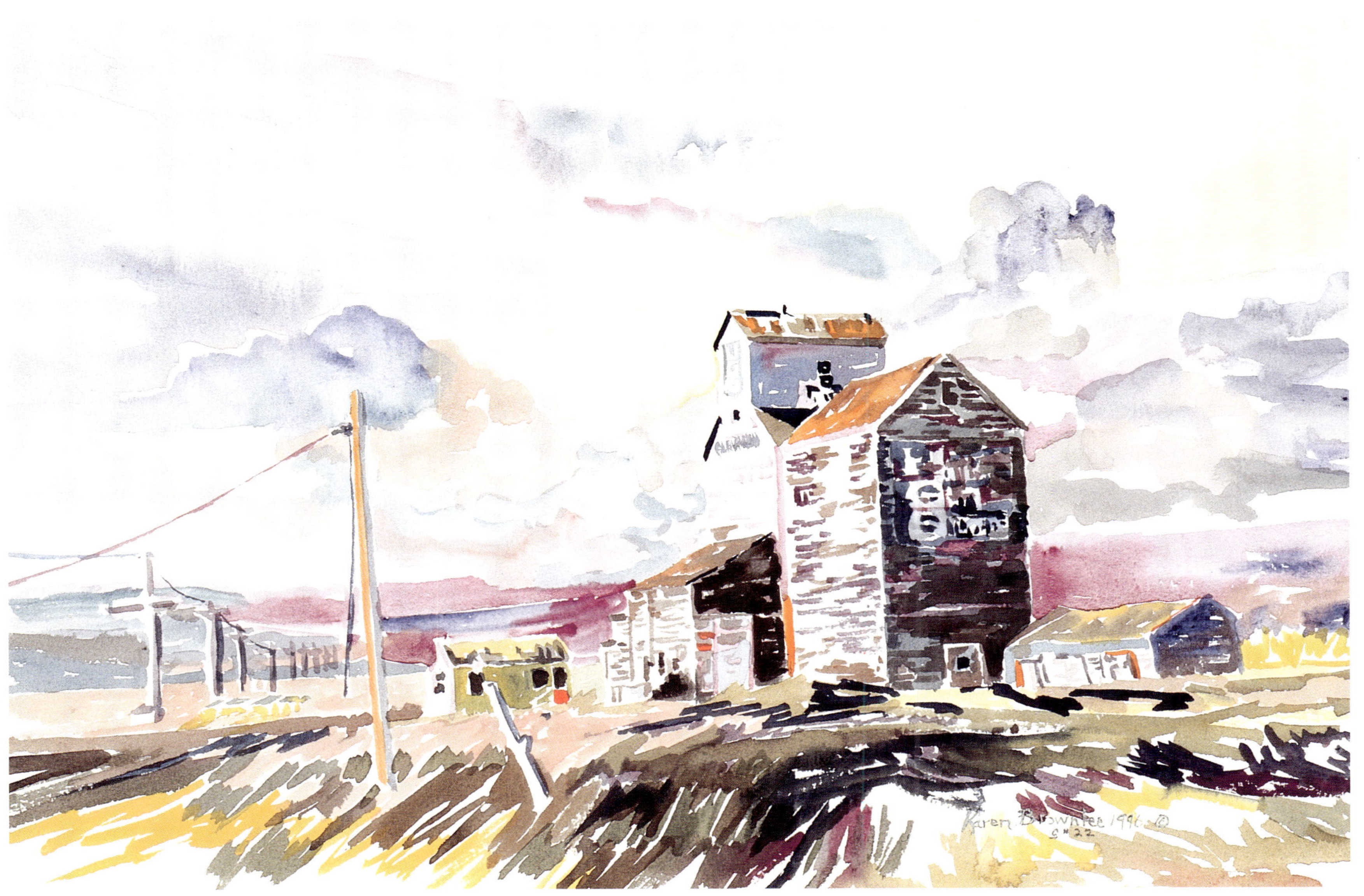

Edward Wood, President of the Alberta Stake when the Latter Day Saints purchased the Cochrane Ranche in 1906, named the nearby small town after his first son. It was originally known in 1908 as Glenwoodville. A meeting to incorporate the village of Glenwood convened on February 15, 1961, at the Alberta Pacific Grain Company elevator, a suitable location since elevators served as early place-name signs.

Glenwood #1, 1996, 18" x 12", circa July 1995.

Named for a master mechanic employed by the Alberta Irrigation and Railway line in 1890, the original spelling (McNabb) of this siding on the Lethbridge to Great Falls, Montana, rail line changed through local usage. Two elevators once stood here, first an Alberta Pacific, then an Alberta Wheat Pool facility. The Alberta Wheat Pool eventually owned both and tore down the earlier of the two.

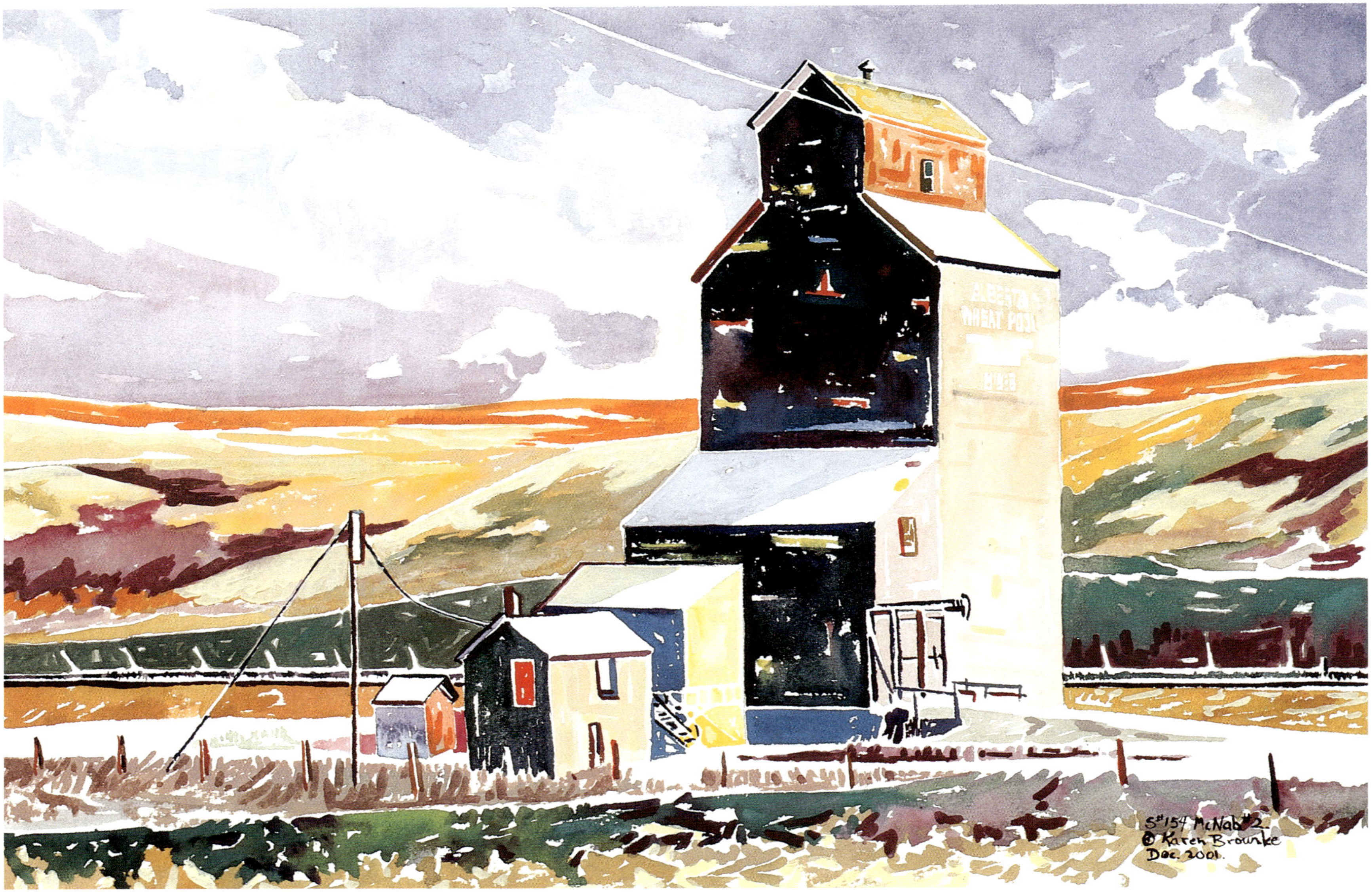

McNab #2, 2001, 18" x 12", circa May 1998.

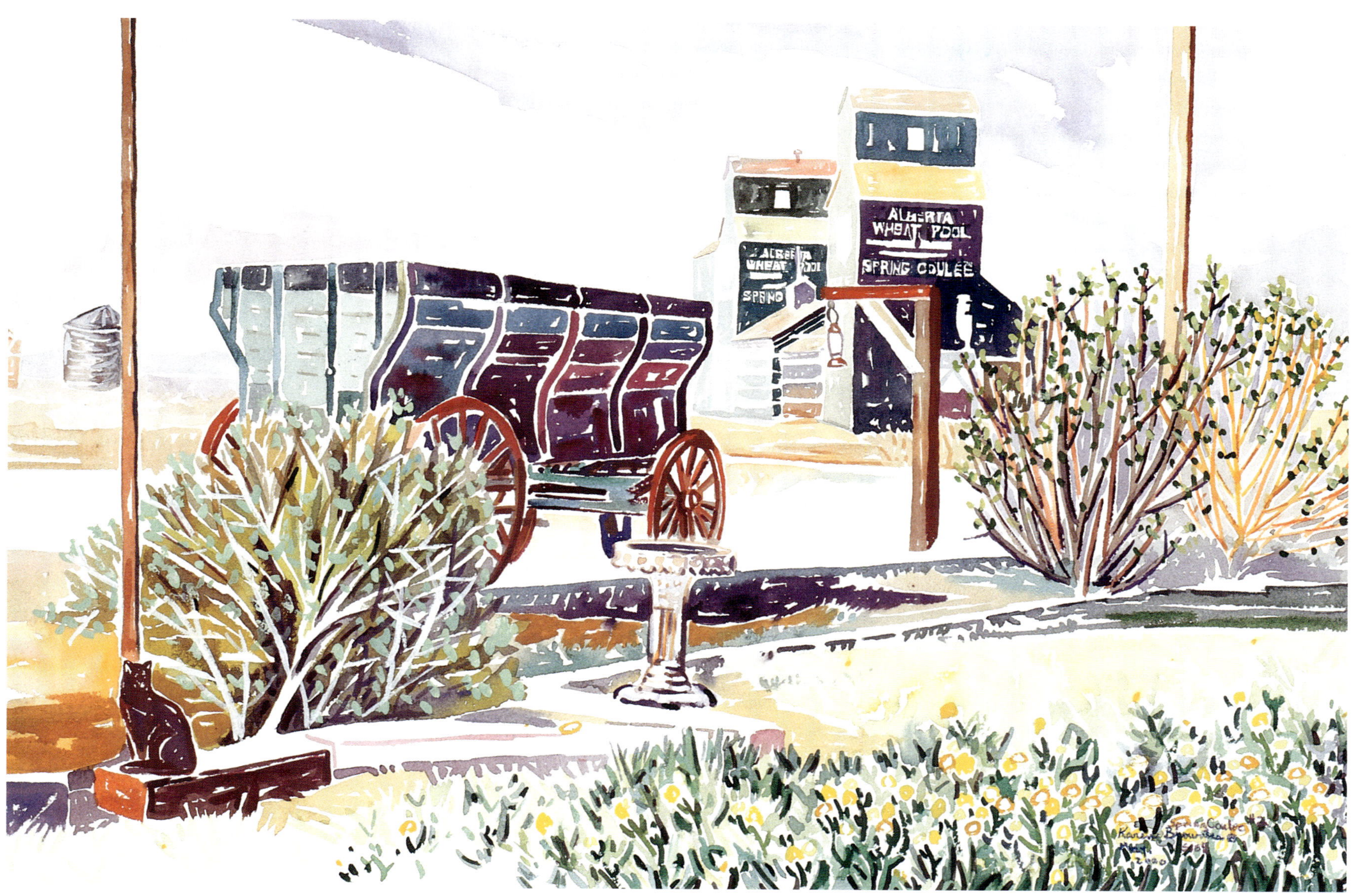

Spring Coulee's four elevators were the Thompson (1905), the Alberta Pacific (1906), the Ogilvie (1907) and the Alberta Wheat Pool (1925). The Thompson burned in 1914 at the start of the First World War. Coincidental fires at Magrath and Raymond caused speculation about sabotage by German sympathizers. Although rebuilt, the elevator was unable to handle the larger trucks rapidly replacing wagons in the 1930s and was demolished.

SPRING COULEE #2, 2000, 18" x 12", CIRCA MAY 1998.

Jones Dill Company of Wabash, Wisconsin, constructed Warner's first elevator in 1909. By 1962 Warner's elevator row, a sure gauge of the prosperity of western towns for many years, boasted eight elevators. Warner had an Alberta first, too. Mustard production, started in the 1930s, prompted the Hadford Company to build Alberta's first mustard elevator here.

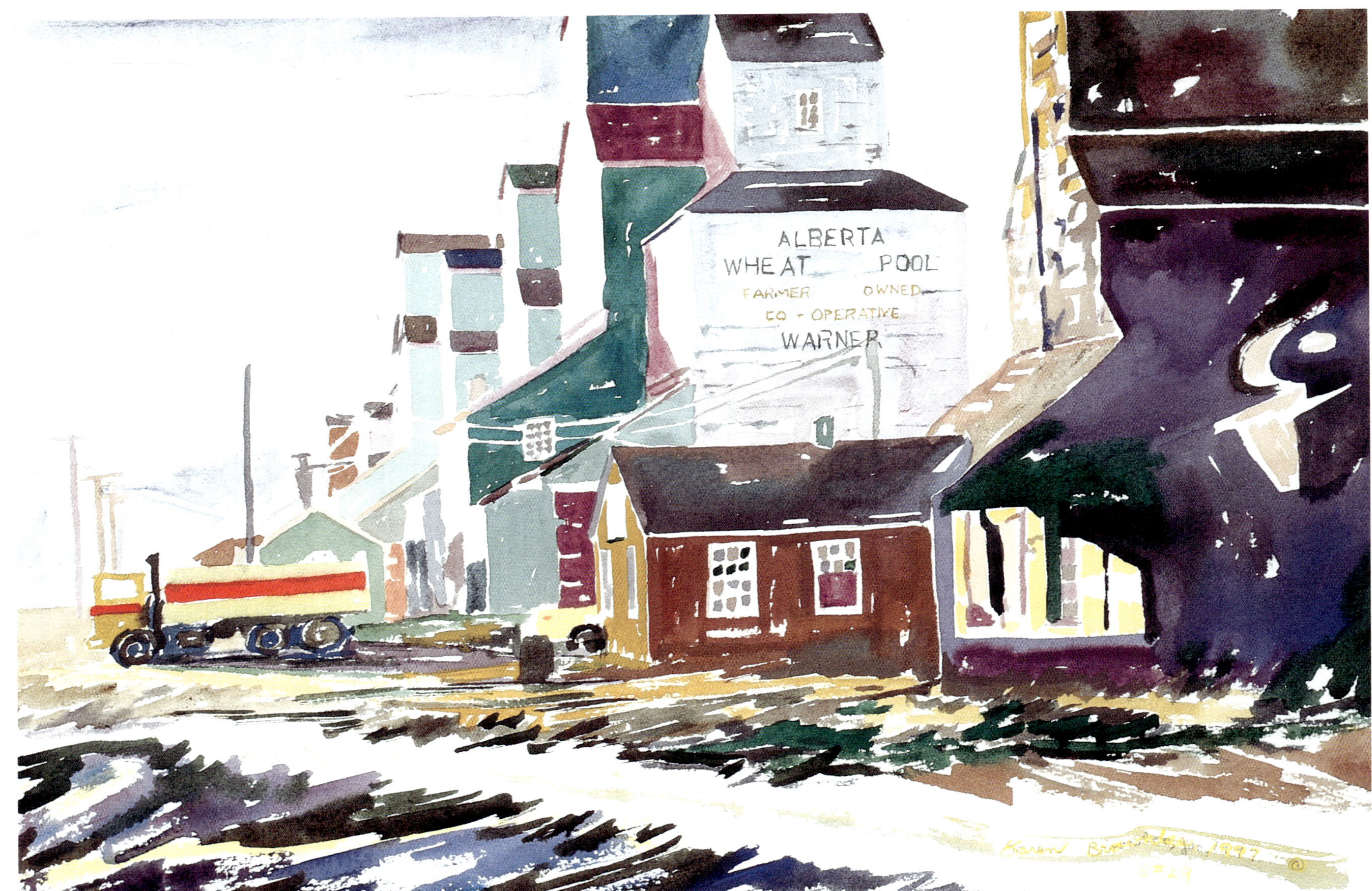

WARNER #1, 1997, 18" x 12", CIRCA NOVEMBER 1995.

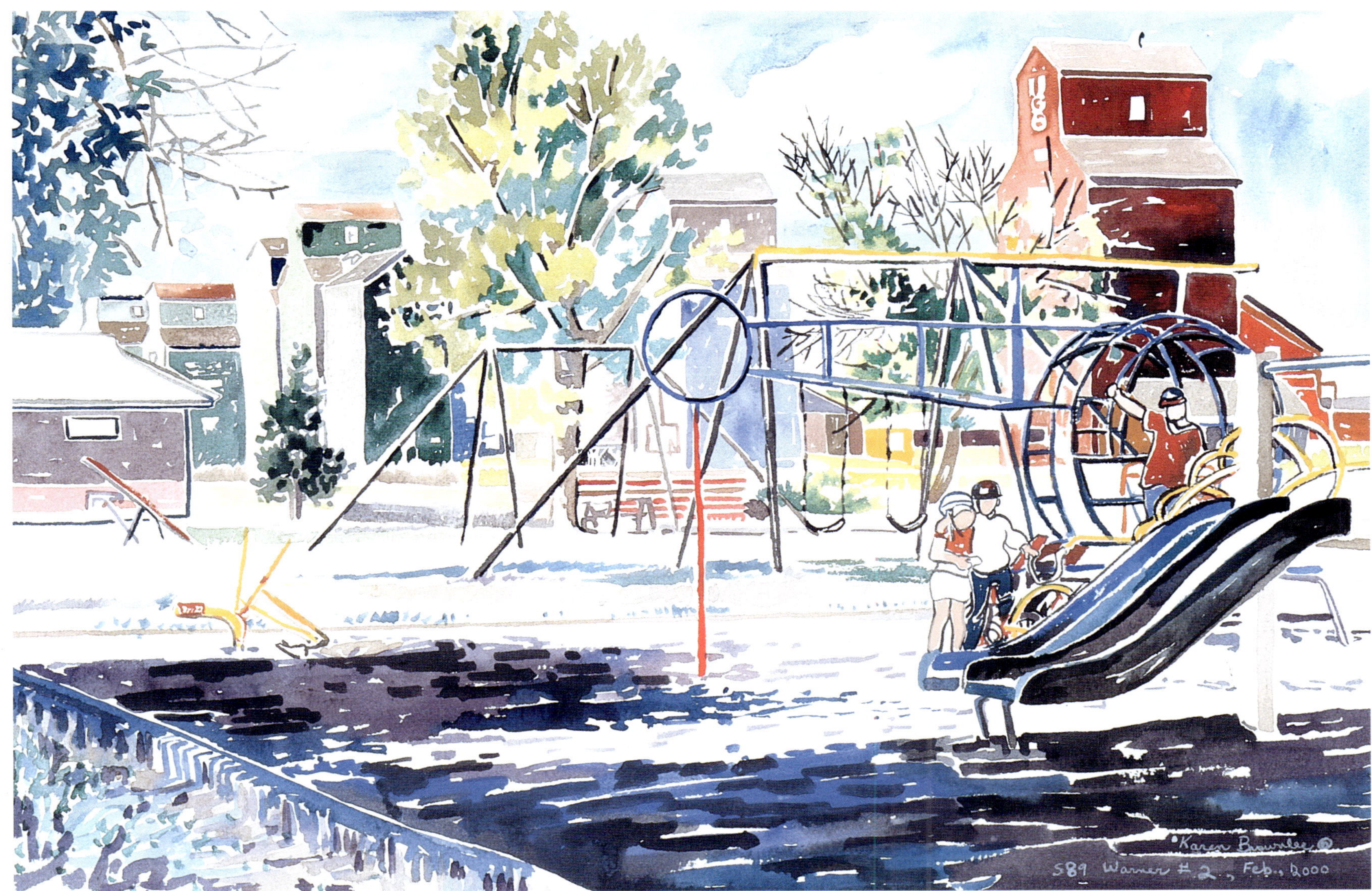

The Alberta Farmers' Co-operative Elevator Company's initial 1913 general meeting in Calgary approved Warner as Local #3, and the company opened an elevator that year. The organization became the United Grain Growers in 1917, then the Alberta Wheat Pool in 1927. The importance of community, reflected in support for cooperative elevators, shows in the town's community playground, where Karen's son, Logan, plays.

WARNER #2, 1999, 18" x 12", CIRCA SEPTEMBER 1999.

Three elevators were built in Cardston after the CPR's 1912 arrival from Stirling: the Alberta Pacific Grain Company, Sunny Belt Grain and Elevator Company, and the Cardston Milling Company. United Grain Growers built in 1918–19. In 1986, when UGG lost two elevators and an annex to Cardston's most expensive fire to date, the facility was rebuilt in time for the next crop season.

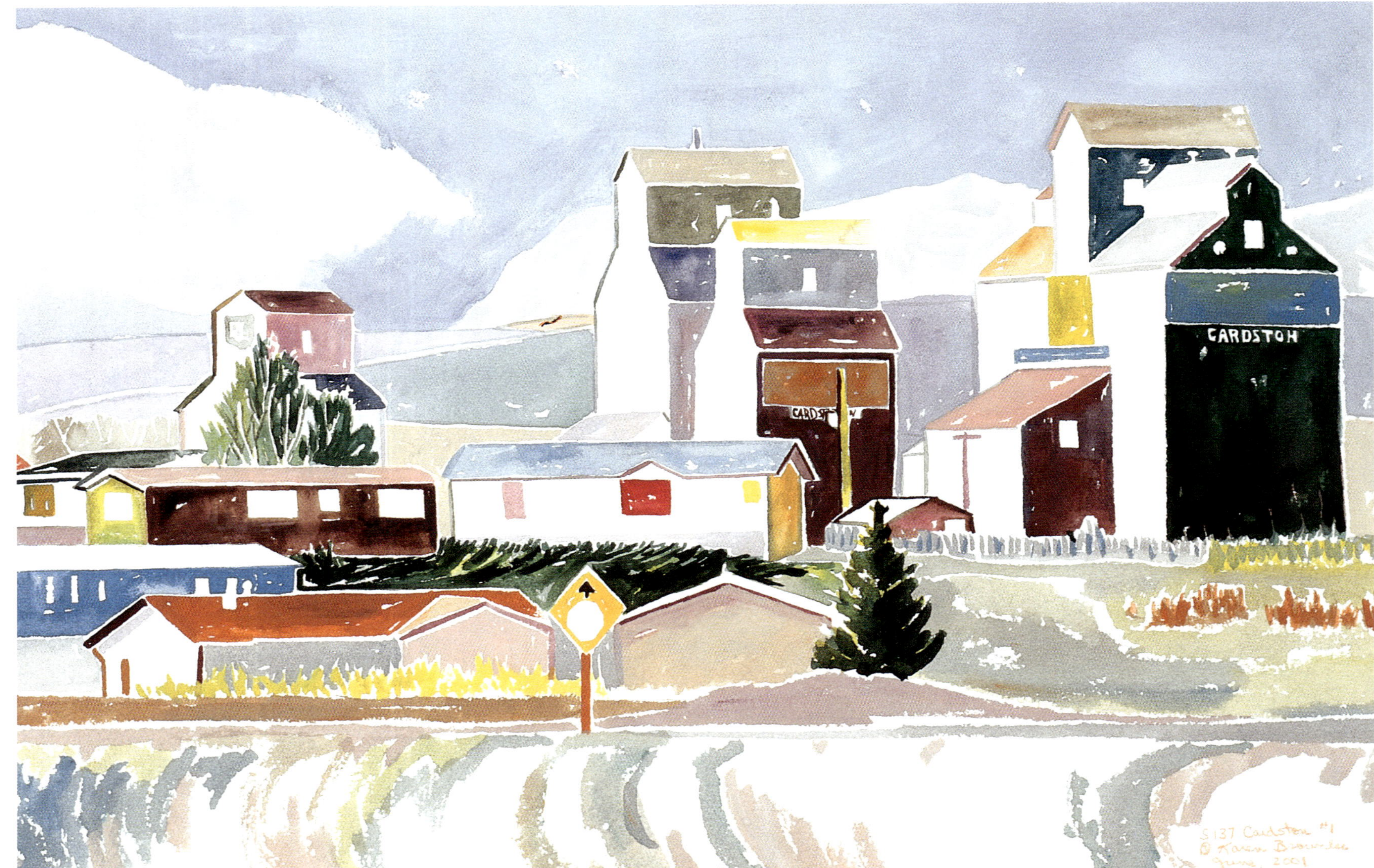

 Cardston #1, 2001, 18" x 12", circa May 2000.

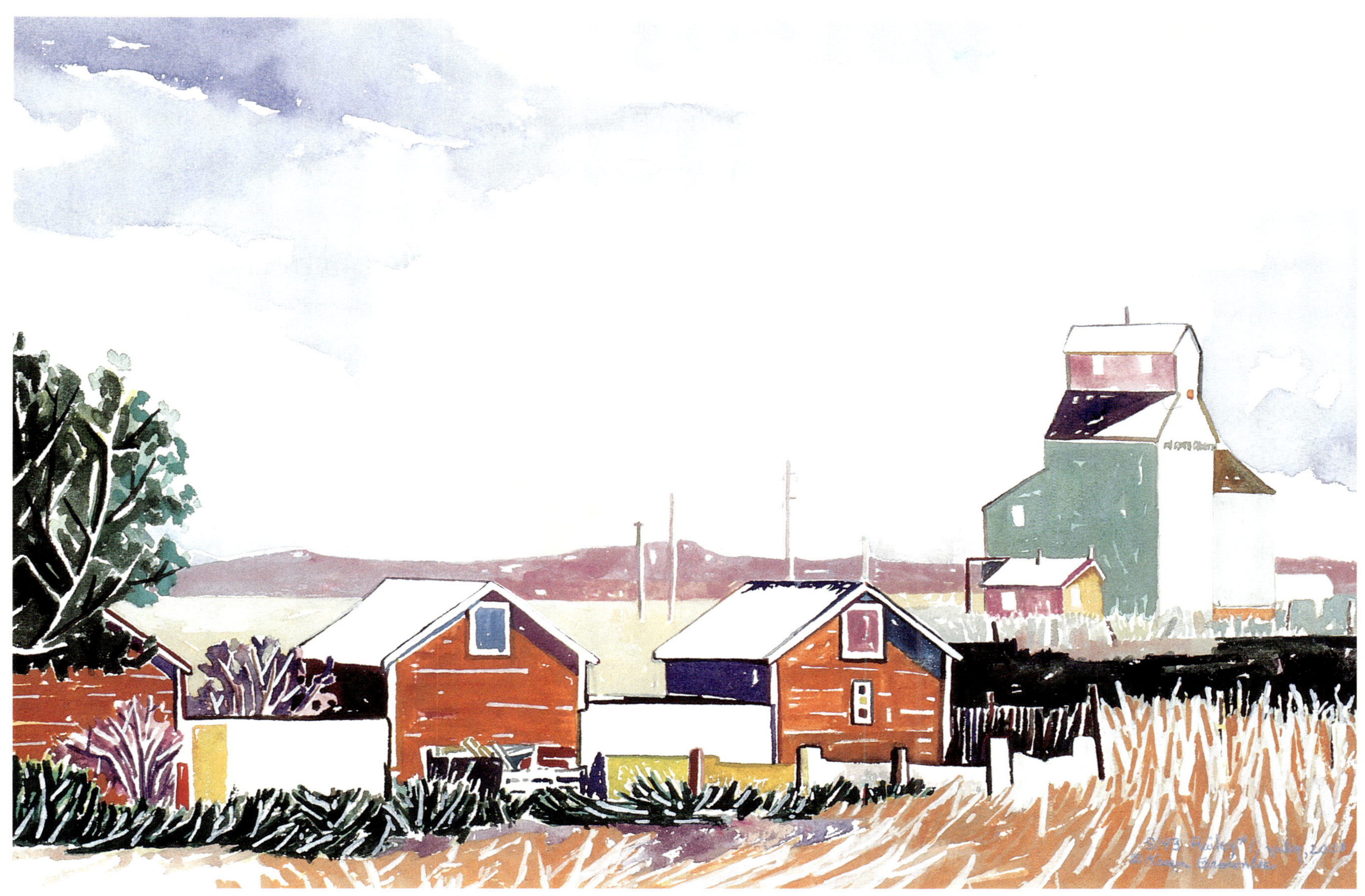

The community of Railey is today marked only by its elevator, which has been converted to private use on a farm. This process at least preserves the older wooden elevators, which are all too often torn down to make way for newer, larger facilities, or demolished as fire hazards.

Railey #1. 2001, 18" x 12", circa May 1998.

In 1805, Lewis and Clark christened the Milk River, the town's namesake, for its resemblance to milky tea. Since 1682 French, Spanish, American, British, Hudson's Bay Company and Canadian flags flew here. Officers at the 1887 North-West Mounted Police post established in present-day Writing-On-Stone Provincial Park in order to stop the whiskey trade, also assisted settlers by herding stray cattle and battling grass fires.

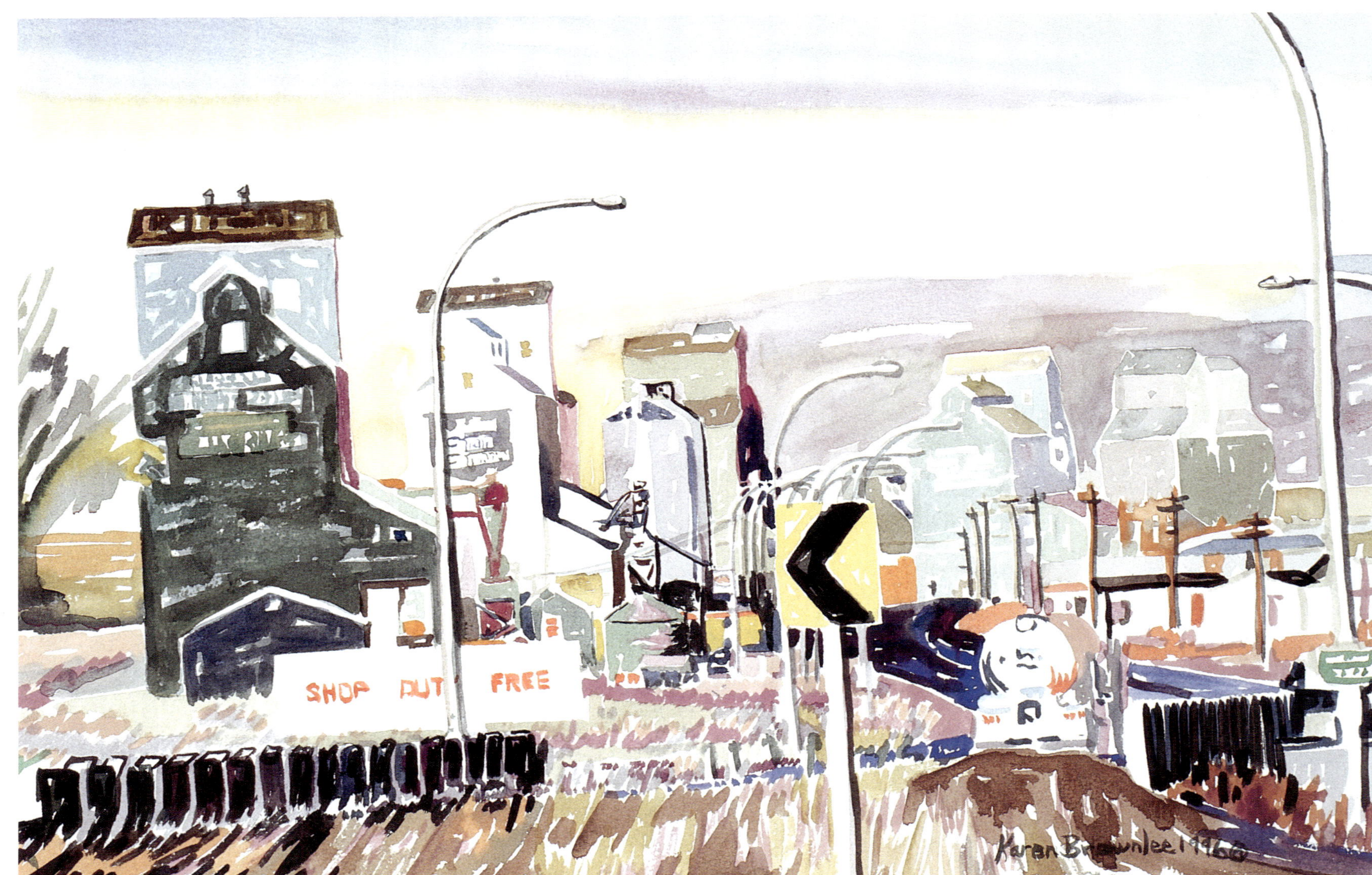

 Milk River #1, 1996, 18" x 12", circa November 1995.

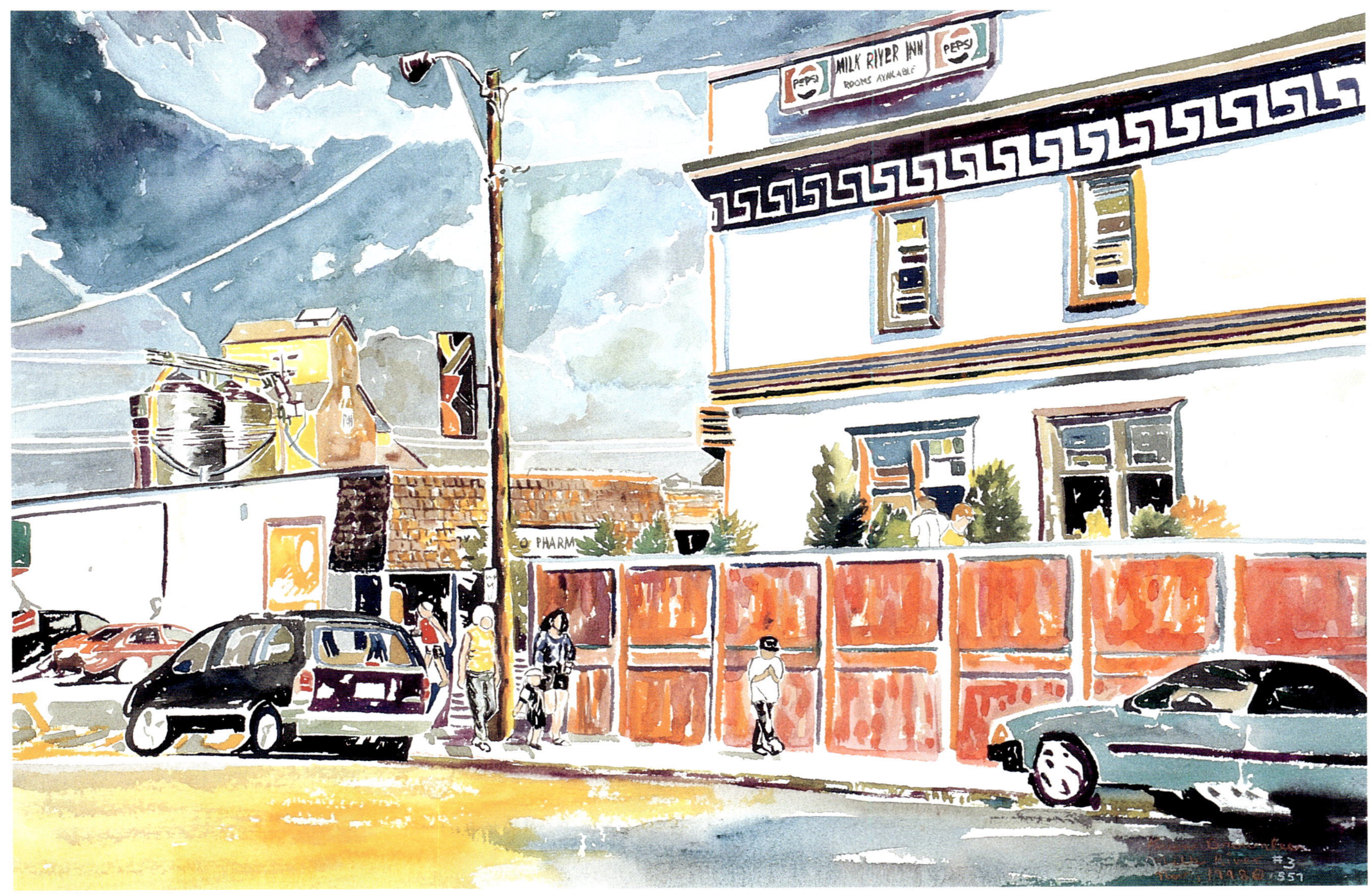

The area's large 1880s leases to the McIntyre Ranch and Knight Sugar were cancelled in 1912. People arrived at the Lethbridge Land Office a month before the 36,000 acres were to be distributed. Eager settlers received numbers corresponding to squares on the sidewalk. On May 1, 1912, an orderly "land rush" assigned 350 homesteads in two hours. Settlement, with buildings and elevators, arrived suddenly.

Milk River #3, 1998, 18" x 12", circa August 1998.

Prior to 1910 farmers loaded boxcars from a platform using scoop shovels. The small, tin-covered Dill and Jones elevator, built here in 1910, was bought by Alberta Pacific, torn down and rebuilt. Taylor Milling Company's elevator, the second constructed, was sold to Ellison Milling and Elevator. By 1969 companies included the Alberta Wheat Pool, Ogilvie and United Grain Growers and a local mustard elevator, P.J. Anderson & Sons.

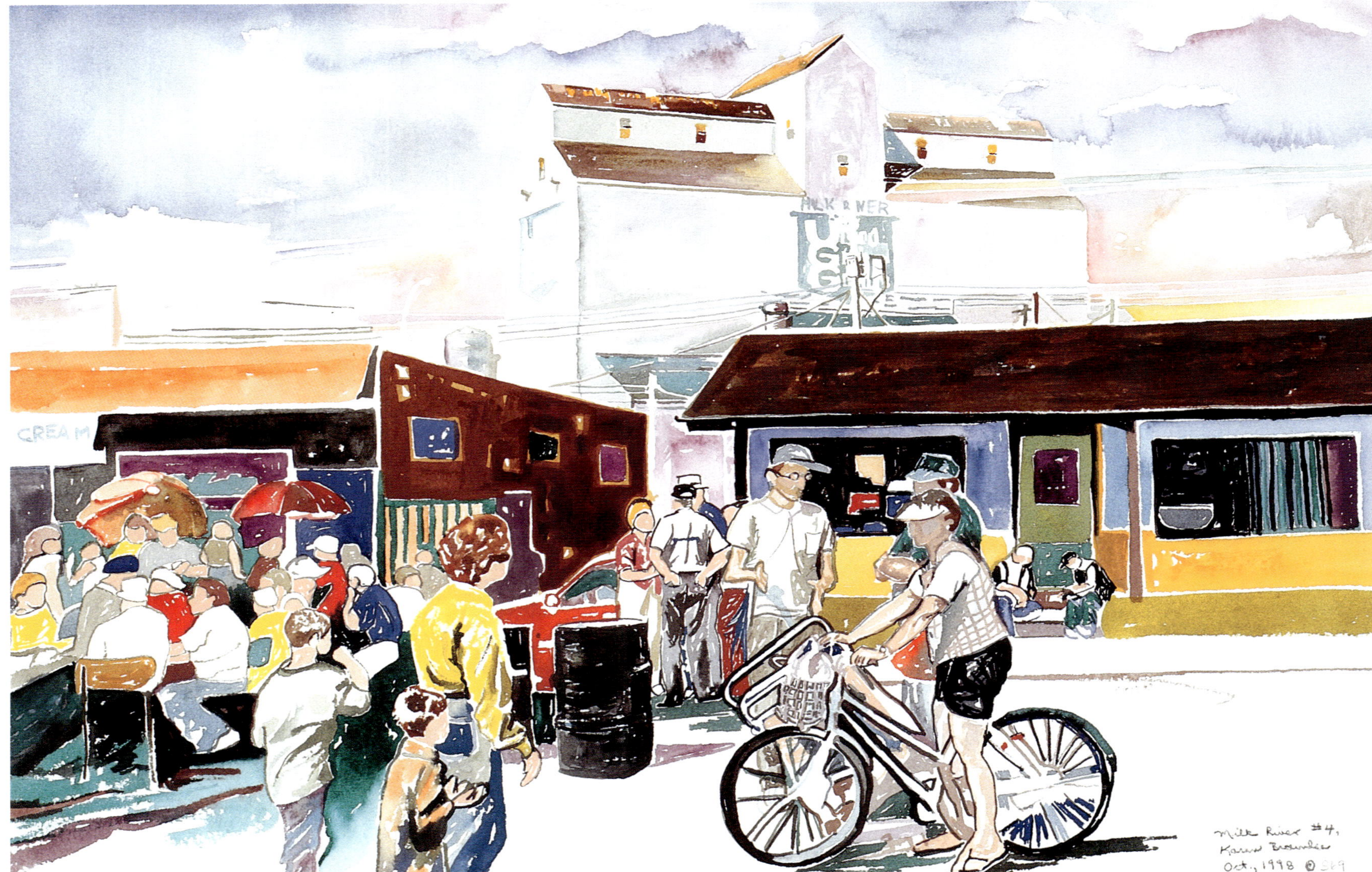

 Milk River #4, 1998, 18" x 12", circa August 1998.

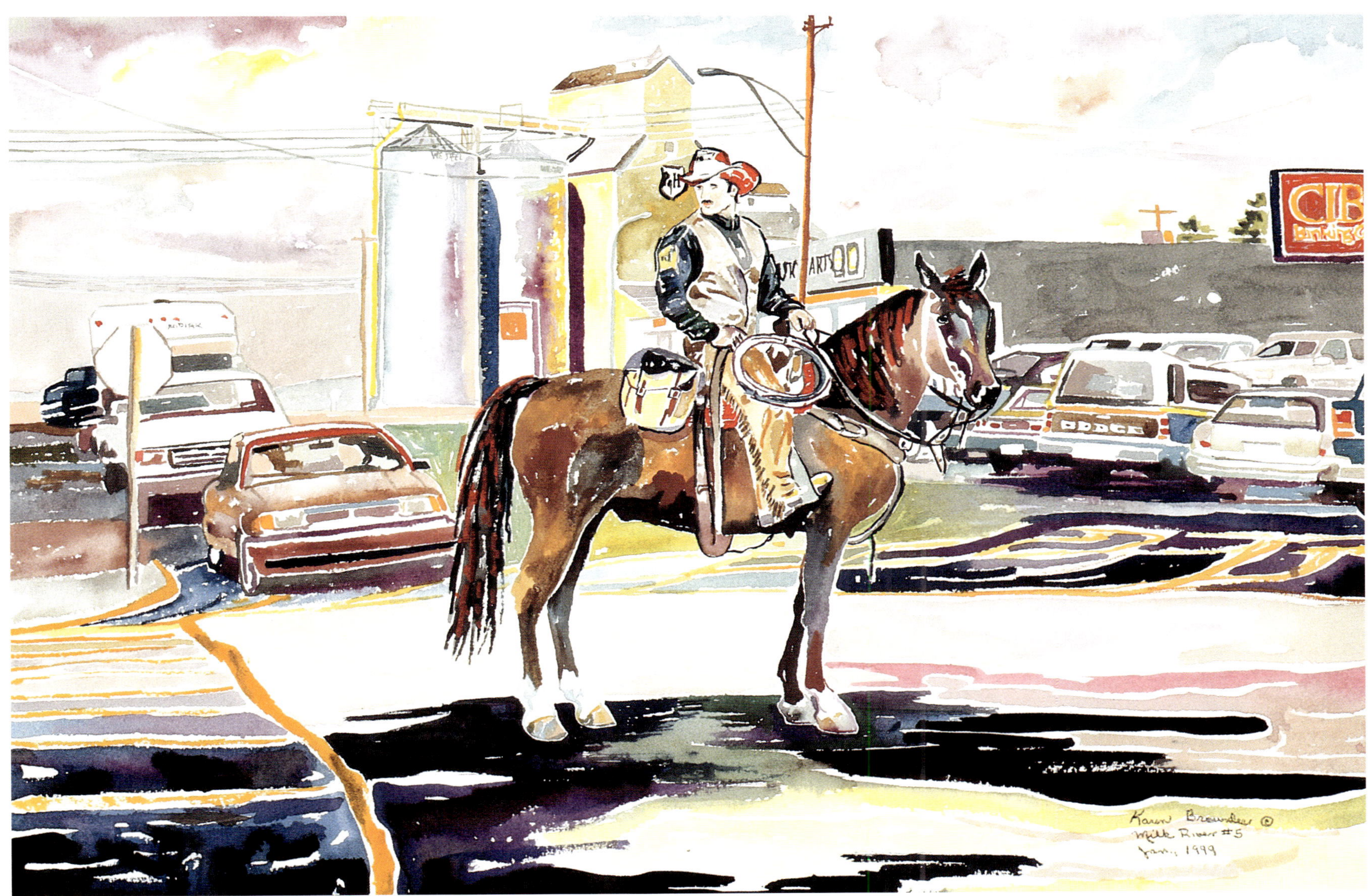

Milk River, the only river in western Canada to flow into the Missouri, has a varied and special past. Petroglyphs bear witness to the long inhabitation by aboriginal peoples before ranchers and homesteaders arrived. The Bonanza Days parade celebrates this diversity. The background elevators recall another enduring bonanza: grain.

Milk River #5, 1999, 18" x 12", circa August 1998.

Coutts, the 1890 A.R. & I.C. Alberta–Montana crossing, saw elevators built during the 1912 land rush. A barn-style elevator was quickly joined by three standard-style facilities: Alberta Farmers' Co-operative (1913), Ellison Milling and Elevator (1914) and Alberta Pacific Grain Company (1915). Elevators are now declining as quickly as they were once built. Of the 1733 wooden elevators operating in Alberta in 1933, only 154 were still licensed in 2001.

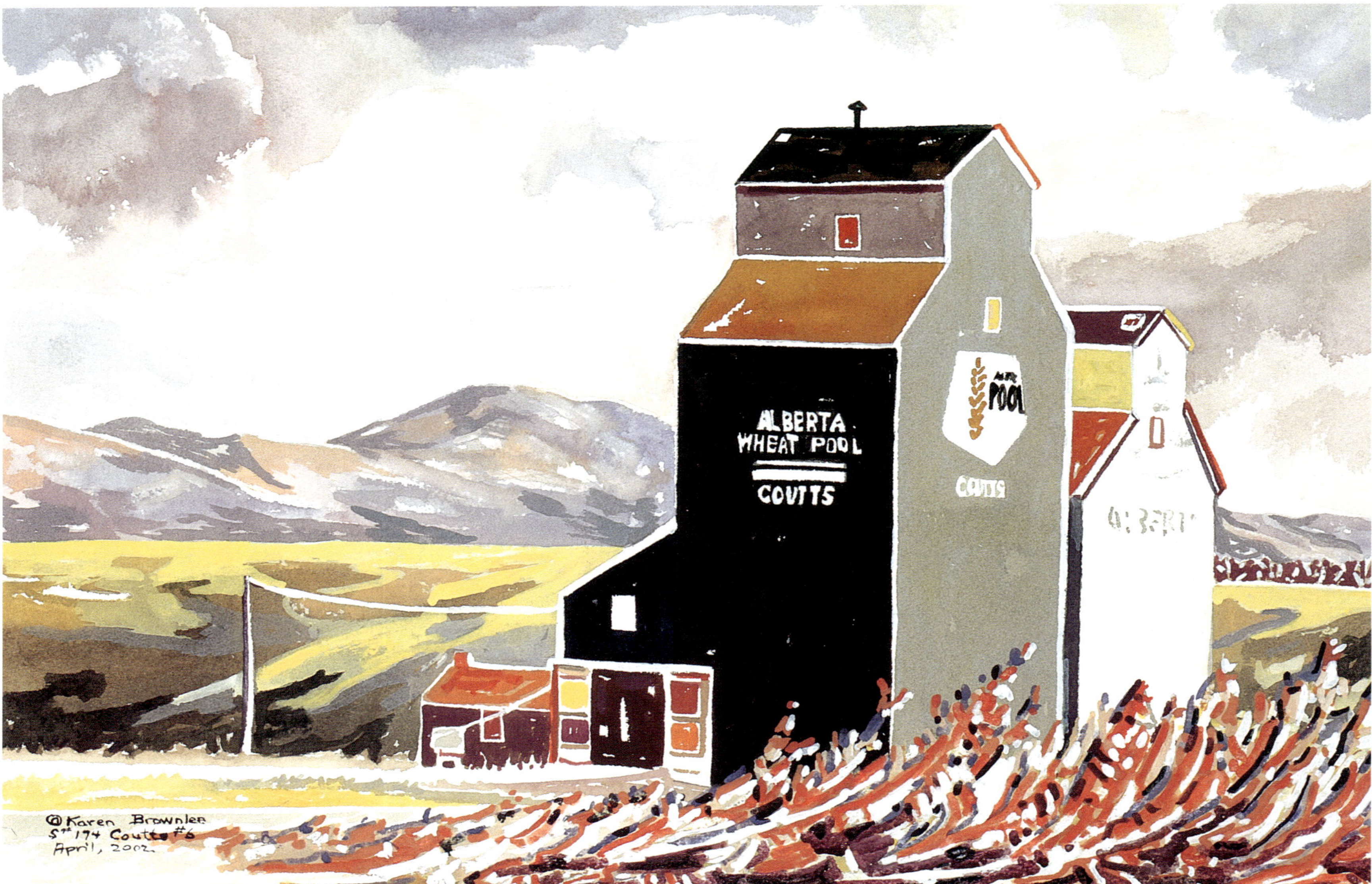

 Coutts #6, 2002, 18" x 12", circa May 1998.

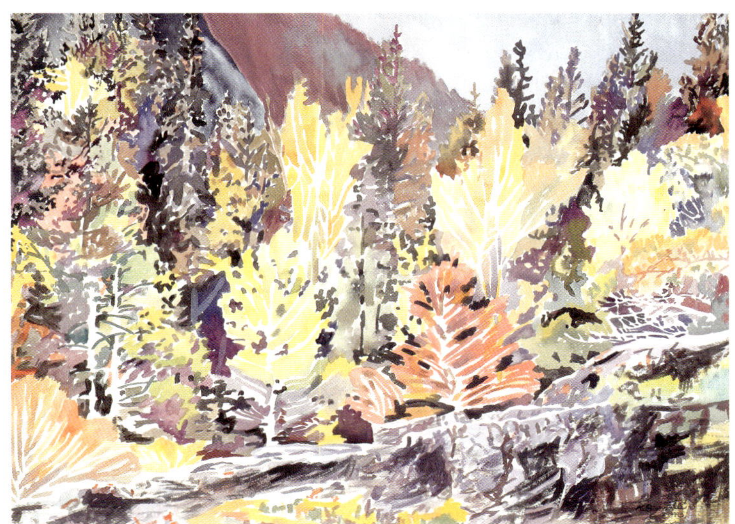

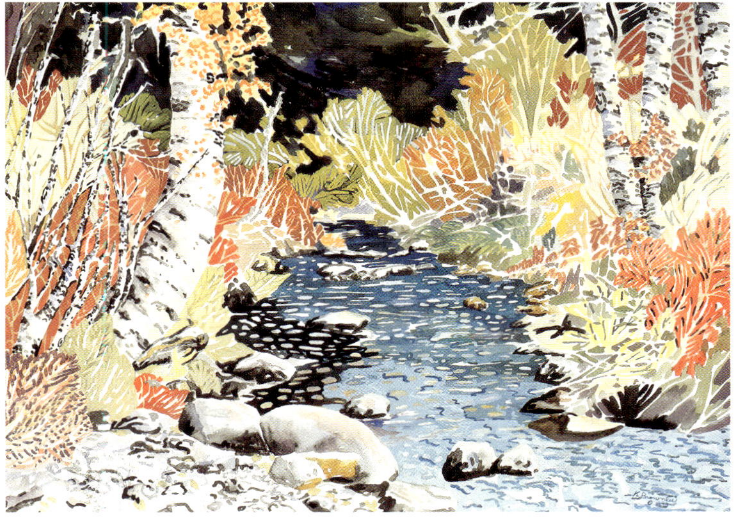

The approach to North Kootenay Pass, Waterton Lakes National Park, was named for its European discoverer, the Palliser Expedition's Thomas Blackiston. Blackiston's 1858 search for a southern railway pass led here, bypassing Crowsnest Pass and changing history. The expedition missed another opportunity. Palliser, seeing drought-stricken land, dismissed southern Alberta as unsuitable for agriculture. Professor John Macoun, with the Canadian Pacific Railway in the wetter 1870s, offered an opposing opinion, spurring settlement.

This creek's name recalls a North-West Mounted Police horse lost here and never found. The scene, in Waterton Lakes National Park, a World Heritage Site, reminds us that while times change, and coal, oil or grain may attract people in turn, some things are forever constant. We may mourn the passing of tipples, derricks or elevators, but the beauty of the Alberta land endures.

Along the Blackiston Trail, 1993, 28" x 21".

Glorious Autumn, Lost Horse Creek, 1993, 24" x 18".

Index of Images